George Negus is one of Australian television's most respected journalists and popular personalities. Apart from his well-known television current affairs pedigree (*This Day Tonight, 60 Minutes, Foreign Correspondent, Australia Talks* and *George Negus Tonight*), he has independently produced documentaries on Russia and children's rights, served on various boards and committees, including the Australian Broadcasting Tribunal's Violence Inquiry, the Federal Government's Environmental Futures Group, the Order of Australia Committee, Soccer Australia and LandCare, and made innumerable television guest appearances on everything from *The Mike Walsh Show* to *The Panel*.

He is the bestselling author of *The World from Italy, Across the Red Unknown* and *By George!*, and co-authored a bestselling children's book series, *Trev the Truck*, with his partner, Kirsty Cockburn. Cockburn, an accomplished journalist and photographer, took the cover photo and the other original photos featured in this book.

D0059468

GEORGE
NEGUS

the world from
ISLAM

A journey of discovery through the
Muslim heartland

HarperCollins*Publishers*

HarperCollins*Publishers*

First published in Australia in 2003
This updated edition published in 2004
by HarperCollins*Publishers* Pty Limited
ABN 36 009 913 517
A member of the HarperCollins*Publishers* (Australia) Pty Limited Group
www.harpercollins.com.au

Copyright © George Negus 2003, 2004

The right of George Negus to be identified as the moral rights
author of this work has been asserted by him in accordance with
the *Copyright Amendment (Moral Rights) Act 2000* (Cth).

This book is copyright.
Apart from any fair dealing for the purposes of private study, research,
criticism or review, as permitted under the Copyright Act, no part may
be reproduced by any process without written permission.
Inquiries should be addressed to the publishers.

HarperCollins*Publishers*
25 Ryde Road, Pymble, Sydney NSW 2073, Australia
31 View Road, Glenfield, Auckland 10, New Zealand
77–85 Fulham Palace Road, London W6 8JB, United Kingdom
2 Bloor Street East, 20th floor, Toronto, Ontario M4W 1A8, Canada
10 East 53rd Street, New York NY 10022, USA

National Library of Australia Cataloguing-in-Publication data:

Negus, George.
    The world from Islam: a journey of discovery
    through the Muslim heartland.
    2nd. ed.
    Bibliography.
    ISBN 0 7322 8048 6.
    1. Islam. 2. Christianity and other religions – Islam.
    3. Islam – Relations – Christianity. I. Title.
261.27

Cover and internal photography by Kirsty Cockburn, except where indicated
Cover design by Christa Edmonds, HarperCollins Design Studio
Printed and bound in Australia by Griffin Press on 79gsm Bulky Paperback White

6 5 4 3   05 06 07

To my incredible and long-suffering Kirst, Serge and Ned who — as they always have — tolerated my erratic work program and its inroads into our life together.

To all my Muslim and Israeli friends and contacts over the years who share the cherished hope that their children will lead the normal, strife-free Middle East life that has escaped their parents.

To Abdallah, an Emirati, and Michelle, an Australian, whose Open Mosque at Jumeira Beach, Dubai, should be a template for breaking down the mutual ignorance at the heart of the differences between our Muslim and non-Muslim worlds.

To Terje Roed Larsen and his wife, Mona Juul, Norwegian architects of the 1993 Oslo Peace Accords, whose passion for a pragmatic solution to the Arab–Israeli conflict was contagious. If it had been left to you two, our friends on both sides of that horrible human divide might have been living that normal, strife-free life years ago!

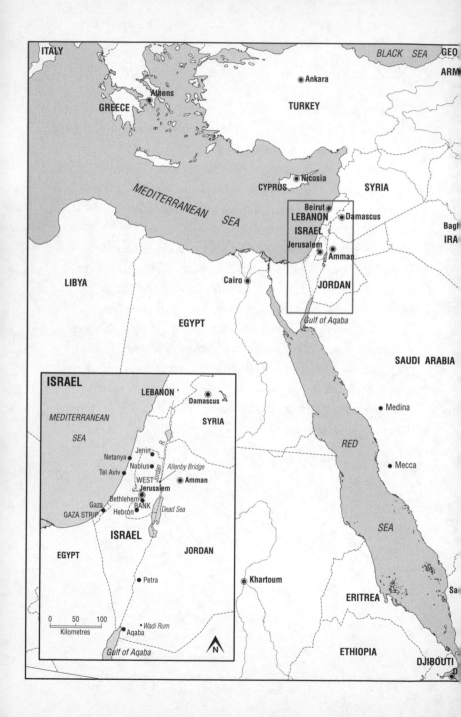

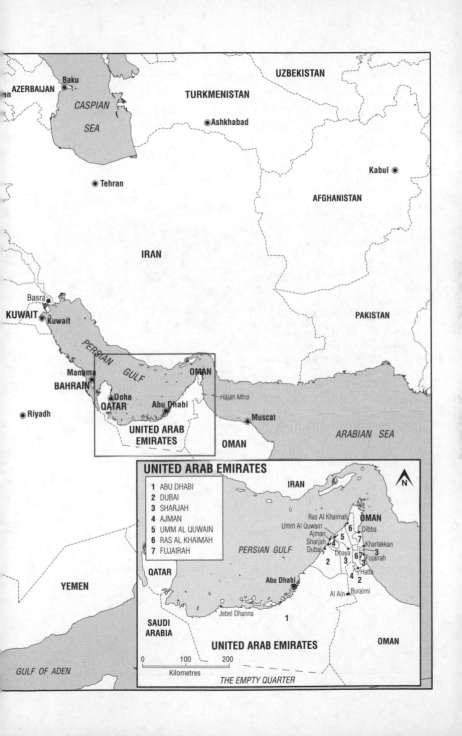

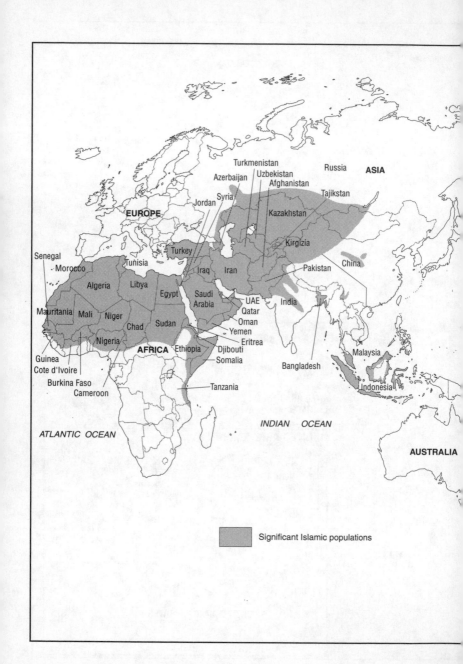

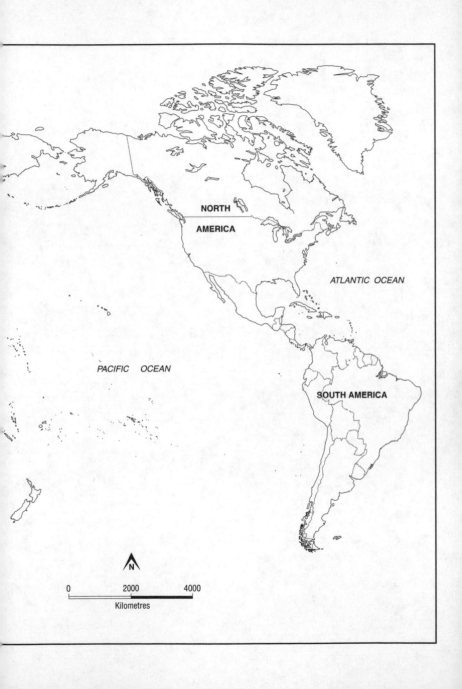

Contents

Author's Note

*T*he *World from Islam* is not exactly a book. It is more a periodical, a journal, in the sense that it is a work by a journalist. It is not written by an author with either literary or academic intent or pretension. In line with the origin of the words 'journal', 'journalism' and 'journalist', it is a series of personal experiences, opinions, observations, interviews, conversations, anecdotes, research and reactions noted and recorded in the course of considerable contact with a wide cross-section of Muslims over the past twenty-odd years. Note and record is what a journalist does, and I am a journalist.

By definition, therefore, this journal is not exhaustive, nor does it claim particular authority. But it is based on personal and professional experience in Islamic countries and contact with Muslims over a considerable period. It is written at a worrying time of unfortunate and arguably unnecessary global tension between the Muslim and non-Muslim worlds.

George Negus
September 2003

A lot of people are looking at contemporary conflict around the world and seeing it as a kind of religious war. And there is no kind of conflict that becomes more intractable than when people are convinced that they alone have access to God's truth and the other side are the people of Satan.

Elaine Pagels, Professor of Religion, Princeton University USA

Update: Post-Saddam

God Must Be the Busiest Guy in Heaven and on Earth!

Throughout history, there've been a few twisted megalomaniacs who actually thought they were God. There have been other misguided individuals who behaved as though they were. But who in their right mind would really want to be God? If you'll pardon the expression, it's a God-forsaken, thankless task.

Take the first week of July 2004. Now, that was a particularly hectic week for God.

Even by his routinely demanding standards, they were heavy-duty days. In fact, it was a non-stop week of prayer and providence. There was literally no let-up in the God-business. And not all of it was business-as-usual.

In Lisbon, the capital of Portugal, and elsewhere in a soccer-mad world, millions of Catholic Portuguese and Greek Orthodox fans were fervently praying for both of their national teams to win the Euro 2004 Cup. In a real nail-biter, the Greeks eventually took out the prestigious title, so we can only assume that the Portuguese had not only been outplayed, they were also 'out-prayed'.

Meanwhile, at the same time and on a more grave note, with the crisis in Iraq refusing to fade into the sunset, in Western capitals such as Washington, London and Canberra, Christians of multifarious theological hues were continuing to ask for His protection and support in that bloody quagmire. On that week's Sunday, like so many others since September 11, 2001, they would have also been beseeching Him for victory in their purported war against unflagging global terror — terror being carried out against Christendom in the name of God in his Islamic guise of Allah, by homicidal maniacs calling themselves Muslims.

At the same time during that eventful July week, thousands of mosques throughout the Islamic world would have been packed with millions of devout moderate Muslims with their heads buried in the carpet and their rear-ends in the air imploring God for a peaceful life for their families, free from what many of them remain convinced is anti-Islamic aggression being perpetrated against them by US-led Christians.

While all this was occurring, just to make sure that the omnipresent Deity stayed on his Providential toes, neither the Jews nor the Palestinians perennially embroiled in the wretched hell-hole that is Israel and the Occupied Territories — almost certainly oblivious to the 'football prayers' of the Portuguese and Greeks — despite a momentary lull in hostilities, had not stopped slaughtering each other with murderous regularity in His Name. The Wailing Wall in Jerusalem and the synagogues of Tel Aviv had not suddenly emptied of prayerful Israelites; futile, deranged Palestinian suicide bombers from Gaza and Jenin had not given up praying before they strapped gelignite to their bodies and headed for an Israeli bus stop or bar — breaking their own God-given Koranic Law in the process.

Obviously, suicide bombers — as well as out-and-out, pseudo-Islamic terrorists — might pray, but they don't appear to wait around for God to answer. If they did, they wouldn't commit suicide, let alone murder innocent, non-combatant Jews, neither of which Allah would ever give his nod to. Then again, on the Christian side of the religious divide, for a while now, God has apparently been turning a blind eye to that old Christian commandment 'Thou shalt not kill.' Apparently, it now reads 'Thou shalt not kill — except under certain circumstances!'

There are, it seems, 'just' wars that God approves of, and others He doesn't.

Needless to say, pretty much all over the globe in that same July week, these were not the only heinous and not-so-heinous acts being carried out with prior reference to some form or other of His Holiness or The Divinity. The religious good, bad and ugly of the human race — Christian, Jew, Muslim or Calathumpian — were up to all sorts of life-threatening tricks 'in His Name'.

They say that God's work never ends, but what a workload! On the strength of Greece's totally unexpected shock win in the Euro Cup final, whichever God those Greek Orthodox folk turned to appears to have had the most success. Whatever His other achievements, on that fateful July 5 2004 in Lisbon, you could say He scored a historic goal — a Greek goal! As for the other prayers that went up that week — the same week, by the way, that the captured Saddam Hussein finally fronted the courts of the now allegedly sovereign Iraq — nobody else scored a winner. Saddam's name having come up, as a God-fearing, self-professing Muslim who has broken just about every rule in the entire Muslim faith and ethos, he also probably muttered a few set-piece prayers before he faced his accusers in that Baghdad Court room.

Confused? Well, in today's confused and confusing world, God Himself must also be getting just a little befuddled about whose prayers He's supposed to be answering. And who could blame Him? What would His reaction have been if a phoney Muslim pretender like Saddam were to plead, not to the Iraqi court or to his American captors, but to Him, as God or Allah? Would Saddam's prayers for mercy and understanding, even for a fair trial, be heard? Quite a question, and almost as important as any answer — if, indeed, there is one?

God 'bushed' by US President!

To believers of whatever faith, these sorts of propositions might sound utterly and preposterously sacrilegious, but, seriously, which God are we talking about here? Is there just one? If so, which one is to be prayed to and believed? Can there be two? In the case of Muslims and non-Muslims, are God and Allah one and the same? If they are not, can they co-exist? Do they ever get their heads together on things — big things, like a predicted decades-long war against terror or the religious Damocles Sword of a clash between the Muslim and non-Muslim civilisations? Bring in the third of the so-called great religions, and ask when Jews and Christians pray, respectively, to the Old Testament God and to the New Testament God, are they exhorting the same God? And where does Jesus, as the Son of God, fit into this unholy theological muddle?

If we're looking for a response — reliable or otherwise — on these sorts of loaded, divisive and ultimately unavoidable questions — how could we possibly go beyond the Man Himself, George 'Dubya' Bush, US President and leader of the Christian free world, the man who categorised the battle with self-appointed Islamic extremists like Osama bin Laden and Al Qa'ida as 'a battle between good and evil'.

In the immediate post-9/11 weeks and months, one of the great worries among even American religious moderates was that the whole US anti-terrorist thing could turn into a religious war, a New Crusades, a war against Muslims. But theologian and social ethicist Professor Jean Elshstain from the University of Chicago thought that it was, in many ways, George Bush's finest hour when he visited the Islamic Center in Washington, DC and declared: 'Yes, Muslims pray to the same God!'

Finest hour indeed — and a finest hour that clears up everything! Hardly. If it is the case that both Muslims and Christians pray to the same God, whose prayers is He answering as things stand? If God and Allah are one-and-the-same, if this is intellectually and religiously so, then God must surely want peace in the Middle East and Iraq and an end to terrorism. So why do these things remain such remote and distant possibilities? Why is He dallying?

The double-bind is this — and deep down, we all know it! Do Christians really believe that God and Allah are the same? When the religious chips are really down — when it's their religion or ours, as it were, do Muslims really believe Allah and God are one? Over the last 1400 years, let alone lately, verbal and other evidence would certainly suggest otherwise.

How Many Gods Does It Take to Fill a Religious Vacuum?

Back in April, 2003, early in the war with Iraq, in Washington George W Bush asked God to 'continue to protect America'. At precisely the same moment, Iraqi Muslims were fervently praying to God for exactly the same protection? Come on! How can this be? God on both sides in this unholy global shambles? Or are we suggesting there are actually two Gods — and, not only that, they are at war? But if the 'one-God' Theory of Life doesn't hold up and there are two or more of them hanging about out there watching over our currently inhuman stupidity and carry-on, then why don't they get their heads together on this whole schemozzle to see if they can sort things out — like, as a good start, death and vengeance being replaced by life and co-existence? As the world stands, the future's not looking terribly rosy for either of their millions of devout followers. In some ways, the crunch question might be this. If George W Bush is right and Muslims and Christians (and presumably Jews) all pray to the same God, how many of the 1.5 billion Muslims in the world would be prepared to convert to Christianity — and vice versa?

But the stupefying fact right now is that both Muslims and non-Muslims carry on as though there are, in fact, two deities — God and Allah — both of them apparently protecting their believers from the wrath of the other side. This means that while God is protecting the Christian and Jewish worlds, Allah is looking after the Muslim sector of Creation. Let's be uncharacteristically honest with ourselves for once, fellow stumbling human beings! This just doesn't make any kind of sense — intellectual, religious or philosophical.

As blasphemous and heretical as it may sound, unless and until we are prepared to even attempt to come to grips with this whole illogical and dichotomous 'God-thing' that's been dividing the human race for close enough to one-and-a-half millennia and is certainly dividing it as we speak, the threat of that oft-predicted 'clash of civilisations' — military, terroristic, religious or otherwise — will not go away. Meanwhile, the 'clash of religions' is already on. Where the world's great religious divides are concerned, everyone still thinks they are right. On the basis of pure logic alone, how can this be? Could it be possible that no one's right?

Muslim or non-Muslim, few of us like putting our religious or even our irreligious convictions under this sort of scrutiny. It is too close to the human bone. But unless we are prepared to put religion, any and all religions, under the intellectual miscroscope, the whole circumlocutory 'my God is better than your God, my religion is better than your religion' dispute is going to drag on endlessly — and violently — for at least another 1500 years. Our kids can't wait that long for us to get our collective heads out of the sand. If we don't, God help us — any God!

He's been accused of 'playing God', but George W Bush is on the record that he believes he's been 'called' by God into public office 'at this hour'. His personal 'calling' from the Almighty is to rid the world of his idea of evil. He is President of the most militarily powerful nation on Earth, he has declared, because God wants him to be. 'We have an obligation to work toward a more free world. That is what we have been called to do, so far as I'm concerned,' are his own words. American religious commentator Jeffrey Brown sees it this way: 'George Bush's language suggests that God is on our side, that it's our God versus their God.'

'The problem with George Bush is not with his sincerity,' says Chicago Uni religious academic Martin Marty. 'It's with his evident conviction that he's doing God's will.' 'When President Bush talks about the war on terror and Iraq, he often uses words that invoke his religious faith,' says theologian Jean Elshstain. 'Especially in times of tribulation, providence is called upon (by US Presidents, including Bush) in the belief that the US is doing God's will, that God's purposes are the US's purposes, that the salvation of the world depends on the US.'

Allah — Defamed by Blasphemous Holy Warriors

In this context, it's a fair bet that some, if not all, of the American troops — the likes of the unfortunately infamous and scapegoated Private Lynndie England — involved in the psycho-sexual abuse of

Iraqi prisoners in Baghdad's Abu Ghraib prison would claim to be God-fearing Christian men and women. It's also a fair bet they believed they were in the frontline in the war of 'good versus evil' and that their enemy's Muslim God was not as 'good' as their Christian one. Indeed, if they took notice of the General heading the Bush Administration's anti-terrorist intelligence gathering operation post-September 11, not only is Allah not as god a God as the Christian God, he is a 'false idol'.

The Abu Ghraib GIs probably also believed that their God would forgive them their sins — if presumably, abusing and 'animalising' Muslim POWs was a sin. Either way, they showed total physical and psychological disrespect for the human and religious sensitivities of their captives, a tactless contempt for their Muslim culture and code. Almost certainly, they had been led to believe that maybe these Iraqi Muslims were not normal human beings. 'They don't believe what we believe; they don't feel like we feel.' Real Christians throughout the West were appalled. Phoney Christians went looking for cover and excuses.

And the other side? The same. Islamic moderates of the Islamic world looked on impotent or silent as their religion and their Allah have come in for a hell of a beating at the mouths and hands of those self-styled Islamic extremists, the so-called 'jihadists', holy warriors, mujahadeen, Al Qa'ida or otherwise, in Iraq or elsewhere.

On almost a daily basis during this visible and invisible conflict, they've been giving the other side every opportunity to use their favourite label for Islam, 'barbaric'. Suicide bombing, kidnappings, torturing, terrorising, depriving, dehumanising and even the grotesque anti-human act of beheading, have all been carried out in the name of God, with utter religious conviction, all for the promotion of sick, perverted extremist and theologically unjustifiable versions of Islam.

As we know all too well by now, George Bush believes he is

carrying out God's will. But, paradoxically, so do his Muslim opponents. As anyone who, like the author, has spent time with Muslims from extremists to moderate on their turf will tell you, dozens of times every day they invoke the most overused term in their entire religious lexicon, '*insh-allah*' — God willing! Indeed, many of them do it, it would appear, without even thinking. They believe that their entire daily existence is governed by God and His will from birth to death, no matter how that comes, in peace or in war. This single, extraordinarily cryptic Arabic word is not just a prayerful entreaty, it's a religious commitment and a way of life that has become an entire cultural identity for a quarter of the world's population. By exactly the same religious token, Christians are equally convinced that their commitment to their faith means they are also doing God's will — what the Muslims call '*insh-allah*'.

In other words, George Bush genuinely believes that he invaded Iraq to take out Saddam Hussein and transform the entire Middle East in America's image because it was God's will that he should. Osama bin Laden similarly believes that sending those maniacs to fly planes into the World Trade Center, killing thousands of innocents was the same, also God's will. Now, if you're able to reconcile those two utterly contradictory convictions, then form your own religion quick smart. The world could really do with a strong leader right now — and you could be it!

You could put it another way, we live in a wilful world, a wilfully divided world in which both sides believe they are doing God's will — even waging war against each other because He has told them to. If the complete lack of logic in all of this wasn't so murderously serious, it would be laughable! That said, this unresolved conflict needs to be recognised for what it ultimately is, a 'religious war' or at least 'a war between religions'. Clear-minded Islamist scholars have already declared all extremist atrocities against Christians and Jews to be against Islamic law, Islamic teachings and the spirit of real Islam. Where the likes of Saddam Hussein, Osama bin Laden and their misguided disciples are concerned, everything about them has to be deemed anti-Muslim, anti-Islamic. What they have been conducting as a so-called 'holy war' is as impossible to justify in Koranic terms as Christian and Jewish attempts to describe their military aggression as a 'just war' in Biblical terms.

Meanwhile, whether or not it ever gets officially acknowledged as at least a religious war of words, unless and until, as a human race, we are prepared to openly and unconditionally discuss the 'R-word', religion, without studiously avoiding open and unconditional reference to the 'G-word', God, this War of the Worlds — the Muslim and non-Muslim worlds — will continue, inconclusively, on and off the battlefield of the Middle East, let alone the borderless global theatre of terrorism.

Whether we want to believe it or not, that sad and sorry Middle East conflict remains both the cause and the effect, the microcosm of the world's gaping, bloody differences over the R-word and the G-word. But, for whatever reasons known best to their psychiatrists, so many are still trying to convince us and themselves that it's not about religion. If it's not, then we must be involved in the religious war the world has when it's not having a religious war!

Ironically, maybe Jerusalem — the accepted tripartite religious home of Jews, Christians and Muslims — could be the wholly appropriate location to thrash out these centuries-old, on-going differences. If Jerusalem turned out to be the preferred venue, God won't have to travel far to chair this 'mother of all debates'. Whether He ultimately turns out to be Jewish, Christian or Muslim — or all three — He's got Himself some pretty impressive pads to choose from in The Holy City of all Three Great Religions.

Man with a Mission

As we were compiling this update to *The World From Islam*, a story appeared in the media about the trial of a bloke accused of trying to hijack a commercial aircraft on a flight between the Victorian capital, Melbourne, and Launceston in northern Tasmania. He was carrying two wooden stakes he'd sharpened at his home, aerosol cans and cigarette lighters he was planning to use as flame-throwers. After a scuffle, in which cabin crew were injured, the man was overpowered, arrested and taken into custody.

In his court defence, the guy's lawyers argued that he was not a well boy, that his outrageous, life-threatening behaviour was due to his impaired mental condition. It was alleged that at the time of his failed hijack attempt, he was in 'a psychotic state'. And what was that psychotic state? He apparently believed he was on a 'mission from God' to hijack the plane and kill all its passengers and that, somehow, this action would 'rid the world of all evil'. In other words, the man believed he was doing God's will! Where have we heard this line before?

The failed Australian hijacker's plan, by the way, had been to take over the controls of the plane and crash it into a beautiful Tasmanian National Park. His target was a spectacular piece of local topography known, by stranger-than-fiction coincidence, as The Walls of Jerusalem.

So, what does this story tell us, allegorically-speaking, about the world's Christian and Muslim leaders who currently believe they are doing the same thing — God's will — by waging war against each other to rid the world of each other's evil? Maybe they should also plead insanity. If they don't, then you'd like to think that history, at least, will record them as such.

George Negus, August 2004

In the West, we have never been able to cope with Islam; our ideas about this faith have been crude, dismissive and arrogant, but we have now learned that we cannot remain in an attitude of such ignorance and prejudice . . .

If the September 11 atrocity leads to a new understanding and appreciation of Islam in the West, something good will have come out of this tragedy.

Karen Armstrong,
Muhammed: A Biography of the Prophet

PROLOGUE

SO WHAT'S ALL
THE FUSS?

An invasion of Iraq is an invasion of the entire Arab-Muslim world.

**Egyptian government official,
ABC Radio's AM program,
26 March 2003**

An Invasion of Iraq or an Invasion of Islam?

On Thursday, 20 March 2003, US Tomahawk cruise missiles in their hundreds — the so-called 'even smarter bombs' — began raining down on strategic targets in the Iraqi capital of Baghdad, home to five million people. But none of the missiles was smart enough to let anyone in the West know whether the ultimate target, the current 'evil man of history', Saddam Hussein, was dead or alive. As that historically high-tech bombardment of Baghdad and the Iraqis dragged on inconclusively, the prescient words of an Arab-Muslim friend, spoken a couple of months earlier in Dubai, rang in my mind.

'If you in the West want to get rid of Saddam, just ask and we will help you,' he said in that sardonic Gulf manner I'd become used to over years of contact with Arab-Muslims. 'But don't expect us to get involved in a military invasion that could mean killing God knows how many Iraqis — Iraqis who also want to see the end of him, including many in uniform.' My friend's proviso was distinctly Gulf, distinctly Arab, distinctly conditional.

Then he added the ultimate in distinctly Arab-Muslim taglines, the ubiquitous *insh'allah*. God willing.

Muslims, you may or may not have realised, believe that everyone's fate, indeed their whole life, is ultimately in the hands of God, or Allah. Muslims live by a sophisticated religious version of 'que sera, sera' — whatever will be, will be. They would never tell you that their lot or yours was written in the cards or will be revealed by the stars. Nor do they adhere to any of the silly forms of predestination. They believe, very simply, that Allah is the ultimate arbiter of their existence — for better or worse. If you don't understand this utterly God-dependent essence of being a Muslim — whether a good Muslim like my Dubai friend or a bad pseudo-Muslim like Saddam or Osama bin Laden — you don't and will never understand Muslims. Islam is not their religion, it is their life.

But whether it was Allah speaking through him or his own intelligent idea, my Dubai friend went on: 'There has always been another way, one that might prevent the slaughter of both soldiers and civilians. They're not just Iraqis, you know, they're Muslims.'

'Are you suggesting that force is not the only way, but that George W. Bush wants to use force?' I asked.

'He'll have to ask his God about that, but there's an approach to the whole Iraqi problem that no one has thought about. Has anyone suggested taking a plane-load of world leaders — Bush, Blair, Schroeder, Chirac, Putin, the Chinese, your prime minister, led by UN Secretary-General Kofi Annan, to Baghdad? Tell the Iraqis they're coming, no tricks, no surprises. No army fighter jets, no CIA. No media. Send an official UN message to Saddam saying, "We're arriving at Baghdad International Airport at such and such a time on such and such a day and we want to meet Saddam. We want to talk with him." Has anyone even suggested it? Anyone? No, they haven't. Why not?'

'Good question,' I replied. 'But what happens when they actually get to Baghdad?'

'If they turned up en masse, what's he going to do? Shoot them out of the sky as soon as they enter Iraqi air space? Arrest them when they arrive at the terminal? Of course he isn't!'

'So what *would* happen when they arrived?' I asked, not entirely facetiously.

'They could take a fleet of taxis — that in itself would be a new experience for many of them — and head off to Saddam's palace compound across the Tigris. If they were to turn up at the main gate and demand to see him, would the Iraqis refuse? I doubt it. After a bit of carry-on, they would eventually get to see him and tell him, "We are here to discuss this mess we're all in, what we're going to do to avoid war. We want to negotiate." What's Saddam going to do — refuse to talk? No way! How could he with the eyes and ears of the world waiting for his reaction?'

The gist of my friend's ostensibly outlandish idea was that Saddam would either talk sensibly to the visiting world leaders about weapons of mass destruction, about any Iraqi links with Al Qa'ida or other terrorist groups, about human rights in Iraq, about democracy, about the Kurds, about a peaceful way out of the impasse — or he would leave the rest of the Muslim world, together with the non-Muslim world, as a sort of Coalition of the More and More Willing, with no option but to use force.

But apparently negotiation was out of the question. And we'll never know if it might have made a difference, if one of the most inhumane periods in recent world history might have been avoided.

Since then, it's become diplomatically and politically acceptable for the West to talk with those other members of the so-called Axis of Evil, the North Koreans, who claim to have nuclear weapons and are prepared to use them, and to self-styled guerillas and thugs in the anarchic Solomon Islands — but not with the likes of Saddam. Curious, at least. At worst, a double standard.

Despite the impression left by Islamic extremists, the overwhelming majority of the world's one-and-a-quarter billion Muslims have never held any brief for Saddam Hussein and his despicable regime. Nor do they support the tactics of Osama bin Laden, or even Palestinian suicide bombers whose cause, not methods, they generally do support. Yet most moderate Muslims have come, rightly or wrongly, to regard the war against the Iraqi dictator and terrorism as virtually and ultimately a war against Muslims and Islam, across the ethnic board. And in that sort of complex, confusing and passionate state of affairs, perceptions count.

Hence the worrying quote at the beginning of this Prologue: 'An invasion of Iraq is an invasion of the entire Arab-Muslim world.' That said, there was never going to be a general Muslim response to the beleaguered Iraqis' call to 'turn every country in the world into a battlefield'. Extremist Islamic minorities, yes. Extremist Islamic majorities, no!

And it's Not About Religion?

With the US battalions storming their way towards Baghdad for eleven tumultuous days, ABC Australia correspondent Geoff Thompson interviewed a couple of young American marines, gunners preparing to rain steel down on entrenched Iraqis in central Iraq. The pair told him how they could fire 88 grenades in one dump on the enemy — precision killing from 30 kilometres, as Thompson described it. 'They drop down and some of them will bounce up and they'll get you chest high,' Sgt Jorge Velasque told him matter-of-factly.

'What do you imagine is happening at the other end of this artillery battery?' Thompson asked the young marine.

'I imagine there's a lot of people out there prayin',' was Velasque's ingenuous reply.

As Thompson was conducting his interview, as sensitively as possible under the circumstances, a military chaplain was leading an improvised church service in the middle of the Iraqi desert. American troops were singing that old Protestant favourite, 'The Old Rugged Cross'. Thompson noted that this bizarre display of prayer and Christian religiosity was taking place in the midst of news that four US marines had just been killed in a suicide car bombing at a nearby checkpoint.

Within hours of going to church, Thompson noted, Lt Col. Charles Robinson was receiving orders to kill people he has never met and whose bodies he will probably never see. So how did he cope, knowing that what he was doing was killing unseen, unidentifiable Iraqis. The young officer's reply was riveting: he asked his Christian God to both protect him and guide his missiles to the 'right' targets. 'Well, you have to definitely know that you're doing the right thing out here — and pray a lot. You have to get that peace from God that you're doing the right thing. You go to church and worship and then you're killing somebody. You know, it's something that causes big conflict.'

Lt Col. Robinson said it was difficult because, 'You know, usually you think about going to church in your nice clothes on Sunday morning at home and going back and eating dinner with the family. But out here, you go to church and three hours later you're sending rounds down, raining shit on people.' Robinson said there was not much emotional conflict for him, 'because, like I said, I think I'm doing the right thing out here'.

A matter of minutes later another reporting colleague, Peter Cave, ABC Radio's international editor, filed a report from Israel documenting the latest bloody Palestinian suicide attack against Jews in the coastal city of Netanya. Cave reported that Hamas, the militant Palestinian terrorist group, had made available to the media a videotape of the twenty-year-old bomber in which he was shown praying and kissing the Islamic holy text, the Qur'an, before going off to blow himself and his young Israeli victims to smithereens. He killed himself, Cave was told, 'as a gift to the people of Iraq and to mark "Land Day", an annual protest at what the Palestinians call the theft of Arab land by the State of Israel'.

Ask yourself: when their time is up, will the young American marines, Valesque and Robinson, their invisible flesh-and-blood Iraqi targets, the pathetic Palestinian suicide bomber 'gifting' his life, and the innocent, uninvolved Israelis all find themselves in Heaven? Will they be together in the same Heaven — or will they be in several different ones? Will they be greeted in the Hereafter by the Christians' God, by Allah or by both? Nasty questions for monotheistic believers, be they Christians, Muslims or Jews, to answer — if, that is, they are brave enough to try! You could say that faith of whatever kind is handy to have while you're alive, to prop you up when you think you might die. But once you're dead and gone to Wherever, what price faith? And what if you picked the wrong faith? You certainly don't get a second chance.

And it's not about religion ... ? Don't let anyone tell you that this all-embracing human predicament, this gulf between the Muslim and Judaeo-Christian worlds brought to a head by the so-called war against terror, is not about just that. As we keep being told, we are not involved in a war *between* religions. But it is a war *about* religion, about personal attitudes, about life values. It might not be, as Samuel Huntington rashly called it in 1993, 'A clash of civilisations'. But it's definitely a clash of ideologies, a clash of value systems, a clash of cultures. And you don't get much more fundamental than that.

In the end, the Great Divide is about what people — Christians, Jews, Muslims, whatever — believe themselves to be. That makes it about ideologies, about purpose, about what people have come to think being a human being means. As my wise Emirati Muslim friend counselled me: 'We cannot and we should not take religion out of it. Only when we take the time to understand each other's religion will we begin to understand each other.'

There's a highly relevant book by an American writer, Benjamin R. Barber, shrewdly entitled *Jihad vs McWorld*. As Barber puts it, the most damaging conflict underlying our times is consumerist capitalism versus religion and tribal fundamentalism. 'These diametrically opposed but intertwined forces are tearing apart — and bringing together — the world as we know it.' If Barber is even half right, getting to know Muslims, their religion and their tribal fundamentalism might not be such a bad idea.

Real Ease and Proper Peace

September 11 is now more than two years behind us; the war against Iraq is apparently over; Saddam Hussein's hated regime may or may not have changed; unlocated weapons of mass destruction apparently still exist; Iraqis and Americans continue to take each other out in the name of cultural sovereignty and democracy; terrorist killers continue to stalk the earth in the name of Allah; the religious slaughter of innocents

at Bali's Kuta Beach is embedded in our national psyche; the
Middle East remains the tinder-box it's been for decades and the
conflict between Jewish Israelis and Muslim Palestinians persists
as the ultimate explanation for global tension and a new problem
has emerged — a barrier of shortsighted self-interest to fence in
the Palestinian Muslims in the Occupied Territories that will
undoubtedly fuel their hatred, frustration and maniac retribution
against Israeli Jews. In other words, the war on terror and the war
on the war on terror rage on!

But in the war that really matters, the one against the root
cause of all of this — the abysmal mutual ignorance between the
world's billion-plus Muslims and the rest of us in the non-Muslim
world — hardly a shot, friendly or otherwise, has been fired.

In this long-time observer's view, only when both sides are
actively engaged in this sort of war, a necessary and desirable war,
will the world begin to be at real ease and enjoy proper peace.
Our mutual ignorance is gargantuan, it is inexcusable — but it is
remediable. This next war should be a verbal war, an unholy war,
an anti-jihad between people on the two sides of the world's
religious divide.

As things stand, religion, no matter whose religion it is —
Christian, Jew, Muslim or Calathumpian — has a lot to answer
for. It's time we stopped pulling our punches with religion and
recognised that it's caused at least as much strife and human
suffering as it's prevented.

Over the last two decades and more, as a journalist I've worked
and travelled in more than a dozen Islamic countries. My contacts
and associates in the Arab-Muslim world in particular are a
virtual human kaleidoscope of Islam — from camel-herders in the
Emirate of Abu Dhabi, Bedouin in the deserts of Wadi Rum in
southern Jordan and former slaves from Timbuktu to Gulf oil
sheikhs, religious mullahs in Iran, Saddam-serving Iraqi fighters,

Islamic scholars, senior Arab politicians, diplomats, sportscar-driving Muslim zealots in Dubai and even Yasser Arafat. On the basis of this regular and varied contact, I would argue that more than 99.99 per cent of Muslims are not, repeat not, terrorists.

The vast majority of Muslims, committed moderates, do not spend their days plotting how to fly planes into New York skyscrapers or bring the United States to its knees. Like the rest of us, they are stumbling forward trying to find a way through life. But even moderate Muslims bear a bitter resentment, often spilling over into studied (as distinct from violent) hatred towards what they regard as the arrogance and cultural imperialism of the West, the United States in particular. If we ignore this antipathy and its reasons, moderate Muslims will never be able to join us in ridding the world of Islamic extremism — and with it the militaristic extremism it provokes in so-called God-fearing Westerners, including their leaders. Have you ever heard the leaders of the Coalition of the Willing ask what actually drives the minuscule minority of Islamic terrorists to do what they do? Sorry, simplistically calling up the tired old 'good versus evil' line just doesn't work! There are good and evil believers on both sides. Information and understanding we need, not blind prejudice and claims to a one true faith. Smart thinking will eventually stop more terrorists than smart bombs will.

As is the case in the Western and non-Muslim worlds, there are Arab-Muslim governments that are incompetent, undemocratic, corrupt, duplicitous; some are violent and dangerous. But we in the West might get further by attempting at least to talk them around, not by berating and haranguing them jingoistically about how superior our Western non-Muslim values are. Bombing them into some sort of questionable pseudo-democratic regime change will not remove their inherent flaws, injustices or their resentment. Coming to grips with our intrinsic cultural, historical and religious differences remains the only plausible approach to removing the mutual human ignorance between us. Until we do this, the 'eye-for-an-eye' killing, the distrust and the tension will continue. The so-called 'Roadmap to Peace' in the Middle East is merely the beginning of a much wider and deeper journey, not the end.

After returning from a refresher trip to the Gulf, reconvinced that really understanding and accepting Islam was the absolute prerequisite to dealing with Muslims, let alone democratising them, the author came across the following exchange in the *Australian Financial Review* (10–11 May 2003) between two longstanding friends, journalist Lyndal Crisp and Sydney-based historian, writer and Catholic priest, Edmund Campion. Just a little leadingly, Lyndal asked Ed if he thought that religion was dying.

Ed replied, 'That's obvious. Religion is shrinking. Many of us haven't really taken this into account. In many ways we're whistling in the wind. On the other hand, an objective observer would have to point to the enormous growing strength of Islam. If the nineteenth century was the century of the British Empire and the twentieth century was the American century, then it's a fair bet the twenty-first century will be the century of Islam. It's a religion with enormous wells of compassion in it — despite the bad press it gets in this country.'

PART ONE

ABDALLAH'S CRASH COURSE IN ISLAM

'From Riyadh to the UN headquarters in New York and Jakarta, there is a growing awareness that militant Islamism is the enemy of established societies — Western and Muslim alike. By widening the battlefront, militant Islamists may have unintentionally created a united front opposed to them.'

Gerard Henderson

The Five Pillars of Islam — and Beyond

Mosques can be overpoweringly imposing and beautiful things. They can be warm. They can be purely functional. They can be big. They can be small. They can be right in your face or tucked away almost shyly, somewhere insignificant. They can be ornate and architecturally spectacular. They can be design-specific or extremely rudimentary. They can be elaborate and artistic; they can be painfully plain. They are built with an astounding array of materials — quarried coral, gypsum, stone slabs, boulders, imported marble, mud, wood and, in the oases, even palm fronds. Almost without exception, they have at least one dome and at least one minaret. But the sky is the limit, depending on the wealth of a community or its benefactors. Unless a mosque is a gift from the government or from a loaded sheikh with excess dirhams or rials, often the case in the oil-wealthy Gulf, it's usually funded and maintained by the locals. But from the Gulf to Casablanca, from Amman to Surabaya, wherever there are Muslims a mosque is never far away.

The Grand Mosque in Muscat, the thoroughly enchanting capital of Oman, is mind-bending. It is no exaggeration to hail it as one of the finest constructions you are ever likely to see. In the author's experienced but architecturally challenged view, it is up there with the Taj Mahal in India and the Duomo in Florence.

There's a lot of it and probably justice cannot be done to it in less than a day.

It was built at the spare-no-expense behest of Sultan Qaboos bin-Said, the Supreme Ruler of Oman who came to power thirty years ago after overthrowing his father in a bloodless palace coup. Qaboos still holds ultimate power in Oman, but if emerging Omani Muslim democrats have their way, Muscat's new and incredibly beautiful mosque — Qaboos' monument to himself — could turn out to be all he is remembered for. But the new mosque could also become a home for the 'new Islam'.

The mosque still under construction outside Abu Dhabi is colossal, multi-domed and many-minaretted. Completed, it will be the biggest in the world. By the starkest of contrasts, the 'traveller's rest' mosque my friend Hassan prayed at off the highway between Abu Dhabi and Dubai was attached to a service station. Just how serviceable can the Muslim faith get? 'Leave the car with me, sir. I'll fill her up and check your oil and water, while you grab a quick prayer.' Islam is truly as much a way of life as it is a religion. In between these extremes is Saeed Marijibe's (we will meet him in Part Five) friendly little community mosque, built by his family for their quiet Omani neighbourhood in middle-class suburban Muscat.

In Dubai there's a very special mosque, one that reaches out to non-Muslims. Abdallah al Serkel, the brain behind Dubai's Open Mosque, is a veritable font of information about his religion and its culture — two things he says are inseparable. We had a number of absorbing conversations during the author's time in the UAE, including one at the mosque as he was attempting to demystify Islam for a bunch of wide-eyed expats and Western tourists.

The mosque is an easy stroll from the Open Beach, a strip of Gulf coast popular with expats, Muslim travellers, Western holiday-makers, and non-Muslim Arabs from the region. The dichotomy of Dubai was evident during several walks the author took at the Open Beach: the elegant minarets of the mosque's towers in the background, bikini-clad sunbathers in the foreground. If the mosque's ambitious Open Doors, Open Minds project takes off, it could well become the portal to the Islam of the future — a far less closed and religiously exclusive Islam.

Abdallah emphasised that he was not a Muslim scholar or anything like that, but a volunteer worker at the mosque. He's also a highly successful businessman. Our chat turned into what I think of as Abdallah's Crash Course in Islam. Read, learn and enjoy!

ABDALLAH AL SERKEL:
The Brain Behind Dubai's Open Mosque

George Negus: What does this loaded word 'Islam' actually mean?

Abdallah: Let me start with how the people from this part of the world think and where that thinking comes from. Islam is a word, in Arabic, which means 'surrender.' If you are a Muslim, you have surrendered, handed over your way of life. You have complied with the 'do's and the don'ts' in God's teachings.

GN: Belief in God is the basis of it all, isn't it?

A: Islam also means oneness, believing in one God, the oneness of God, the one and only beloved God. In general, whoever believes in the oneness of God — you can call him Allah, God, by whatever name you like — you are a Muslim. Muslims believe that what will save you on Judgement Day is believing in the one and only Creator.

GN: The Five Pillars of Islam — what would you call them?

A: Let's start with the *shahadah*, the declaration of faith. When in a person's heart they reach the conclusion that there is one Creator, that's the first step. You don't have to stand in the main square in the city of Dubai or Abu Dhabi or anywhere else and shout in front of everyone: 'I have reached this conclusion.' That is not the way of Islam. Islam is something that comes to your heart and then you plan your life on it.

GN: And the Second Pillar?

A: The Second Pillar of Islam is prayer, *salat*. Muslims pray five times a day, starting before sunrise, the time we call dawn. About an hour and a half before the first signs of light appear on the horizon, that's the dawn. That's the time when, every day, people pray their first prayer. The second prayer is the noon prayer, which at this time of the year is around 12.15. You can pray this prayer anytime after that time. You have a period of about three hours until 3:30.

GN: So you don't panic and go into a flat spin when you hear the Call to Prayer?

A: No. If you're at work or if you have a business, many places have their own prayer rooms and you can just finish whatever you have to do. If you're a doctor, you don't drop your tools in your patient's stomach and go to prayer!

You can wait until you've finished and then go to the prayer room. The 3.30 or 3.45 prayer depends on the time of the year. That's the optimal prayer time and it has a limit also, until sunset, again a period of two-and-a-half to three hours. The sunset prayer is the fourth prayer. That has a limit of about thirty minutes, because that's when it's getting dark. We should pray while it's half dark, half light. The last prayer is the night prayer and at this time of the year, that's around 8.00 or 8.30. Anytime before dawn, you can pray the night prayer. You don't have to rush once you hear the Call to Prayer. But you do get a reward if you walk to the mosque or if you pray on time.

GN: Given that Islamic society is tax-free, what's the Third Pillar about? Is it a sort of tax substitute?

A: In a way. The Third Pillar, called *zakat*, is the purifying of your money. It's something you have to do once a year, every year, at a set time. If twelve months have passed on the value of your property, your capital, your assets, then you're required to take out $2^1/2$ per cent of the total money that you own and pay it to people in need. There are eight categories specified that cover the needy side of the community, starting with your closest relatives, then your closest neighbours and so on.

GN: The Fourth Pillar — your annual fast? Most non-Muslims are really intrigued by that idea.

A: We're talking here about the month of Ramadan when Muslims fast from dawn until sunset. We don't drink or eat during that period. We don't do 'the husband and wife thing' during the daytime. You would understand what I mean? Who should fast and who shouldn't? Is it compulsory? Well, fasting is for those who are healthy and can normally fast between dawn and sunset.

GN: Any exceptions?

A: Women who are pregnant and women who are breastfeeding don't have to fast. If you have some kind of illness, any kind of illness or surgery, you don't have to fast. But you have to make it up later. With diabetes, for example, you don't have to fast at all if it could seriously damage your health. If you're travelling, you don't have to fast, but again you have to make it up some other time. Because we follow the lunar calendar, Ramadan might come in the middle of summer when it's very hot, so some Islamic scholars have said construction workers and people like that shouldn't fast on those hot summer days. So they have to make the fast some other time.

GN: What about the once-in-a-lifetime Hajj? Is that the ultimate Islamic commitment?

A: The Hajj is the Fifth Pillar — the pilgrimage to Mecca. I get many questions: why Mecca? Why not Pakistan? Why not Jerusalem? Why not anywhere else? This actually has to do with the first man and woman — Adam and Eve, as you call them. We all know that the first astronaut in the history of mankind was Adam. As Muslims believe, when Adam and his wife Eve were sent by God from Heaven down on Earth, they landed in a place called Mecca on a mountain called, in Arabic, *Arafat*, or the mountain of mercy. So that's why Muslims gather there for a whole day, once a year. At least once in your lifetime, as you say, a Muslim — he or she — must visit Mecca and go through the pilgrimage, which is actually the story of the great men and women, the prophets — Abraham, his son Ishmael and his second wife, Haja, the mother of Prophet Ishmael.

GN: Abdallah, what do Muslims think of other religions? Dismissive? Tolerant? Or what?

A: God said in the Qur'an: 'We have honoured the sons of Adam.' He didn't say we have honoured a Muslim. He didn't say we have honoured a Jew or a Christian. He said we have honoured mankind.

GN: The Prophet was to all intents and purposes a normal man?

A: Prophet Muhammed was born, raised and lived normally until he was forty years old when the Qur'an was revealed to him by the angel Gabriel in the mountains near Mecca. Then he started preaching to his people, telling them to neglect whatever was making them slide, to get them closer to the higher principles, to link them with their Creator, and to look forward to the next life. The authorities of the day objected to him and tried to control his movements. So he moved with his followers to a city called Medina near Mecca. His first rule was that everyone living in Medina was a citizen of the new government. He did not specify Muslims only. There were Christians. There were the Jews. There were non-believers and there were the Muslims. They were all citizens. They had their duties and they had to comply with the rules of the new government.

GN: Do you think non-Muslims understand what you Muslims and your religion are about?

A: When Islam ruled in many parts of the world, there were lots of misconceptions. But, today and in the future, we always should look for the common ground where different cultures and religions meet so we can solve our problems. There are good and there are bad Muslims. I always say the wrong do not wear a turban or a cowboy hat. They could be in any culture, any religion. That does not mean that a certain religion is all wrong or that all of its members think the same way.

GN: So other religions are OK?

A: In the religion of Islam, we emphasise freedom of religion — especially for people who are sharing the life and living under Muslim rule. The Verse says that there should be no compulsion of religion for non-Muslims or anyone sharing life with Muslims. I am taking this from the teachings and the books of the Muslim religion. Non-Muslims can have freedom of speech, freedom of religion, freedom to own property, freedom to build their own worship places. They have the right to be treated kindly and nicely. Their poor have the right to a share of the charity and donations, even *zakat*, one of the Five Pillars of Islam. They have a share in it. They have the right to be a neighbour with a Muslim.

GN: So you would say there are misconceptions about Islam?

A: There are a lot of these misconceptions, not just among non-Muslims but also among Muslims themselves. Many Muslims don't understand how we should behave with others. It's part of the ignorance that the Muslims have — nowadays, it's probably equal with the ignorance of non-Muslims. We all share ignorance. We share selfishness and we share the greediness. We don't give time to understand each other.

Touché Abdallah.

PART TWO

MUSLIMS LOVE THEIR CHILDREN TOO!

Jordan

Jordan is a delightful place to visit, made more so by its
truly friendly people, who continually call out to you,
'Welcome in Jordan' — and they really mean it!

Lonely Planet

Jordan: The Land of the Friendly Arabs

If you've been to more than one of them, you'll know what I mean when I say there are Arab countries and there are Arab countries. Even Arabs themselves will agree that some of the places they call home are nothing to write home about. The stereotypical view is that more often than not they're overcrowded, dirty, oppressive and unwelcoming. In some cases, this is not entirely inaccurate. But even when they do fit the classically negative Western stereotype, you'd have to be a very ordinary traveller not to find them interesting, even alluring. Like all places worth going out of your way to get to, the very fact that they're different — even if negatively so — is what makes them appealing. It's this difference, in all its forms in the idiosyncratic and distinctive Islamic world, that this book celebrates.

If you're looking for a pleasurable place to begin a discovery tour of Islam and its inhabitants, you probably can't go past the regally named Hashemite Kingdom of Jordan. You'd have to say that it's had some fairly bad press of late related to so-called 'honour killings', a reprehensible form of premeditated domestic violence that arguably stems far more from barbaric Bedouin tradition than from the Islamic faith. But most Jordanians I've had contact with over recent years either deplore or, given the opportunity, would deplore this despicable minority practice. And Jordan — wedged gingerly between Israel and the Occupied Territories and Egypt, Saudi Arabia, Iraq and Syria — is known with good reason as 'the land of the friendly Arabs'. In the main, the inhabitants are an identifiably amiable people and have remained so over decades of conflict and tension that have characterised the dangerously brittle relationship between the Arab nations, Israel and parts of the West. Usually the Jordanians have played a clever balancing game in one of the trickier geopolitical situations of the world. For this reason alone you have to admire them. They don't appear to fear; they don't appear to loathe; they have always worked to overcome their ignorance of the non-Arab world — and wish we would reciprocate. Under the late King Hussein, they even signed a peace treaty of sorts with Israel, the Arabs' sworn enemy across the not so mighty River Jordan.

The level of mutual ignorance throughout the world being what it is, the reaction of most Westerners on their first contact with Muslims, of whatever nationality, is usually cautious. Clearly someone — probably his parents — must have forgotten to tell this to Serge, our terrifyingly normal but insatiably inquisitive son, then ten years old. When he met his first Muslims on their home turf in Jordan, not only was he unfazed but he immediately took to the people themselves and their mysterious Muslim ways.

His first association was with Khalil, an uncomplicated Jordanian friend who drove us from Amman's Queen Alia Airport across the Eastern Valley and up on to the plateau to the capital. Later he was to take us to other unforgettable places in his less than extensive country. Khalil is the classic helpful, good-natured Jordanian of the guidebooks. He and I worked together on my earlier journalistic stays. As we had done, he and Serge became instant mates.

Serge's second encounter of the Jordanian-Muslim kind was quite different in terms of the people involved. Our hosts, Ranya Khadri and her husband Ardi, were well-educated, financially comfortable middle-class professionals. Ranya is a super-smart media 'fixer' with a law degree; Ardi is a quietly proficient private-hospital executive manager. You could describe the Khadris as bicultural: with their two delightful kids, they are steadfastly Muslim yet quite westernised.

Most of the other Muslims Serge met in Amman were people in shops, on the street, in restaurants, in the bazaar, at the pharmacy, the hairdresser's or the ATM; wherever people were he took to them easily. Given Amman's infectious Arab hustle and bustle, he also instantly liked the capital, with its million-plus perpetually busy inhabitants. Sure, he couldn't help but notice that some of them, the women in particular, were different. They dressed differently, often in long dresses that completely covered their arms and legs, with scarves that covered their hair. Some even wore veils over their faces. They spoke what was to him a strange language. They ate mainly from roadside stalls rather than restaurants and mostly shopped in the souk, the city market, not in supermarkets or normal shops. They took buses rather than driving cars. And early on he noticed many of them trudging along the side of the road like hitch-hikers, though they didn't seem to be after a lift.

We hoped he was enjoying the everyday differences, the ordinary people doing much the same as anyone in Australia but not doing it in exactly the same way — not so much a cultural divide, more a narrow cultural cleft. In Amman's frenzied market district with its bustling crowds, its hawkers and its never-take-no-for-an-answer merchants flogging gold, silver, jewellery, rugs, cheap clothes, shoes, handicrafts and live animals, he was agog.

But there were other, massively unfamiliar goings-on for him to handle as a non-Muslim youngster. Most of them, significantly, had to do with religion. At certain times of the Jordanian day, weird high voices, half-singing, half-caterwauling, came from those exotic spires he had noticed everywhere in the city. We'd already told him the 'spires' were minarets and the buildings they were on were mosques. And he learned that wherever they happen to be, Muslims are called to prayer five times every day. They pray to Allah, their name for God. Sometimes, immediately after the prayer calls, he noticed men kneeling, often bent forward, prostrate on small colourful mats. They all seemed to be facing in the same direction — towards Mecca he was told, not that Serge, even after a crash course in Middle Eastern geography, knew with any certainty where Mecca was.

None of this strangeness appeared to bother him. Indeed, the more glaring the differences the more they seemed to captivate him. The fact that they were Muslims was far less significant than the fact that their daily lives as a people, Islam-dominated, were so different.

The Valley of the Moon

It was a clear, crisp spring morning in late March when Kirsty, my journalist–photographer partner, the constantly curious Serge and I set off from Amman in the pre-dawn light. With those wonderful early morning sounds of a city growing louder around us, we wound our way through modest rectangular homes clinging to the nineteen hills of the capital. We were headed down Jordan's ancient King's Highway. One of the most historic and scenic routes in the world, these days it's a sealed road, making for a more comfortable journey than it offered in the old days of camel and caravanserai. We could have taken the much newer and quicker Desert Highway to the west along the Dead Sea shore, but we wanted a more leisurely adventure.

We had two exciting Jordanian destinations in mind, both in the parched stony desert down south on the route to Aqaba and the Red Sea. One was the legendary Lost City of Petra, the 'rose-red city half as old as Time', as the poem has it. Petra, which I'd visited before, is an unqualified 'must'. Second, and a little further south, was Wadi Rum. Wadi Rum! How could you resist a magic name like Wadi Rum? Inveterate traveller or otherwise, you could not fail to go there if you were anywhere in the region. Wadi Rum is the epitome of the stark, arid beauty that characterises the entire Arab peninsula.

But what, you must be asking by now, is a wadi? It is an ages-old dry riverbed. They're everywhere in predominantly desertified Jordan. But having wandered about the vast pointed and domed sandstone hills on two earlier occasions, let me tell you that Wadi Rum is the wadi to beat all wadis! It also happens to be one of the best places to come to grips with any anti-Muslim fears or phobia lurking in you. Spend a bit of time with Wadi Rum's laid-back Muslim inhabitants and you won't be able to imagine them giving much serious thought to terrorism — other than reading about it or seeing it somewhere on cable TV.

But where Wadi Rum's renowned 'stark, arid beauty' is concerned, don't just take my word for it. Many who know about these things — admittedly most of them Arabs — will tell you that Wadi Rum is the most spectacular desert landscape you're ever likely to see, not just in the Middle East but anywhere on the globe. 'Unsurpassable scenic grandeur' is not putting it too high. And possibly more importantly, at least at the human level, it is also home to most of Jordan's enduring 40 000-odd nomadic Bedouin, the region's intriguing Muslim desert folk.

The locals don't call Wadi Rum the Valley of the Moon for nothing. It's more like the surface of some remote celestial body than part of our own planet. Indeed, someone has suggested that the combination of its immensity, its colour and its awesome shapes creates a setting that is almost supernatural. Wadi Rum thumps both the mind and the eye with its massive maze of cream, tan and rust-coloured granite and sandstone almost devoid of vegetation as it rises from the desert of southern Jordan. At daybreak it's mind-blowing. Known as jebels, sheer columns and huge mesa-like curiosities thrust themselves dramatically thousands of metres from the desert floor like walls or waves of unbroken rock. 'Built sectionally, in crags like gigantic buildings along two sides of their street,' is how T. E. Lawrence saw them. Yes, *that* T. E. Lawrence — the 'Lawrence of Arabia' captured so brilliantly on celluloid by Peter O'Toole.

In his much-read, revered and even rubbished account of the Arab Revolt, *Seven Pillars of Wisdom*, Lawrence recalls that his little party of men 'grew self-conscious and fell dead quiet, afraid and ashamed to flaunt its smallness in the presence of these stupendous hills'. Small is certainly how we three felt when we first set eyes on the jebels of Wadi Rum. Small and insignificant — except our Serge. Straight away, he wanted to get up there among their precipices, down their narrow alleys, into their nests of domes and gaze in awe at their high caverns. He wanted to be up close and personal with these amazing formations and to explore them. 'Landscapes in childhood's dream were so vast and silent,' was the way the literary Lawrence put it. Confronted by them, you knew he was right.

This is the area where the desert scenes in *Lawrence of Arabia*, David Lean's epic movie, were filmed. The 'Seven Pillars of Wisdom' of Lawrence's equally heroic book are said to be a rhetorical reference to the first seven jebels, or hills, that come into view as you turn east off the King's Highway, after coming from Amman, and head across the scrubby sand towards the western entrance to the wadi.

Bedding Down with the Bedouin

About thirty Bedouin families, together with sundry camels and dogs, reside in the dusty local village of Rumm, which scores a second 'm' for effect. All up, there are some 4000 Bedouin throughout the Wadi Rum area as a whole. Aptly-rated for real travellers, the 'half star' Government Rest House at Rumm offers tourist information, a café-cum-restaurant, a campsite and al fresco rooftop accommodation. Since my last visit a few more less-than-salubrious stores, *dhokans* in Arabic, had bobbed up in ramshackle Rumm selling rudimentary budget-traveller supplies — local pitta bread, canned food, dried fruit and the like, with the odd bit of desert craft the only other obvious sign of commerce. If you're one of those touristic anti-heroes or an ageless back-packer, Rumm is your kind of place.

The uniformed constabulary are a bona fide local feature. In their heyday the men of the legendary Desert Patrol (DP) were colourful and camel-mounted. But these days they seem to do little more than hang around their base at the small fort on the outskirts of town. Why is it, you wonder, that relics of bygone colonial officialdom always seem to have those meticulously white-painted rocks at their boom-gate entrances and lining their gravel driveways? A sign, maybe, of too little to do now that their glorious past has, well, passed.

In that more glorious past, the DP patrolled Jordan's sparsely populated eastern borders for smugglers and drugs. They also kept watch on any toey, independently minded tribes in Jordan's desolate south. Now, though, they don't do a huge amount of patrolling, preferring instead to show off for tourists. Four-wheel-drive vehicles fitted with machine-guns have replaced the trusty camels and basic rifles, daggers and bandoliers. The DP men mightn't really make it as swashbuckling movie extras these days, but for a few dinar they'll dust off the old gear and their old swagger, treat you to a glass of black cardamom-flavoured coffee or very sweet tea brewed over an open fire in the outdoor officers' mess and tell tall tales about their constabulary exploits out in the wadi. They'll pose with their stand-about camels and, if you're unlucky or stupid enough, even take your photo after hoisting you up on board the uncomfortable hump of one of those unfriendly buggers — after, not before, it had crankily come down from its great height and spreadeagled its spindly pins at the DP officer's equally cranky command.

As fundamental as it is to Arab-Muslim life generally, there may well be something lyrical about the nomadic desert life, but it can also be a pretty rugged one. When we were there in 2000, the Bedouin families in Rumm were not actually living in the government houses but in their traditional camp tents — outside the houses. Centuries-old habits can die extremely hard. Interestingly, they were using the rudimentary houses for storage and as feed sheds for their most prized of possessions — their slobbering, grunting, obnoxiously nasty camels. Camels, of course, are always slobbering, grunting, obnoxiously nasty characters whether you're in Rumm or any other place on Earth that keeps, uses or tolerates them. Even Serge, an unquenchable animal-lover, couldn't find much to love about the proverbial 'ships of the desert'. Can't imagine why!

But what he did warm to were their owners, including Abdullah, one of the raffish young town blokes Khalil introduced us to. At a price, naturally, but not an outrageous one, Abdullah offered to take us in his Toyota ute out into the wadi. Toyota utes, by the way, are rapidly replacing the humped dromedary as the first choice for transport in Middle Eastern desert lands. 'I can take you to some special spots I know,' he said, making it sound as though there was something exclusive about his offer, though we knew there wasn't. They mightn't have been all that exclusive but they were certainly worth the trouble of a sweaty few hours bumping about in Abdullah's four-wheel-drive in the dry wilds.

It was mid-afternoon as we headed east, out into the wadi, our slightly banged-up ute dragging itself through the sandy, almost treacherously rutted wheel tracks. On our left, the mighty east face of the Jebel Rum rose wall-like. Serge and I were in the back with the bags, his mum up front with Abdullah. While we could still make out the shapes of the modest buildings of Rumm whenever we looked behind us, we didn't feel isolated by the desert's vastness and heat. But as soon as we turned north at a Y intersection and lost sight of Rumm and habitation, we began to feel really 'out there'.

About forty minutes out of town we left the truck and were soon clambering excitedly up cool, narrow jebel canyons. Every few metres or so, it seemed, there were old scratched drawings, scrawled inscriptions and small stone enclosures to ponder. Anything between 1500 and 3000 years old, they were put there by the Nabataean and Thamudic peoples, among the original nomads of the region. Battered by time and the elements, there are also Nabataean ruins throughout the wadi. One of them boasts scrappy bits of what was once obviously a splendid temple, dedicated, Abdullah told us, to Allat, the revered goddess par excellence. Not difficult to see that word, Allat, as the feminine of Allah? Allat was 'the treasured one', the principal goddess of the North Arabian nomads. It must have been the combined allure of Allat's temple and the fresh water from perpetual springs in the neighbourhood that attracted the original nomads to out-of-the-way spots like the Wadi Rum.

Without getting too carried away, it really did feel as if we were walking with antiquity — because we were. The

Nabataeans were an ingenious bunch and we would hear about their ingenuity again in a few days' time as we were gaping incredulously at their old capital, Petra. The lost city carved out of the rocky jebels is only a couple of hours north of Wadi Rum.

A couple of hours later, with Serge still asking those tricky questions we usually couldn't answer and the sun getting closer to the jebel tops, we reached our overnight destination. We weren't sure about the veracity of Abdullah's promise to take us to a typical Bedouin family encampment where we could stay overnight. But there it suddenly was, ahead of us, a cluster of interconnected black tents called *beit sha'ar* — literally 'house of hair' — their durable, naturally weatherproof fabric handwoven from black goat's hair.

They are not at all like Western tents. They are much longer and lower than the usual holiday tent back home and, as we were soon to discover, have only just enough headspace for you to stand up in. There's always a hefty central pole to support what is a pretty large, heavy cover; sometimes a number of poles if the owners are wealthy enough to afford more than one. Serge couldn't wait to explore his desert accommodation — no running water, no electricity, no bathroom or toilet. But it had to be at least seven stars. Why? We were about to bed down with the Bedouin!

When you bother to look up their Arabic origins, you find that the word *bedu* means what you probably expected it would, nomad, and similarly *bedouin* refers to desert-dwellers. No one knows exactly how many of them are still around these days. Possibly as many as several hundred thousand are scattered throughout the entire Arab region; maybe forty thousand of them are in southern Jordan. But by 2002 only a few could be described as real nomads living 'the old way' — moving every few months from spot to spot, re-erecting their *beit ash-sha'ar* each time, tediously grazing their precious herds of goats, sheep and camels until the measly fodder was gone, and then moving on.

It's a tough, dry, repetitive but paradoxically unsettled existence. But out here in the wadis, the location is 'to die for' and the rent zilch. Nevertheless, many Bedouin have given the nomad thing away and opted for either town or city life; others have taken to tilling whatever fertile soil they stumble across to grow crops. They see this as an easier alternative to herding their animals around the wadis on the perennial fodder-hunt. I reckon it would have to be a toss-up. A lot of the time, these Bedouin camps are occupied by just one family, as ours was at Khasm Mizmar. But at others, often there would be three or four families, usually related; more like tribes within a tribe.

Abdullah went off to fix things with the family — or at least with the women of the family, who were the only ones at home in their marvellous 'house of hair' when we arrived in the late afternoon. The father had gone to Rumm in his Toyota four-wheel-drive, possibly with the family's private 'ship of the desert' uncomfortably crammed into the back of the ute. Arabs always want others to know when they are the proud owners of stock, particularly of the dromedary variety. The old man's sons, we gathered, were also away from home, out on the wadi shepherding the goats.

The Muslim Curtain

The men being away from the camp was a bonus for us. It meant that Mrs Bedouin and her three daughters — aged between sixteen and the late twenties, we figured — were a lot bolder in dealing with their strange guests than they might otherwise have been.

We unpacked our knapsacks from the back of the ute and were escorted by Abdullah into the men's section of the tent, also the public area for entertaining guests and travellers. For the moment, the four women seemed to be hiding away in the *haram*. The *haram* is the forbidden area where strangers — people like ourselves — are not permitted. If you're thinking, as you well might be, that the Arab word *haram* is very like the word 'harem' then you're right. It has the same derivation and connotation, but different spelling.

The 'Muslim Curtain' is a very different one from either of those other great cultural divides, the Iron and Bamboo Curtains. But it has pretty much the same effect. The Bedouin tent-home is basically cordoned off into two parts, usually by an elaborately patterned curtain, the *sahah*, or by a beautifully handcrafted rug. One section is the men's domain, the *al-shigg*, and the other is the women's. Interestingly, the 'good side' of the patterned divider — the side where you don't see all the scraggy knots in the weave and the like — always faces the men's section. The women get the scraggy side. You can read into that what you will.

But this deliberate gender-divider down the middle of every Bedouin tent does not, in fact, cut Bedouin women off from much at all; arguably quite the opposite. Often it places them in a position of far greater knowledge and influence in male-dominated family affairs than their physical separation might have you believe.

Indeed, as you learn if you've travelled a bit in this part of the world, Muslim women being present but apart, pretty much not seen and not heard, does not mean they are or even see themselves as second-class citizens. Anything but! In actual fact, the whole issue of the role of women in Muslim society is far more complicated than the widespread image of oppression and subjugation would suggest. That is not to say that the treatment of Islamic women by their men is acceptable — but it does have its explanations, as unpalatable as those explanations might be.

Despite his ostensibly alien surroundings, the sheer fun of being with people who 'camp out' daily enchanted Serge. Being his ingenuously curious self, the questions flowed — and not just ferociously practical ones about how they got their tent together in the first place. He got straight down to the differences between them and us. Like, why does there have to be a special area for the women? Who says so? Do they mind being on the other side of the curtain? Are they allowed to talk to us? Why are we in the men's section? You're a woman, Mama. Why aren't you across the other side of the curtain with the Bedouin ladies? Some of the questions were tricky, but that last one was easy enough to answer. Because she's not a Muslim, buddy, and they are!

For several hours until the father got home later that balmy desert evening, the girls talked excitedly to each other and to their mother as they prepared food for us, giggling delightedly at the idea of guests in their home. Soon they popped their heads over the dividing rug and the eldest occasionally ventured onto our side for some very stumbling attempts at conversation. The mish-mash of Arabic and English conversation might have been pretty ordinary, but the desire for communication was palpable. And as the evening wore on, it became even more of a learning experience.

After a brilliant pink dusk, the shadows from the towering jebels in our Wadi Rum backyard lengthened and the dark desert night closed in. As it did, a thought occurred there in the quiet remoteness. Could the curtain between Bedouin men and women symbolise a much wider and higher curtain between Muslims and non-Muslims? The curtain is there, but how hard have we worked to find a way around it or to see over it? In their own way Bedouin women have done this.

Well, we certainly ate pretty well that evening — albeit just a tinge tentatively. The mind was definitely willing, but the stomach was a little weak. Besides, the cooking took place on the women's side of the curtain and we had no real idea of matters of health and hygiene. There was a fire, of course, but other than that the preparation of the food — let alone its age or the last time, if ever, it had seen a refrigerator — was a mystery. Best we didn't know. What we did know was that we were hungry and none of our local knowledge suggested that the Bedouin made a habit of sending their foreign guests home with food poisoning! After we'd settled in on our side of the curtain on the well-worn floor rugs, almost certainly woven at one of the family's campsites somewhere in the surrounding wadis, from the other side the girls, heads covered and giggling ever so cutely, delivered our flat pitta bread, pan-roasted chicken and saffron rice with sultanas on large wooden platters used both for serving and eating. No cutlery. In most Arab places, hands, as most know, are the preferred culinary tools. More later about the myths and facts about which hand Muslims use for what human activity, but not while we're eating — or are on the subject of food!

You quickly discover in moving among them on their own turf that hospitality is a matter of honour with Arab-Muslims. It's at the heart of their everyday domestic culture. As Rosalyn Maqsood, a convert to Islam who's travelled widely in the region puts it, desert code and the precepts of Islam demand that if a stranger cannot expect to be 'fed and watered and granted rest, lodging and protection', then the whole Bedouin group at that camp is shamed. It's not quite as big-hearted and charitable as Samis and Inuits offering their wives as cuddly eiderdown substitutes on freezing Arctic nights, but, as we say in the West, never look a gift horse in the mouth.

On a Mat and a Prayer

Every Sunday morning in so-called Christendom — weather or pressing family, social or sporting commitments permitting — devout Christians go to church. Devout Jews in Jerusalem go to the Wailing Wall daily; if they don't live in the Holy Land, they go to the synagogue. Five times a day, every day, devout Muslims kneel on a mat and pray. Like nominal, less devout Christians and Jews who don't necessarily go to church on Sundays or to the synagogue, nominal, less devout Muslims don't necessarily pray five times a day. But for most Muslims, praying every day is one of the Five Pillars that literally and metaphorically 'prop up' their Islamic faith, and they're expected to pray before sunrise, just after noon, in the late afternoon, immediately after sunset and finally at night. *Salat*, it's called.

Shortly before dawn, deep in the wadi, we stirred in our borrowed camp beds, rubbed our eyes and tried to make out the astonishing shapes and masses of our arid back yard. As we ventured out through the tent flaps the first thing that came into focus was a couple of kneeling figures a hundred metres or so from the camp. Out here in the desert of southern Jordan we were seeing for ourselves from a respectful distance the private pre-sunrise prayer. Intruding any closer would probably have been sacrilegious — or at least insensitive if not rude — a bit like bursting into the local Methodist Church in the middle of the congregation reciting the Lord's Prayer or Psalm 23. Perched on a rocky hump away from the tents, our Bedouin hosts praying in their breathtaking desert environment, religion-related thoughts streamed into the head.

What the heck is prayer anyway? Do you have to be religious to pray? Whether they are Muslim, Catholic, Baptist or Calabloody-thumpian why, in fact, *do* people pray? What are they actually doing when they pray? Do they believe that someone is listening to their prayers or even hearing them? If they pray out loud, are they really just thinking out loud? If they don't pray out loud, are they merely thinking — maybe more precisely and pointedly than they normally do — but merely thinking? If this is what prayer is, what do they think about when they are 'prayer-thinking'? Do they ponder the real meaning of life and death, the difference between good and evil — or what?

Do Muslims, Jews and Christians ask the same things when they pray? When Muslims pray to Allah, Christians to Jesus as the son of God and Jews to the Old Testament God, are they praying to the same or different deities? In the Muslim context in which we found ourselves, do Muslim prayers have more or less chance of being answered than Christian or Jewish ones?

The early Greek Christians apparently saw praying as some sort of psychosomatic activity. The thesaurus button of your laptop will tell you instantly that 'mental' and 'emotional' are both synonyms for 'psychosomatic'. As any dictionary will tell you, common usage of the words 'mental' and 'emotional' makes them almost contradictions in behavioural terms!

Other students of prayer see praying as getting a 'virtual' image of God. But wouldn't forming a mental image of God while you're praying almost certainly mean that you've missed the whole point of God as a spiritual rather than temporal Being? As with trance-like yoga, some early Christian students of prayer talked of 'stripping their souls naked'. They reckoned that prayer demanded the total shedding of thought. On the other hand, the good old Catholics take an entirely contrary tack. They would have us believe that their version of God can only be reached not after emotional carry-on, but after great effort by the mind. Sounds a lot like heavy thinking, even mental gymnastics?

So what about Muslims? What are they up to when they pray? They certainly do it often, more often than most of the globe's religious adherents — with the possible exception of Buddhist monks and the Greek Orthodox recluses of Mount Athos. It's one of the rituals they claim transform their basic religious beliefs into reality. Regular prayer — like the other four pillars — is a constant reminder of a Muslim's duty to Allah. And Muslim believers pray, no matter where they are — indoors, outdoors, at home, work, school or play. If they live in decent-sized villages and towns or cities, they get a noisy nudge to kneel from the traditional Call to Prayer, *azan* in Arabic.

The kneeling couple in the distance had gone there in the silence of the desert to pray. It is different in the towns. I heard my first *azan* in, of all places, East Jerusalem, the Arab quarter of that religiously riven capital of the religiously riven nation of Israel.

Hearing it for the first time, out of the early morning blue, was an arresting, memorable experience. Eventually, the Call to Prayer becomes almost indelible, one of those special sensory responses you identify with a particular place, even people. In this case, the Call to Prayer, coming from the minaret of a nearby local mosque, will tell you like nothing else that you are in an Islamic country and among Muslims. It's just like the early morning pealing of the bells at any *chiesa* or *duomo*, that distinct sound that tells you, if you had any doubt, that you are in Italy.

As the Islamic explanation of the *azan* goes, Muhammed, Allah's earthly messenger, wasn't impressed by the call-signs of other religions. Bells, horns, whistles, tinkly things and drums were not his bag. Being Muhammed, with what he regarded as more or less his own private, direct line to Allah, he didn't need to be called to prayer. He just prayed and asked God for guidance. He reckoned he got it. In Medina, a neighbour told him of a dream in which he saw 'a man calling out phrases in a loud voice', telling people to come to prayer. It seems that was enough for an alert, down-to-earth character like Muhammed. He figured God had spoken to Muslims again, this time through the night-time reveries of his neighbour. As American Muslim convert and scholar Yahiya Emerick tells it, Muhammed then instructed the dreamer to pass the words he'd heard onto an African slave who had recently converted to Islam and happened to have a divine voice, just what the proverbial doctor ordered for a religious call to prayer. When he'd got the words right, Bilal, the slave, got himself to the top of Medina's tallest mosque minaret and let fly with them. They sound more fitting in Arabic than English, but the call is the same one you still hear five times a day everywhere in the Arab world. Will it be an international hit? Remains to be seen, but it certainly is already with more than a billion Muslims wherever they reside all over the world.

> God is greater, God is greater. God is greater, God is greater. I declare there is no god but God. I declare there is no god but God. I declare Muhammed is the Messenger of God. I declare Muhammed is the Messenger of God. Rush to prayer. Rush to prayer. Rush to success. Rush to success. God is greater, God is greater. There is no god but God.

The guy who gets the *azan* gig, the *muazzin*, apparently not a particularly special office or even a holy role, is about as notable as the bell-ringer at St Luke's C of E in Birmingham. But Muslims would be lost without him. Not surprisingly, only Muslim *males* get the call 'call', as it were. Having an agreeable voice and strong vocal cords are probably the sole qualifications. These days, loudspeakers make life easier for the *muazzin*, but can you imagine how tough it must have been when the old larynx was the only means of making yourself heard.

Yahiya Emerick, despite his personal bias in favour of anything Muslim, is spot on when he says no trip to an Islamic country is complete 'until you've been awakened in the early morning to the sounds of the *azan* floating over the landscape'.

Whose Truth is it Anyway?

Two disparate but strangely connected things occurred in mid-2003.

One, the debate about the link between Islam and terrorism was raging after the war in Iraq and two, in Australia, the word began to seep out, via various media outlets and scuttlebutt, that this work-in-progress was underway. With less than an inkling of what *The World from Islam* was on about, a number of ostensibly well-meaning folk made contact with the author to offer their views on Islam. Some were aggressively defensive of other religions, particularly Christianity. Others were aggressively offensive towards Islam.

Some Jewish folk offered reasonable, justifiable opinions from their Semitic perspective, but a number of evangelical Christians went so far as to add to my considerable library of books on religion. One of them, by an American, Reverend Don Davidson, was passed on by a sub-continental Christian convert. Reverend Davidson's openly anti-Islamic treatise asserted that Islam was an inherently violent religion. He quoted numerous verses from the Qur'an to back up his thesis.

As I read his selected quotes I could not help thinking of all that Old Testament stuff about biblical characters 'slewing' people with the jawbone of an ass. More pertinently, I found myself wondering how Christians — including the leaders of the

United States, the United Kingdom and Australia — found a way of defining what they called their 'just war' in Iraq?

It will come as no surprise to hear that the Qur'an — like those other reportedly holy books, the Bible and the Jewish Torah — is treated with what even the most irreverent cannot deny is due reverence. In Arab-Muslim countries, most Muslim families have one either wrapped in a protective fine cloth and kept out of harm's way high on a shelf or cupboard top or stashed somewhere to be toted out on special religious occasions. You can usually gauge the level of a Muslim family's devotion by the prominence or otherwise that the Qur'an gets — a bit like some Christian families you must have known and their display of the Bible in their living room.

Cleanliness being so close to Islamic godliness, a Muslim's not supposed to touch the Qur'an unless the hands are clean. So that the book itself never touches the floor or the ground, they're taught to read it from a stand or some other safe resting place. During their lifetime, most Muslims will read it from cover to cover and rote-learn great slabs of it, as part of their Islamic education for life. One particularly devout Omani friend, Khalfan al Esry, told the author he read it, cover-to-cover, once a month. During a lengthy conversation with Khalfan in Muscat in late 2002, he was able to quote lengthy, relevant passages. Muslims like Khalfan who know the whole voluminous thing by heart are known as *hafiz*, noted people. Like all Muslims, Khalfan believes that Allah spoke to the world in Mecca via the Angel Gabriel to Muhammed. That, he says, makes the Qur'an's 114 chapters the 'word of God' — curiously, another belief he shares with believers in other religions. As our Muslims friends told us repeatedly, the Qur'an is not just some ethereal religious text, it is also immensely practical, a 'handbook for Islamic living'. Hints from what to eat and drink to what not to eat and drink, family life, divorce and dress to sex and care of elderly relatives. Name it and it's probably there somewhere.

The word 'qur'an' itself is Arabic for 'recitation'. When Muhammed did his preaching thing, it is said that he spoke, not in tongues, but in rhyming prose. His words were said to be so lyrical and poetic they could only have come from God — which you can be pretty sure Jews and Christians would also have you believe about their holy scriptures. As we've found ourselves repeating, the three so-called great religions can get perilously close to agreeing on all sorts of matters theological. All three are founded on a belief in one God and claim that their sacred books have recorded his teachings and edicts for humankind. All three demand that their followers behave kindly, justly and care for the poor and weak. For all three, Abraham — Ibrahim to the Muslims — was a vital early prophet in the same way that Jerusalem is a three-faith holy city.

But these common roots can get terribly, terribly tangled. The Jews, we know, will not have a bar of Jesus. But, Isu as the Muslims call him, is respected in Islam as a prophet and a teacher. The rub, of course, is that Muslims don't believe that Jesus, their prophet Isu, is the Son of God. Paradoxically, this is a conviction they share with the Jews. Told you it's a tangled religious web! Muslims don't believe that Jesus died when he was crucified or that he rose from the dead on the biblical third day and ascended into Heaven to sit on the right hand of God, the Father. To utterly confuse this issue — just when the claims for a scientific basis for Islam were looking pretty good — for some reason probably best known only to Muhammed himself, Muslims believe that God removed Jesus directly from the cross and took him straight to Heaven.

Wouldn't it be a heck of a lot easier on everyone if the Big Three disagreed completely and on all the key historical, let

alone theological, points. But they don't! For their part, Muslims
are convinced that from the Garden of Eden days of Adam and
Eve, God has dispatched any number of prophets to Earth to
teach the human race how to behave decently towards each
other. Muhammed, they believe, was the lucky last, the so-called
'seal of the prophets'. They believe he was chosen to pull a sinful
world's religious loose ends together. And to do this, he called on
teachings from the other spruiker-messengers before him — even
Jesus. But, it's the Jesus-not-being-the-Son-of-God bit, of course,
that's always really bugged Christians — enough to fight wars
over it!

The 'Rose-Red City Half as Old as Time'

Petra in Jordan's southern desert is one of those rare places on
earth that have to be seen to be believed. As with nearby
Wadi Rum, the postcards just don't do Petra justice. Nor do
cameras of any kind capture its unparalleled 'difference'.

Petra is extraordinarily special whatever way you look at it. Its
magnificent physical splendour, its architectural exclusivity, its
captivating cultural history and its Bedouin cave-dwellers
combine to make its very nature different. Essentially, it's the
ruins of a mysterious ancient city hacked out of precipitous
sandstone cliffs that have been stained various shades of
succulent pink and brown, tawny and maroon reds, even whites
and yellows, by centuries of iron oxide action and water
weathering. You enter it through a very deep and narrow cleft in
the valley wall, known as the Siq Gorge.

Petra's a great tourist money-spinner for the Jordanians, but why mention Petra here? Does it have any particular significance in the overall scheme of things Islamic? Has it played a part in the schism between the Islamic and non-Islamic worlds? Well, not really, but it might have. For a while a few years back, Petra was symbolic of a potentially monumental change. In 1997, when the author was there for the first time, reporting for the ABC's *Foreign Correspondent* program, he came across a unique sight in that dodgy part of the world: Muslims, Jews and Christians standing together, shoulder to shoulder, camera to camera, gaping incredulously at the Lost City's ancient architectural wonders carved ingeniously out of the area's rose-red cliffs.

Three years later we travelled there on a family treat. At a mere twenty Jordanian dinars each, it proved one of the most memorable days of our lives. Ten-year-old Serge was rapt, clambering up the long staircase to the Al-Deir Monastery, running across the still intact 8000-seat amphitheatre, and exploring the maze of multicoloured caves for hours on end. Is it any surprise that he didn't want to leave? The other tourists — Muslims, Jews and Christians — didn't want to leave either. They were doing the same thing, having one of those special times in their lives, together.

But today there is no shared marvelling at Petra by these three incongruent groups. Things have changed; they've changed across the River Jordan in Israel and the Occupied Territories and they've changed in the rest of the Middle East region — for the worse.

The hopes of peace so graphically symbolised by those Muslims, Jews and Christians, contentedly coming together in one of the most staggering settings of history left on Earth, have faded. In fact, they're so dim they can't be seen except by a few super-optimists. In the United States, the government and leadership have changed — and maybe they shouldn't have. In Israel, governments and leaderships have changed — and maybe they shouldn't have either. In what the Arab nations call Palestine, the government and the leadership have not really changed — and maybe they should have. In Iraq, the government and the leadership had not changed, but in the most brutal fashion the Americans and their supporters in the Coalition of the Willing have embarked on their own form of 'regime change'.

What's my point? It might be drawing a long bow, but when my son can again stand alongside Muslims, Jews and Christians posing in front of the Al-Khazneh, the magnificently pillared façade of Petra's Nabataean Treasury building — which they may well have seen, would you believe, in *Indiana Jones and the Last Crusade* — then things will have changed once more, and this time very much for the better.

Like Father, Like Son — the Voice of Moderate Islam

Although it's not all that obvious while you're there as a visitor enjoying Jordan's cultural, historical and geographical delights, let alone soaking up its Islamic origins, over the decades the Jordanians have had their anxious moments. Under the quasi-democratic rule of the brilliantly diplomatic late King Hussein, and now his son and quietly canny heir Abdullah II, the Hashemite Kingdom has tried to be a bridge, a broker, in the whole ungodly Middle East mess. In 1994 the king flew in the face of everything by signing a truce with the

Israelis. This was a very brave move considering that it was the Israelis who seized the West Bank across the Jordan River after the Six Day War in 1967 — one of the triggers for the ongoing and all too bloody Middle East deadlock.

Throughout the conflict, right up to the most recent explosive times in Iraq, the Jordanians have walked a dangerous diplomatic, political and even religious tightrope. Their position has always been an invidious one — around a million Palestinian refugees living in their land of five-million plus, with tetchy Israel just across the Jordan River and Saddam, the devil incarnate, their next-door neighbour on the eastern side. And when an American diplomat was assassinated in Amman after September 11, it dragged Jordan closer to the vortex in the event of an attack on Baghdad, which occurred nineteen months later.

The Jordanians have always steadfastly refused to allow America to use Jordan as a base for any such attack, in fact for any sort of base. During the notorious Operation Iraqi Freedom launched so ruthlessly in March 2003, the dubious honour of hosting the US base went to nearby Gulf states, including lowly Qatar, a place much of the world had never heard of until America's Hollywood-designed Centercom media unit for the invasion of Iraq was set up there.

Against this background, what might King Abdullah say to Serge to make the boy feel better about the 'great divide' between his new Jordanian friends and the non-Muslim world?

Whatever the reason — blatant stupidity or equally blatant bias — in the Western media we almost never get to hear what prominent moderate Muslims like Abdullah have been saying. Yet since September 11 he's been a voice of sanity in Washington, London, Paris and other Western capitals. And his family claim to be direct descendants of the Prophet Muhammed and say they have served the Prophet for no less than 40 generations. So

Abdullah's credentials are not to be sniffed at when it comes to providing a Muslim perspective. He wrote the piece I'm quoting below shortly after the annual Muslim holy month of Ramadan, a time when Muslims throughout the world pause to reflect on their faith. The article, which appeared in the *Washington Post* and other newspapers in 2002, begins: 'Compassion, goodwill and respect for others — these are core ideals in Islam. Our religion calls on us to live and work for justice and to promote tolerance. Daily we share God's blessing: *Salaam Aleikum* — Peace be upon you.' Then it continues:

> This is the true voice of Islam but it is not the voice that Americans always hear. Instead they hear the hatred spewed by groups mistakenly called Islamic fundamentalists. In fact, there is nothing fundamentally Islamic about these extremists. They are religious totalitarians, in a long line of extremists of various faiths who seek power by intimidation, violence and thuggery.

In other words, extremist violence flies in the face of the moderation and openness that Islam is based upon. These better qualities, Abdullah says, make the Muslim world 'the home of diversity and tolerance'. And then he adds, in an unequivocal denial of one of the great myths surrounding such extremism: 'Nor does their violence constitute jihad or holy war. The greater holy war is not against others at all but against one's own failings — the war against ego.' Abdullah quotes the Prophet's disciple and immediate successor, Abu Bakr, who told his Muslim troops in their early, genuinely holy wars: 'Do not betray, do not deceive, do not bludgeon and maim, do not kill a child, nor a woman, nor an old man, do not burn, do not cut down a tree.' Furthermore: 'If you come across communities who have consecrated to the (Christian) church, leave them.'

These persuasive words are part of the basic religious education received by all Muslim children, in whatever Islamic nation. As Abdullah says, he was once one of those children. He goes on: 'So when today's terrorists target innocents, they provide direct evidence of their real agenda — power politics, not religion. In fact, long before so-called Islamic terrorists began attacking the West, they were targeting fellow Muslims. The goal was to silence opposition and obliterate the Islam of peace and dialogue.'

'For decades' the moderate Jordanian leader says, 'many Muslims thought that because they had nothing to do with this criminal fringe, they could ignore it. September 11 2001 changed that kind of thinking.' Like probably the majority of the 1.2 billion Muslims who share his moderate stance, Abdullah was aghast at the homicidal antics of Al Qa'ida. 'The idea that anyone would exploit our religion to sanction the killing of innocents outraged Muslims everywhere. To my knowledge, every Muslim country, every centre of traditional Islamic scholarship and every major Islamic organisation condemned the September 11 attacks absolutely. They did so not out of diplomatic nicety, not out of fear of the United States, but because their faith demanded it.'

Abdullah's great fear appears to be that Muslims themselves are not doing enough to guarantee that 'the real voice of Islam' is heard outside their own Islamic world, a line I've heard elsewhere in the troubled region. 'Today, Muslims must speak out boldly in defence of a dynamic, moderate Islam — an Islam that upholds the sanctity of human life, reaches out to the oppressed, respects men and women alike and insists on the fellowship of humankind. This is the true Islam of the Prophet.' It is the Islam that terrorists seek to destroy.

Abdullah's remarks would reassure young Serge. But the king had one more comment to offer. 'Nowhere,' he said, 'is our help needed more than in the Holy Land, where Palestinians and Israelis alike are crying out for peace, stability and security. We must urge their leaders to hear the voices of reason, end oppression and occupation, stop the violence and create a future of hope.'

PART THREE

THE PROBLEM IN A
SEETHING NUTSHELL

Israel and Palestine

We need to summon the will to turn our vision
into a concrete reality that touches the deepest
aspirations of both people. That means terrorism
and violence must stop.

**Terje Roed Larsen, in *Haaretz*, the Israeli-Jewish
daily newspaper**

Israel and the Occupied Territories: Bridging the Gap

In the past twenty years or so covering the Middle East conflict, the author has crossed the Jordan River on that famously unpretentious British military construction, the Allenby Bridge, on numerous occasions. Bridge or no bridge, the reality is that crossing the Jordan is a symbol of crossing swords as well as crossing from one culture to another, given the ongoing fractious antipathy between Arabs and Jews in the region.

The Jordan is a quirk of both geography and history. For starters, to call it a river is probably a misnomer. Its near lack of water makes it more of a riverbed. Its thoroughly desolate location is daunting, its dodgy geopolitical location even more so. Thanks to geographic happenstance and religious rivalry, it has become one of the flimsier dividing lines in a tinder-dry region. But its biblical history is epic in scale.

Over the past two years, the situation in Israel and the Occupied Territories has deteriorated so badly that these days there's no way any self-respecting parent would consider taking an uninvolved ten-year-old to that region. But less than three short years ago, we did — with little concern or apprehension. The place felt relatively peaceful. On both sides of the Jordan, the locals seemed uncharacteristically relaxed. But I remember commenting to Serge and his mum at the time

that most things, most of the time, are 'relative' in this part of
the world.

With backpacks and handbags, we strolled across the Allenby
Bridge, leaving behind the Jordanian officials who were being their
usual jocular, half-efficient Arab-Muslim selves. Despite arriving
late for the last crossing that Saturday, the Jewish Sabbath, the
Israelis were sanguine and welcoming enough, their customarily
thorough bag search lacking the usual suspicion and aggressiveness.

We were actually walking, not being driven, across the bridge.
Previously, in a dozen or so crossings as a journalist, I had only ever
been driven. Even Serge, a hard to impress young boy, seemed
excited at crossing one of the world's most hazardous frontiers, the
shallow dry river gulch between a peaceful and a warring Middle
East, on foot! His questions flowed, some prompted by his mum,
others off the top of his own inquisitive head. Why the barbed
wire? Is it to keep people in or out? What's a landmine? What's all
the open space without any buildings or people? — this query
asked as we passed through the Jordanian–Israeli no-man's-land.
What does no-man's-land mean? Why do they have to have one?
Are we still in Jordan? When do we get to Israel? Why are the two
checkpoints so far apart? Why do we have to have our passports
checked? Why is there a frontier? Why can't people just come and
go from one country to another? How can it be two different
countries? — it doesn't even look any different on the other side.
Do the Jews speak Arabic? What's Hebrew? Why are people from
Israel called Jews? What does being Jewish mean? How come they
have to have separate religions?

A few hours later at our Italo-Austrian friends' home in East
Jerusalem, we remarked on how interested Serge had been
throughout a pretty momentous journey, and how unconcerned
about his and our safety he appeared to be. But his mood had
changed once we hit the outskirts of hilly Jerusalem. Coming

from an easygoing society, he was noticeably perturbed by the prevalence of military hardware, the checkpoints bristling with soldiers, the heavily armed street patrols, and wondered why we hadn't seen these things back across the river in Jordan. Jordan's anger and fear were beneath the surface or around the corner; but in Israel these things were in his face and he didn't like it much. But in the same way that he'd come to the Muslims in Jordan for the first time knowing next to nothing about Islam, he was just as unpresupposing about Jews, Judaism and their state of Israel. It wasn't the people who bothered him. I guess it was the situation in which they — and now he — found themselves.

The Battle for Bethlehem

After making it to the legendary Holy City from the Jordanian frontier, having a now identifiably gun-shy ten-year-old with us meant that we spent less than a week with our friends in Jerusalem. But we did get young Serge to most of the spots. One of our friends worked on the reconstruction of Bethlehem for UNESCO and we spent a wonderful day with her and her two sons in that memorable place, discovering Christian holy places like the Church of the Nativity and its crypt containing what is said to be Christ's manger, his birthplace.

Sadly, not long after our thoroughly safe visit to Israel, trouble re-erupted in the region. After a few Oslo Accord years of comparative peace, another Palestinian intifada and a new and even tougher Israeli response to it became a daily experience — more and more rock-throwing and suicide bombings by Palestinian youths and girls, more and more heavy-handed Israeli retaliation in the Occupied Territories. It was certainly not a place to take a kid, or to bring up a kid. But that's what both the Palestinians and the Israelis have been doing and are still trying to do, knowing full well that Israeli policies will turn Palestinian kids into suicide bombers, and Palestinian policies will mean that they will, in turn, kill Israelis young and old.

On almost the same daily basis, the world's media was preoccupied by serial suicide bombings by Palestinians. Provocation and retaliation by the Israelis occurred with the same demoralising regularity. In a conflict in which each side has always accused the other of casting the first stone, it was, as usual, impossible to tell which came first, the chicken or the egg. Blame was met by counter-blame. Heavy-handed military barbarism by the Israelis guaranteed further sacrificial terrorism by the 'Pals'. Atrocity and frustration preoccupied both sides. Escalating fear and insecurity were constant and worsening. Love, you could say, was lost on an hourly, daily and weekly basis as the bodies were counted — Israeli Jews blown apart by lone suicidal attackers, branded 'Muslim terrorists'; Palestinians shot or buried alive by uniformed troops in tanks and armoured personnel carriers, who others condemned as 'state terrorists'.

In a period of scary tensions and horrible possibilities, April 2002 was to become a regrettably memorable time, with some religiously curious spinoffs for Jews and Christians. One of the major (and unlikely) battlegrounds, as the Israelis pushed into the Palestinian West Bank area, was Bethlehem. Bethlehem had always been something of a religious battleground, but now it was a military one as well. And not just the town of Bethlehem, forty minutes drive from Jerusalem, but biblically awesome locations such as the Church of the Nativity.

The domed holy place — its cavern-like basement in particular — is said to be the very spot where Mary and Jesus dropped into the village of Bethlehem on that December night two thousand or so years ago; the place where, it is said, the baby Jesus was born. At the height of the exchange in late March–early April 2000, some 200 or more Palestinian fighters took refuge in the historic church adjacent to Manger Square.

The fact is that something like 5000 of the Palestinians living in Bethlehem are Christian Arabs — not Muslims. This paradox appeared to escape the media pack huddled on the edge of the town and being fed information as the 'hallowed' place was being systematically taken apart by the Israeli militia, most of whom you would have to say couldn't have given a flying dropkick about Bethlehem's sanctified status for Christians, Arab or otherwise.

In the region, and elsewhere, the pessimistic talk was of the conflict spreading, of enraged neighbouring Arab nations coming to the aid of the Palestinians. Heightening this pessimism was what appeared at the time to be a slightly unhinged possibility canvassed by the United States of a pre-emptive attack against Saddam Hussein in Iraq — a member of the trio that President George W. Bush had earlier labelled the Axis of Evil, along with North Korea and Iran. This was a terrifying adjunct to America's now declared war against terrorism. The Middle East was a bloody mess, literally and figuratively.

In the month of April 2002, news coverage all over was saturation stuff. It was one of those crunch periods, even in the turbulent geopolitics of the region, a moment of serious truth. The acute deterioration in relations between Muslims and Jews in Israel was becoming violently obvious. The relative peace, the lull, we had seen and enjoyed earlier was no more. And there were very few encouraging signs for peace around. Talks, tricky at the best of times, had broken down pretty much completely. Fragile truces fell apart almost before they began. A terrifyingly topsy-turvy two years down the track, in Israel and the Occupied

Territories, things were as bad as they'd been for years, if not worse.

As we watched the mutual mayhem on television, safe in our distant home, Serge remembering his happier hours in Israel, we could only imagine the pain and anguish of our friend Costanza in East Jerusalem as her dreams of a New Bethlehem for Christians, Muslims and Jews were desecrated by Palestinian gunmen and pulverised by the Israeli military.

How do you explain that sort of thing to a young boy? You can't really, given that it makes no sense to people much, much older. The adults of this world have a lot to answer for!

Whose Eye and Whose Tooth?

If you're Jewish, the blame for the violence and hostility in the Middle East, particularly Israel, is ultimately attributable to the Arabs. If you're an Arab — particularly a Palestinian Arab — the responsibility for decades of unabating, deadlocked bloodshed rests with the Jews and their Western supporters, the United States in particular. In reality, though, who could possibly sort out the evolution of such a protracted conflict with such impeccable accuracy that they could say with certainty which side fired the first shot? The horrible fact of life in this part of the world is that you *can't* say. Little wonder that the bitter recriminations go painfully on between the two sides, despite all the valiant peace efforts. The length of time — all up, more than half a century — that their extremists have been failing to wipe each other out must surely have told them something of the futility of the whole gruesome exercise. Both from a distance and close-up, it all appears so heart-wrenchingly pointless — until you remember the explosive mix of religion and race that is part of the equation.

Religion, whoever's it is, and if it's anything other than self-delusion, fantasy and fear of the unknown, particularly death, is probably mostly about humankind's stumbling attempts to explain the inexplicable and make sense out of life. But how can confusion and ignorance justify consciously knocking off people who don't share your particular brand of doubt or confusion?

In this context, the irony of the Israelis' attack on Bethlehem during their Operation Protective Wall in April 2002 was a three-way irony: Jews overrunning a Christian holy place, the Church of the Nativity, with Palestinian Christians resisting them on behalf of their Palestinian Muslim brethren. Mull over that! Was this a battle for territory or a battle between three versions of the soul? Would the last one on their feet go to Heaven? And who would be there to greet them — God, Allah or Jesus? It's all a bit ridiculous, but don't say that in the wrong Jewish, Muslim or Christian circles.

So what about race? If religion tells us what we believe, what does race tell us? Rather than telling us anything, maybe it makes us what we are, makes us physically and (more importantly), culturally different from others as we scramble to make our form of sense out of life. Like gender, which is an even more basic human characteristic, race and religion are about a fundamental form of identity. A sense of self maybe? 'I'm a Jew, that's what I am — a Jewish male.' Or 'I'm a Muslim woman, a Palestinian Muslim woman.' Or 'I'm an Arab, a Christian Arab.'

As soon as you introduce land, a place, a location, a country or a nationality, things start to get tricky, even messy. Each of the above identities — our Jewish male, our Muslim woman, our Christian Arab — could come from Israel. They could all call Israel home (or, since 1967, at least its Occupied Territories). That's what makes the situation problematic, delicate and, in places like Bethlehem at the wrong time, risky and even dangerous. If religion and race are about identity, land is where we can 'be our race' and where we practise our religion. It seems that you cannot be a race or have a religion unless you have land where you can be and practise it.

In a few words, what are we saying? Is the Middle East conflict about race, is it about religion, is it about land — or is it about some deadly conglomeration of all three? Answer? Yes! Yes! Yes! And Yes!

The Nordic Couple Who Won't Give Up on Peace

There was a time when the Australian Government — not the present one from whom we hear practically zilch in the way of policy or even attitude towards the Middle East conflict — advertised this country's official position as 'even-handed'. Maybe the explanation for the lack of an even-handed approach these days is that the current Australian Government invariably waits for pronouncements from Washington on these matters before following suit. We don't have a powerful Jewish financial and political lobby as America does and if there was an active Islamic lobby in Australia we would almost certainly ignore it. All of this makes it hard for most Australians to work out where they stand on the whole 'blame thing' in the Middle East.

The Oslo Peace Accords of 1993, unknown to many and initiated and engineered by a quite remarkable Norwegian husband-and-wife team, Terje Roed Larsen and Mona Juul, were a brave attempt to break the self-defeating politico-religious nexus in Israel. Juul and Larsen were convinced that only a dumping of the eye-for-an-eye pattern of mutually destructive behaviour could unwind the cycle of violence and desperation of ordinary Palestinians and Israelis. As I write this, Larsen is still working as UN Secretary-General Kofi Annan's special envoy in the Occupied Territories. The two indefatigable Nordic optimists have made viewing 'the world from Islam' and the world from Israel their life's work.

The Oslo Peace Accords were famously signed for all the world to see on the White House lawn in September 1993 by Yasser Arafat and Yitzhak Rabin, under the watchful eye of the then US president, Bill Clinton. Despite a heavy politico-personal leaning towards the Palestinian position — mainly because he sees poverty-stricken and culturally and socially imprisoned Gaza as the crux of the entire problem — Larsen is consciously 'even-handed' when it comes to the violence in Israel and the Occupied Territories. The professional peacemaker, who I have the privilege of knowing as a friend as well as a journalistic contact, somehow manages to take religion out of his Middle East equation.

A look at his utterings on this atrocious two-sided battle puts the whole 'blame thing' into a different perspective. During the March/April 2002 attacks on Palestinian citizens in Bethlehem, Gaza and particularly the crowded refugee camp in Jenin by the Israeli Defence Forces, Larsen, in his official role, was scathing in his criticism of the Israelis. But a few months and a number of atrocities later, he took aim at the Palestinians, in the Jewish daily newspaper *Haaretz*.

Spurred into verbal action by suicide attacks in both Jerusalem and the north of Israel — 'in this era of unimaginable attacks that rip through the bodies of innocents, the fabric of communities and the tattered remains of a peace process' — Larsen reiterated his and the UN's longstanding and unwavering tenet — the principle of non-violence — which he had embodied in the Oslo Accords. Somehow, despite what he has seen over the years, Larsen still believes there is 'a way out of this madness, a negotiated agreement that creates two states, Israel and Palestine, living side by side in peace and security'. In our talks about this — on camera, lazing over a beer at the beachside UN Club on the Gaza Strip or pontificating in the late-night cellar bar at the wonderful American Colony Hotel in East Jerusalem — Larsen has always maintained that negotiators have continued to see the solution as far more complicated than it needs to be.

That said, his August 2002 tirade against Palestinian terrorism was unequivocal. 'When it comes to the bloodshed that stretched from the campus on Mount Scopus to the hills of Galilee, let me be clear: terrorism has absolutely no justification on any level. Only one word describes indiscriminate attacks against men, women and children: murder. Terrorism has wreaked havoc on Israel and must be stopped. The Israeli people need to know that when they board a bus, visit a café, mark a religious holiday or, yes, even go to school, they will not be victims of heinous acts of violence.'

And then came the political, the strategic, rub, the real basis for any railing against Palestinian suicide attacks against Jewish citizens, and also the ultimate rationalisation for an even-handed analysis. 'Moreover,' said Larsen, 'terror attacks have also been extremely counterproductive for the Palestinian people. They have deepened the occupation of their land, which remains the core of this conflict. They have helped provoke a severe Israeli response of closures, curfews and military attacks that have created a humanitarian crisis in Gaza and the West Bank. Sadly, this deprivation is driving the type of extremism that often leads directly to more terrorism.'

This is Larsen's version of the cause-and-effect dilemma. As he sees it — and he's seen it now for more than a decade — the fact is that those guilty of spilling the blood of innocents have been dictating events in the region. They are actively undermining any efforts to forge peace. So, where to from here if an enduring peace is to ever be achieved? The international community must play a central role in ending the violence and brokering political settlements. Larsen points to an important new alliance, The Quartet — the US, the EU, Russia and the UN — as the main international actors in the peace process. These four acting together are the vital players working for 'the right of Israel to exist in full and permanent security free from terrorism, free from attack and free from even the fear of attack [and] second and with equal vigour … the Palestinian right to independence and self-determination'.

A logician rather than an ideologue, Larsen expresses this two-pronged goal in the Middle East more simply and clearly than probably any other participant or observer. 'The two beliefs,' he says, 'can be reconciled in one common vision — two states living in peaceful co-existence.'

Ultimately, that's what the whole mess is about, the individual struggle for existence, for land, that must eventually become a single — though double-faceted — goal. And despite everything and his close-up experience of the mutual hatred and unabating violence by Muslim Palestinian on Jewish Israeli and vice versa, Larsen can always see a glimmer of light at the end of the region's long, dark tunnel. Listen to some unwavering even-handedness:

Despite the recent waves of violence and the fear and anger they engender, recent polls continue to show that the clear majority of Israelis support peace plans based on Israel's withdrawal from occupied territory. Moreover, despite severe deprivation and daily violence, there are strong calls from Palestinians, including some from erstwhile extremists, for a ceasefire that also leads to a two-state solution. This is heartening and we must build on such sentiment. Now we need to summon the will to turn our vision into a concrete reality that touches the deepest aspirations of both people. That means terrorism and violence must stop.

Larsen, of course, is far from alone. Kofi Annan shares the same even-handed vision of both the problem and the solution. As he put it at about the same time last year, one side — the Palestinians — resorts to indiscriminate terror and the other — the Israelis — responds with retaliation that is equally devastating in its effect on ordinary people. 'Each feeds the anger and hatred of the other and then yet more lives are swept away in the backlash.' If only the Larsen–Annan view was shared by a Bush-led US which, for its own strange, probably parochial reasons, has chosen to sweep away the Oslo Peace Accords in its vainglorious attempt to wrest the mantle of Middle East peacemaker from its wearers. If it wasn't so absurdly tragic, it would be funny.

Larsen, by the way, is a great late-night companion. But his mind is never far from what (other than his pressured relationship with his beautiful and intelligent diplomat wife) has become the main purpose of his existence. And some of his most illuminating insights come over a glass or two of something wet and fine. He is certainly no angel but no one has so far managed to clip his dove-like wings. Life has become one long shuttle between Oslo, Tel Aviv, Gaza, Jerusalem, New York and anywhere else he needs to be in order to keep the peace train on the rails.

Perhaps the Most Fascinating City in the World!

The area immediately inside the history-laden Jaffa Gate, one of seven so-called 'open' gates to the stone-walled Old City of Jerusalem, has to be one of the world's great places. Don't ask me why it's great, it just is. You can't be there without feeling that you're really somewhere that matters.

The heavily cobbled, centuries-old road leading through the gate and into the square on the southern edge of a splendid Arab bazaar is polished smooth and shiny by the years — no, by the ages. The tyres of the heavily dinged Mercedes taxis squeal as the cars spin round to park and wait for late-night fares, most of them tourists or visiting journalists.

Late one night, sitting on one of the square's hard, cold but brilliantly located traffic control bollards, sipping popular Macabee beer, an Australian television colleague of Croatian background and I were musing about 'the future of the human race', a not uncommon subject for travelling media types to muse on. At one point, assisted by the icy Macabee and peering vacantly into both the Middle East's ancient past and its uncertain present, the author uttered one of those truly distinguished inanities: 'There are walls and there are walls — but that's a wall! There are places where worlds meet and there are places where worlds meet — but this is a place where worlds really do meet.'

Jerusalem is that kind of city, no matter where your religious dice fall.

It's no accident that Jerusalem was always going to be the sticking point in any resolution — military, political, peaceful or not so peaceful — of the Middle East stalemate. Jerusalem is where the Christian world, the Jewish world and the Muslim world literally cross paths. But the Jaffa Gate is a specific meeting point. During a couple of hours and three or four Macabees, you can see the whole world and most of its religions pass by.

The Good, the Bad and the Ugly

To stand on the Mount of Olives and look across the narrow valleys of Kidron and Jehosophat to the Old City of Jerusalem, with the gleaming gold of the Dome of the Rock as its centrepiece, is an experience close to overpowering.

Despite the rare historic splendour, your first look at Jerusalem doesn't *feel* like the first. For this consciously 'lapsed' Christian, the city more than lived up to all those old Sunday School expectations. Those tiny Holy Land stickers they used to hand out to you for being quiet during the reading of the lesson didn't do justice to illustrious Jerusalem, where reality beats the hell out of art, imagination and fantasy. The timeworn stone walls recall the multitude of human episodes they have enclosed. You don't have to know the detail.

The good, the bad and the ugly history of this city that is more than just a city is obvious. Fixing your eyes on it from the Mount's fabulous vantage point, even for a moment or two, opens your observer's mind to more than your eyes are seeing. X-ray-like, your astonished gaze takes your mind into this unfathomable city's savagely divided soul. And you know from others' experiences that its peace is so easily shattered in a violent split second. Its three disparate worlds have many more than three faces.

Not so long ago, another besotted traveller described Jerusalem as 'perhaps the most fascinating city in the world, as well as one of the most beautiful and surely the holiest city of all'. Regardless of your point of view, 'yes and no' would have to be your rejoinder to that word picture. Holy it may be, but 'unholy' is not exactly an inappropriate adjective for 'the highly disputed capital of Israel', as the same traveller described this town of perpetual tumult. Jerusalem, many believe, will be the final battleground in a death struggle between Jewish Israelis and Muslim Palestinians, with the rest of us caught up in their fight for a city they both love for different reasons.

But that timeless cliché about beauty being skin-deep was made for beautiful Jerusalem. It has a most unattractive underbelly that all too often has made itself evident. And yet religious pilgrims and even non-religious visitors have been spellbound, as it were, by something dubbed the 'Jerusalem Syndrome' — the curious psycho-emotional impact the place can have on unsuspecting and impressionable visitors. There are many extremely odd instances of apparently stable folk who come to believe they have been drawn to the Holy City 'by divine command'. In its three-religion garb, it's about the same thing — humankind's eternal quest for God, whatever that might mean. It's also about very different versions of that God. The Christians get closer to their God here than anywhere else and the Jews get closer to theirs. And it is, for reasons just as curious, a holy place for Muslims. Work that out! It can't be just geographic or even religious happenstance. Are they feeding off each other at the same time, in two cases anyway; killing each other, both in the name of their God? Jerusalem is a beautiful, entrancing place, one of the most beautiful and entrancing in the world. But it can also be ugly, very ugly.

Killing Each Other — It's Just Stupid!

Rewinding the tape, as Kirsty and I, with Serge, took a worse-for-wear Mercedes taxi to Jerusalem from the Jordanian frontier, we tried to explain to him why people were living in those Bedouin shanties in the dry riverbeds and why those brand-new apartment blocks on the steep rocky peaks had guards on the roads that led up to them. I said we tried. How do you explain that nonsense to yourself or any other less informed adult, let alone an impressionable child?

We tried, in our stumbling parental fashion, to explain the human silliness, the ridiculousness, the illogicality, the irrationality — all those very adult behavioural characteristics — of the way the Jews and the Arab-Muslims living in this apparently God-forsaken land treated each other. But I suspect we didn't get very far. And why should we? No one else has — even if they had a lot longer than the hour it takes to get from the Dead Sea to the outskirts of the so-called Holy City.

We tried to explain why the Arab-Muslim Palestinians claim this as their homeland and why the Jewish settlers make the same claim. Try explaining why Israel is 'the only Jewish country in the Middle East and has a religion that stands alone in a sea of Islam'. If you can, your Nobel Peace Prize is in the mail!

Next day, as we drove from the crowded, hazy, gutterless streets of Palestinian East Jerusalem, past its shanties, past the bustling New City and the ritzy modern apartments looking across to the old walled city, we tried again to explain it — not just to Serge but in our own heads. As we wound our way from the hectic area of the Damascus Gate, with its hawkers and animal sellers, into the claustrophobicly magnetic Arab bazaar, we tried to explain the Old City. What its four quarters, the Armenian, Christian, Jewish and Muslim, were all about. On the 'centres of the world's religious gravity': the Temple Mount, the Haram ash-Sharif, the location of the unavoidably brilliant Dome of the Rock and the Al-Aqsa Mosque, the Jewish holy shrine, the Wailing Wall, a giant walk-in, open-air synagogue open twenty-four hours a day, and the Church of the Holy Sepulchre, said to be where Jesus was crucified, buried and resurrected. All very heavy places and all within the lyrical stone's throw of each other, living on each other's religious doorstep.

Needless to say, we weren't sure that Serge understood all of our necessarily simplified explanations. Or maybe he did. His response was to the point and eminently recordable, particularly when we carefully talked together about the death and misery that the ongoing Palestinian–Israeli conflict had caused. 'They're all people. Who cares if they're Jews or Arabs — or Muslims or whatever they are?'

Many Ways to the Top

One early morning we stood atop the Mount of Olives, with its famous biblical sites of the Garden of Gethsemane and the Tomb of the Virgin Mary. As we gazed east, open-mouthed, across to the panorama of the Old City, that hairy old thought tumbled into my mind. You know it — the one about how there are supposed to be many ways to the top of the mountain. A short while later, strolling around the ramparts of the Old City, the thoughts kept tumbling. Here in perplexing and paradoxic Jerusalem, there are also many roads leading to God's three

Houses: the revered Muslim mosque, the revered Jewish Wall and the revered Christian sepulchre — but almost everyone seems to get lost navigating religion's back alleys.

Serge didn't get lost, mainly because he didn't know where he was going. And who really does? As irreligious as it may sound, the path to Heaven is littered with lost souls who thought they knew where they were going. Serge loved the crowded claustro-labyrinth of the Arab bazaar in the Old City of Jerusalem. Then again, he didn't know that bombs had regularly gone off there over the horrible years of conflict and killed people as they headed off to pray — Muslims in their flowing garb, sandals and Arafat-like stubble, flocking to the mosque five times a day; orthodox Ashkenazi and Sephardic Jews in their funny hats, ringleted hair and stockings on their way to the Wall; and Christian pilgrims in their jeans and T-shirts saying 'Coca Cola' in Hebrew and Arabic finding their way along the Stations of the Cross on the staggered Via Dolorosa.

We told him about the bombs and deaths in the bazaar, in Jerusalem's bars and restaurants, its buses and bus stops. He never got to the Gaza Strip. His reply was one we'd heard from him before: 'That's stupid!' So what do you call that — a universal truth maybe?

Gaza: Shrine or Dirt-Poor Prison?

As the reputed burial place of the Prophet Muhammed's grandfather, Gaza is an Islamic shrine. But for other reasons it's also a dirt-poor prison.

People — and by design rather than accident they're all Palestinian Muslims — don't live in Gaza, they survive. Situated at the southern end of the country's coastline, the narrow, cramped Gaza Strip is hemmed in by either well-off Israeli settlers and heavily armed Israeli forces. The Palestinian authorities who run the place are often inept or corrupt, or both. Human rights are a dice game in Gaza — a virtual toss-up, depending on which Palestinian faction you support or don't support. It's not exactly the most desirable or attractive real estate in the world, nor among the more sought-after Middle Eastern neighbourhoods. In fact, while it's better than the cardboard-box-on-the-footpath existence of Calcutta's ghastly slums, that's about it.

Strip or city, Gaza is incontestably a poverty trap. By any standard used to evaluate that global human quandary, Gaza is at the wrong end of the rich–poor spectrum. It's the pits, affording a mere existence to those Palestinians who still somehow manage to call it 'home'. There is no way you would live the way its inhabitants do unless you had no choice or had a profoundly political reason for doing so. The million and more Palestinians who scrounge an existence in this dry, dusty, dilapidated, often bombed-out place fall into one or other of those categories. If Arab poverty and politics don't keep them locked in their squalid Strip, the Israelis do. As Anton La Guardia wrote in Holy Land, Unholy War in 2001: 'Gaza is a cul-de-sac, an appendix that nobody wants. Its railway runs from nowhere to nowhere; the tracks were ripped up by the Israelis to raise high fences around their army camps.'

It is the problem in a seething nutshell — not just the Middle East problem, but the much wider one between a quarter of the world's population and the other non-Muslim three-quarters.

It's a revealing comment on this destitute Mediterranean enclave that after the Oslo Peace Accords were signed in 1993, Terje Roed Larsen, co-architect of the Accords, felt it necessary to persuade his government in Norway to donate US$8 million worth of paint to spruce up the dreary Strip — as a fillip for the generally depressed Palestinian masses. They painted everything that wasn't moving — buildings, paths, fences, rock walls, the lot — mainly white to make the long Omar al-Muktar Street, which runs four kilometres from the Israeli entry checkpoint right to the seafront, look cleaner and less run down. It's also no accident that Larsen declared that if there was ever going to be peace in the Middle East and Gulf regions, then alleviating the abject poverty and angry hopelessness that pervades life in Gaza was the main priority. Get that right and support for Hamas and other Palestinian terrorist groups would evaporate. But somehow, between 1993 and 2003, that simple plan got lost, and the peace process suffered. The Saddam Husseins and Osama bin Ladens who provoked the war against terrorism have both claimed at various times to be fighting against the imbalanced US support for Israel and on behalf of the Palestinians in places like Gaza. Hence Saddam's scary financial support of the Strip's suicide bombers. More on the bombers shortly.

To be honest, it's so obvious that you don't really have to live in Gaza's daily nastiness to recognise the roots of Palestinian Muslim enmity and hatred. But it helps to have seen it, smelled it and experienced it even for a brief period of time. Seeing, as they say, is believing, and believing just might provide understanding. The Palestinians are not angry and vengeful for no reason. 'Cause and effect' applies there too.

The statistics say that as many as six out of ten Palestinians in the Occupied Territories, other than those living in the relative economic ease of East Jerusalem, are unemployed. This figure hasn't really changed for years. Many of those people must be living on less than the widely accepted global poverty benchmark of two US dollars a day. Barricaded in as they are, there isn't a great deal they can do about this invidious situation. In the meantime, they ponder their plight. They fret. They fantasise about a better life. They question whether they even have a right to exist. They become angry. They become angrier and some do silly, irrational things — like blowing up themselves and a few innocent Israelis and thinking that that will alter things for their fellow Palestinians, that it will take down the checkpoints, create jobs and even bring about a civilised future for them and their kids. As I say, it's irrational, but verging on the understandable.

A Brave Optimist

One of the saddest things I came across in looking for a Palestinian view of 'the world from Islam' was the official website of the then mayor of the City of Gaza, the late Nasri Khayal. If you've had any doubt about the inherent, even foolhardy positivism that humankind can display in the face of nonstop adversity and insuperable odds, read these few sentences from a man who died late in 2001.

It's my pleasure to welcome you to our website which was initiated recently to provide you with information regarding the City of Gaza.

Almost seven years ago, the Israeli occupying forces left Gaza and parts of the Gaza Strip and the West Bank as part of the peace process which brought the return of the Palestinian Authority under the leadership of President Yasser Arafat. Much has been achieved during these seven years and the city enjoys a healthy environment, a beautiful beach and rehabilitated neighbourhoods. Quite a change from the dark days of the Israeli occupation.

However, the Gaza Strip still suffers from the Israeli blockade, which deprives the Palestinians from free movement and trade. This is the major factor causing high rates of unemployment and poverty, as part of the official Israeli policy.

Like other people of the world, the Palestinians have their dreams of prosperity, stability and freedom. This can be achieved only when justice and mutual respect prevails between the parties. We look to the future with optimism to establish our independent Palestinian state with Jerusalem as our capital. Thank you again for your interest and support.

Obviously Mayor Khayal was simultaneously a master of hyperbole and understatement, managing perfect 'pollie-speak' despite the appalling destiny of his people. In the months following his death, the Israelis inflicted close to US$400 million worth of damage to his city and to Arab towns on the West Bank in their military and air incursions, usually following yet another pointless Palestinian suicide bombing of a non-military Jewish target.

Since the beginning of the 2001 intifada — and obviously these are not the latest figures — a reported 6500 Palestinians were taken prisoner on the grounds of both accurate and allegedly spurious terrorist associations in Arab towns and villages such as Gaza itself, Nablus, Jenin and Bethlehem. In late May 2002, rumours emerged of a draconian Israeli plan to 'fence in' all of the Occupied Territories within a year. If this plan were to go ahead, commentators remarked, it would completely cripple the Palestinian economy; one Palestinian sympathiser facetiously replied: 'More than it's crippled already?' The fence would isolate eight major Arab towns from one another and from the outside world. Probably unheard of in the so-called civilised world, including Germany with its Berlin Wall and South Africa in its dim, dark pre-Mandela apartheid years, such a barricade would prevent the normal movement of people, goods and services between Palestinian towns that already exist more like refugee camps than like places of proper human habitation. This deprivation of any really free movement and transportation by the Palestinians has been in place for the thirty-six years since the Six Day War of 1967.

Suicide Bombers and Terrorists Don't Go to Heaven

Guided by some internet surfers living in the region, I discovered another website called The Middle East Media Research Institute — and what a discovery! If you're after a moderate Muslim view of the world, this is the place to find it. In one article, a Palestinian Muslim, Ashraf al-Ajrami, dealt in some detail with the suicidal behaviour of Palestinian bombers in Israel and the Occupied Territories and how they might be stopped. Remember, he himself is a Palestinian Muslim, not an antagonistic Jew.

Why do they do it? he asked. Is there a root cause? Al-Ajrami began on the disturbing note that the phenomenon of martyrdom — in the now notoriously regular suicide attacks — was on the increase, particularly among Islamic youths and children. 'The Palestinians' distress from their lives of difficulty and degradation under the occupation pushes many to disdain life and seek the shortest way to the Hereafter, in order to free themselves of reality and reach Paradise,' he wrote. 'The honour and esteem that the Palestinian people give to the martyrs has, no doubt, had a crucial effect on the emergence of this phenomenon.

'Likewise, the funerals of the martyrs and the celebrations held in their honour have always been accompanied by talk of life everlasting and the eternal serenity in Paradise, making people think: "Why wait and go on living a life of misery when Paradise can be reached by the mere press of a button or even by coming in range of Israeli shooting?"'

Whatever your reaction to this explanation, it pours cold water on any suggestion that the bombers carry out their atrocious acts for no reason or because of some innate homicidal tendency or uncontrollable hatred of Jews. As a Palestinian himself, al-Ajrami recognised the danger of nationalistic sentiments among young Arab-Muslims being exploited by encouraging them to martyr themselves 'for nothing', as he said has happened in the Gaza Strip. 'There, children have recently risked their lives to be martyrs and to attain life everlasting, or at least a hero's funeral and festivities in their honour, as are held for martyrs. Some Gaza children are influenced by the schools, the mosques or the gatherings attended by many children at which praise for sacrifice and martyrdom is voiced.'

Al-Ajrami acknowledged that some extremist groups are prepared, in return for money, to arm kids with pistols, hand grenades and readily available pipe bombs that cost just a few shekels. 'These brainwashed children are imbued with motivation to approach the nearest settlement,' he went on, 'where they are shot dead by the soldiers of the occupation. Our data indicate that a considerable number of the children who martyred themselves in the Gaza Strip went to the settlements in broad daylight. In 90 per cent of the incidents, they faced danger.

They were armed with grenades, pipe bombs, and similar objects purchased with their own money.'

As al-Ajrami saw it, the negatives for the Palestinian cause — let alone the wider image of Muslims — are obvious. 'The children's suicide martyrdom promotes the hostile propaganda from the enemies of Palestine. It particularly reinforces their claims that Palestinians send their children to the front line. These are false claims aimed at justifying the indiscriminate shooting at all the Palestinians, shooting that has caused the deaths of many children throughout the months of the intifada. It constitutes a danger to the lives of Palestinian youths whose homeland will need them when they grow up and are able to serve society.'

Interestingly, he reckoned that the suicide phenomenon tends to cause Palestinian children to rebel against their parents. Following the spread of the self-killings, it was noticed that children were threatening their parents that they would martyr themselves if the parents did not meet their demands or failed to turn a blind eye to the children's bad behaviour at home. In another equally disturbing revelation of the domestic repercussions of the suicide practice on family life in Gaza and the West Bank, Ashraf al-Ajrami commented that some Palestinian kids have actually been known to use pipe bombs during arguments among themselves, 'as has happened in more than one place'.

No Dark-Eyed Virgins

Is there a moderate Palestinian response to children's suicide attacks against the Jewish enemy they grow up both fearing

and loathing? Do the Palestinians really believe that the
homicidal violence triggered by this ultimate in mixed emotions
can ever be contained? According to al-Ajrami the only way to
curb, let alone stop, this suicide phenomenon would be 'a
supremely collective effort' beginning at home, where the
children should be supervised, cared for and in particular have
their moral needs met. Their activities and movements would
have to be monitored, not just at home but also at school and at
the mosque. Al-Ajrami argued that this collective effort has to
be the responsibility of the local governing body, the Palestinian
Authority. 'All activities having an ill effect on the children's
emotional stability, pulling them in directions outside the normal
matters of children, must be monitored. The schools should take
it upon themselves to engage the children in developing hobbies
and utilising their time for positive activities that help develop
their character, reinforce their reason and free them from the
negative influence of the events happening in the homeland.'

At the same time, al-Ajrami said, the Palestinian security
apparatus has to apprehend arms traffickers and collaborators
preying on passionately patriotic Arab youth in order to make
money. As things stand, they are wiping out many of the current
young generation of Palestinians with their nationalist
enthusiasm and will to take on the enemy. 'These arms traffickers
and collaborators should be severely punished,' he added. Then
he said something remarkable. He would even attack the
problem at the contentious level of religion. Islam itself, he said
bravely, could be part of the Palestinian problem. 'It is important
to stop the mosques from engaging in exaggerated political
activity that provides fertile ground for anyone who wants to
abuse the minds of youths and minors.'

You might have noticed that the Jews, traditionally the sworn
enemy of the Palestinians, have so far not rated a mention. But

the Palestinian and Arab media don't escape al-Ajrami's broad broom. 'The media,' he said, 'have an important role to play in refraining from broadcasting pictures affecting the emotional state of the children, and in refraining from exaggerating in reporting tragic news that arouses among the children feelings of frustration and despair. Similarly, children's programs must constitute a proportionate part of the entire broadcasting, and they should be broadcast frequently in times of emergency.'

I don't know about your reaction, but none of this sounds like the irrational ranting of an Islamic fanatic. Indeed, al-Ajrami concluded on a somewhat wistful note. 'We all must keep in mind that the current situation is temporary, and that the future will be better. The future, at any rate, belongs to the youth, the generation of tomorrow.'

Let's hope that in that future they feel no need to destroy themselves.

In the meantime, we have the consolation that suicide bombers and terrorists don't go to Heaven. They don't get to sit at the right hand of Allah. If they're men, they can forget about those 57 dark-eyed virgins that are supposed to be a reward for Muslim martyrs. Suicide and the killing of innocents and noncombatants are, in fact, against Qur'anic teaching. That is why moderate Muslims condemn such acts.

Gaza First, Then Maybe Jerusalem!

Back in the early 1990s, Terje Roed Larsen and his wife, Mona Juul, pulled off an amazing coup. Somehow, they managed to get warring Israelis and Palestinians — academics, bureaucrats and politicians — together in Norway. Secretly, for nine months, as the BBC's Jane Corben puts it in her book *Gaza First*, 'in country mansions and homely log cabins, far from the prying eyes of the media and critical forces within their own communities, Israelis and Palestinians ate, drank, walked and laughed together in the process of hammering out a peace deal'. As Corben reported and Larsen confirmed to the author in any number of convivial chats in Oslo, Tel Aviv, Gaza or Jerusalem via satellite TV hook-up, 'there were moments of high drama, screaming matches, resignations and sometimes farce'.

It was apparently a roller-coaster — euphoria one moment, depression the next. But both sides were determined not to look back into their mutually troubled history or blame each other or let the talks stall. 'They would only look forward,' according to Corben, 'to the future of their own children and the generations to come.' The 1993 Oslo Peace Accords were the climax of this incredible breakthrough between not just the Palestinians and the Israelis, but the entire Muslim and non-Muslim worlds.

In more recent times, while he's still very much involved, Larsen's immeasurable influence on the Middle East peace process has been somewhat bottom-drawered. The US has become a player via the Roadmap to Peace and old-fashioned, counter-productive point-scoring and grandstanding are the order of the day. But it's fair to say that the two Norwegians and the 'peaceniks' on both sides they sponsored got bloody close to pulling off the impossible.

When I originally met and spoke with the couple in February 1994, they were convinced that alleviating the poverty in Gaza was the number one priority, the only way to bring an end to Islamic extremism and terrorism in the region and the world. Hamas and the other Palestinian extremist/terrorist groups fed off the deprivation and hardship of the Palestinians caught in the Gaza poverty trap. Unlike the PLO, they offered both physical respite and hope of freedom from the Israeli yoke. But the Norwegians also openly acknowledged that ultimately the trickiest aspect of any overall solution was not Gaza, but Jerusalem.

'There has to be a solution on Jerusalem,' Larsen told me later that year after he'd hosted an unprecedented lunch between Palestinian leader, Yasser Arafat and Israeli leader, Shimon Peres. Arafat was his next-door neighbour in Gaza. 'There will be a solution,' he said, because their historical forces are so strong that neither of the parties can live for long with the Jewish–Islam question unsolved.'

So how do you think it's going to be solved, I asked. 'I can envisage a solution on Jerusalem. Go back and look at what Yasser Arafat said one year ago about Gaza and the West Bank. Look at what the Israeli politicians said. They were far apart. Now they are talking like you saw for yourself at my home in Gaza. It will take a long time. It will take years. But, in the end, I think they will find a solution, hopefully a compromise between their two positions.'

In Gaza working on an ABC *Foreign Correspondent* report on the progress — or otherwise — of 'Oslo', as it is still referred to colloquially in the region, Larsen set up an interview for me with the remarkable Suha Arafat, the French-born Christian wife of Yasser Arafat. Our discussion took place at the heavily guarded Arafat compound, walking distance from Larsen's UN residence, set back from the Gaza seafront.

Larsen had insisted he live cheek-by-jowl with the PLO leader so he could maintain both regular personal contact and, you might say, political surveillance of the man regarded by many as a terrorist, or at least an instigator of terrorism. Their two houses were close enough to borrow the proverbial cup of sugar and to link up on Sunday mornings for family tennis. Larsen and Juul played; the Arafats were keen spectators.

On arrival at the Arafat villa for the interview with Suha, we were thoroughly searched and I was escorted into the *majlis*, the traditional Arab-Muslim reception area for guests. How do you explain a *majlis* to non-Muslims? It's a room and then some. Basically it's a formal sitting area off to the right of the entrance foyer where Muslim men — and men only — meet and greet guests. It's part of the whole Muslim hospitality thing that allows unexpected guests to arrive and stay for three nights before being asked why they're there! Many Muslim houses, including Bedouin goat-hair tents out in the desert, have a *majlis*.

In my thirty-minute wait for Suha, I enjoyed a bizarre experience, even for that bizarre part of the world where almost anything can happen and often does. The room was full of armed PLO fighters in combat gear, laughing, chatting and introducing themselves to me. One of them was babysitting the Arafats' quite recent addition, bouncing the happily gurgling infant on one knee, balancing his Kalashnikov on the other. Bizarre indeed!

Recalling this with Larsen later over a Jewish Macabee beer, he probably summed up the humanitarian instincts that motivated him to voluntarily take on his go-between role in the Middle East, coming at the problem mainly from the Palestinian perspective. 'They are human beings before they are Palestinians and Muslims,' he said. He could have said that they are Muslims before they are fighters — or even terrorists. Despite everything, they love their children too. Larsen told me how he insisted that both the Palestinians and the Israelis who took part in his highly successful and secret 'Oslo Back Channel' brought their wives and, most importantly, their children with them during the most tense of their deliberations. 'Just to remind them what it's really all about.' He smiled sheepishly. Not the past, not even the present: the future.

Ten years later, the debate is still raging. The Israelis remain adamant that Jerusalem is not negotiable and the Palestinians continue to claim it will be the capital of the new state of Palestine — on the face of it, totally irreconcilable positions. You could say that the work of Larsen, the gentle Norwegian persuader, is clearly far from over.

That said, no matter who or what was to blame for their breakdown — the assassination of Yitzhak Rabin by a Jew, the election of Benjamin Netanyahu, the sacreligious invasion of the Al Aqsa Mosque in Jerusalem by Ariel Sharon, Yasser Arafat's intransigence, Israeli persecution of Muslims in the Occupied Territories or maniacal Palestinian suicide bombers — this long-time observer cannot help believing that had the Oslo Peace Accords been able to continue their five-year plan, peaceful co-existence may have broken out in the Middle East before this, and as a direct consequence relations between Muslims and the rest of the world would be very different. But we'll never know.

PART FOUR

SHOPPING AROUND
FOR A COMPROMISE

The Gulf

Islam is more than just a religion. It is a way of life that governs even the minutiae of everyday events, from what to wear to what to eat and drink.

Dubai Explorer

The Gulf: Dubai, the Islamic Straddler

If you're into travel, flying anywhere even vaguely new or different is always a buzz. Coming into a place like Dubai, the gleaming high-rise hub of the United Arab Emirates (UAE), after a twelve-hour flight from Perth in Western Australia, is one of those experiences. You can tell you're passing through a cultural frontier, on a latter-day magic carpet ride. You're travelling from a still emerging Australia to the new–old ways of Arabia. Perth and Dubai, separated by the near-empty blueness of the Indian Ocean, are distinctly different but strangely similar. They both have that peacock-like boldness of New World urban youthfulness about them. They're both coastal but sit on the edge of vast tracts of arid, semi-habitable desert stretching endlessly from their modern urban outskirts.

If Perth is unlike any other Australian city, Dubai is a different planet when held up against just about any of the other Arab cities in its Gulf and Middle East region. 'The Hong Kong of the Gulf' is one way of describing it these days. It's a big call. Often those sorts of fashionable clichés miss the mark. But if wildly wealthy locals and almost an entirely immigrant workforce are any sort of measure, Dubai, an Arab bastion of almost-anything-goes capitalism, is not just figuratively but literally a shining example of the petro-dollar fairytale of the latter half of the 1990s. In just a little over three decades, Dubai has careered from desert rags to cosmopolitan riches, from a simple, seldom-mentioned Arab village to a millionaire-magnet and international talking-point.

So why come to a place like Dubai and the UAE when you're working on a journal aimed in part at demystifying Islam? For starters, for someone returning to a global hotspot like the Gulf, Dubai's special geopolitical location is almost reason enough. From this place there's a good chance you'll get a fresh, different perspective on 'The World from Islam'. This is New Islam. It's one of seven Arab sheikhdoms of the United Arab Emirates, part of that alluring cluster of smallish, non-aggressive Islamic nations on the Arabian peninsula. Its giant southern neighbour, however, is that great Muslim mystery, Saudi Arabia — powerful, reclusive, the origin of the Arab race, language and religion, intensely Islamic. Not far away, past Bahrain to the north-west, is Kuwait, these days totally reinvented after Saddam Hussein's invasion and the Desert Storm campaign that rescued it from his clutches in 1991. Nor is Iraq itself, a sea journey up the Gulf, all that distant. Smack on the UAE's western border is Qatar, where late in 2002 the Americans spent a quick billion to set up the tiny, little-known Gulf state as a base for the then mooted final onslaught against Saddam.

As far as geography goes, you could say that Dubai is close to the action in the Gulf and the Middle East. But despite this it's still regarded as safe. Why? Because somehow, since they got together as the UAE in 1971, the proudly Arab Muslims of Dubai and the other six emirates — Abu Dhabi, Sharjah, Ajman, Umm al-Qaiwain, Ras al-Khaimah and Fujairah — have managed to straddle the *human* gulf, the one that divides the Muslim and non-Muslim worlds. This factor, with Dubai as some sort of coincidental compromise between Islam and the West, helps to make it an intoxicating place to spend time in.

According to the *Dubai Explorer*, the local guide:

> Dubai's culture is firmly rooted in the Islamic traditions of
> Arabia. However, in contrast to the image, the UAE is tolerant
> and welcoming; foreigners are free to practise their own
> religion; alcohol is served in hotels and the dress code is liberal.
> Women face little discrimination and, contrary to the policies
> of Saudi Arabia and Iran, are able to drive and walk around
> unescorted.

But how does the reality of Islamic life in the 'new world' of
Dubai match up with the official literature? Can it really manage
to be both Arab-Muslim and modern, almost 'westernised',
simultaneously? In a way, that's what we were here to explore;
and Dubai, the Straddler, turned out to be an intriguing and
revealing, predictable and unpredictable possibility.

'Up the Creek' with a Very Different Kind of Islam

With its avant-garde architecture leaping pubescently
skywards from the desert floor, Dubai is physically and
visually quite amazing. Half a century ago it was an unremarkable
backwater, nothing more than a fishing village with a few small
farms scattered nearby. Now its worldwide reputation for
uncharacteristic Arab modernity precedes it. Mention Dubai and
everywhere they'll tell you it's about oil, near-obscene wealth,
migrant workers, golf courses in the desert — and maybe an
emerging new Islamic way.

By coincidence, the Straddler also straddles the Creek, as the locals call the stretch of spring-fed water dividing this astonishing city in two. To understand how this modern Gulf metropolis actually functions on a day-to-day basis, they say, you have to take this famous Creek into account. It's a relatively narrow waterway that starts on the outskirts of Dubai and curves through the city on the way to its mouth, where it becomes a brackish inlet on the Gulf.

From the ruler, Sheikh Muhammed bin Rashid Al Maktoum, down, Emiratis regard what happens on and around the Creek as a bit like their version of the Thames, the Danube, the Nile or the Volga. The Creek, they tell you, shaped old Dubai. But these days new Dubai, with its miraculous greenery of trees and parks, its towering office blocks and splendid golf courses, has quite literally reshaped the Creek, tunnelling under it, bridging over it and crisscrossing it with water taxis.

To see Dubai via the Creek, a cheap water taxi, an *abra*, is the way to go. It's not Paris from a *bateau* on the Seine or Venice via *vaporetto* on the Grand Canal, but you know what I mean. From its relatively shallow waters, the city is all there before you — from the ancient wind-towers near its mouth to the architectural forest of this unblushingly commercial place's high-rise skyline, a skyline punctuated by the slender minarets of the city's similarly unapologetic mosques. Two cultures in one. At the wharves, old fishing dhows and wooden trading craft vie for mooring space with tacky pleasure boats and the work vessels servicing the Emirate's lucrative offshore oil fields. You could say that if being Islamic is the 1400-year-old soul of modern Dubai, being Arab is its flesh and bones and oil the financial lifeblood coursing through its otherwise constricted veins.

From the air, with the outlines of its towering sculptured buildings dawn-grey, its floodlit streets following the curvature of the Creek, it almost takes on the look of a nocturnal adult theme park. On the ground, from the moment you leave the stylish international airport via a labyrinth of turnpikes and freeways, it feels eerily like LA, that other adult theme park — also another desert-edge city. But there's a more mature style, distinctively Arabic, about Dubai. It might be a bit movie-set deliberate, but you'd be far more likely to make movies about Dubai than to shoot one in it.

Oil-Rich Spoilt Brats?

For ages, even by the Gulf's rapidly emerging modern standards, Dubai was a reasonably successful trading centre. During its 6000-year history, meagre as most of that might have been, it apparently imported and exported with the best of the Gulf's legendary merchants. But then the oil rush hit them like a large bag of black gold. After they picked themselves up out of the desert sand and dusted off their Bedouin past, the Emiratis discovered that their perpetual struggle to survive was well and truly behind them. They grew like a fast-blooming desert flower in an irrigated dune. As Sheikh Hamdan bid Rashid Al Maktoum, a member of the ruling family and the country's deputy leader, puts it, 'There has probably been more change in Dubai in the last three decades than in the whole of the preceding six millennia.' In the early 1950s, Dubai's exports totalled — wait for it — a mere US$6 million. By the late 1990s, this figure had risen close to a staggering US$20 billion.

Oil was discovered offshore from Dubai only in 1966 and, as the oil flowed, so did the country's income. Bouncing off the massive injection of wealth, the Al Maktoum family, the ruling sheikhs — at their best, what we might call generous benevolent despots; at worst, not-so-generous benevolent despots — poured their petro-dollars into other money-making ventures. Dubai's fortuitous geography was hardly a disadvantage. It's propped more or less halfway between Europe and the Far East, beautifully positioned not just in terms of the Gulf and the Middle East but also in relation to the old Levant region, the Indian subcontinent, Africa and even the untapped post-communist markets of the CIS, the defunct Soviet Union.

If the accusation can be made against many Muslim peoples throughout the world that they have not 'modernised', this is hardly true in the case of Dubai and most of the UAE sheikhdoms. The negative is that, in terms of modern politics, they all have what can only be described as a benign oligarchy maintained undemocratically by an unopposed family dynasty. As in so many Arab-Islamic states, democracy, in any of its lauded but variegated and inconsistent Western forms, has not even flowered, let alone flourished. Looking across the Gulf towards Iraq, articulate English-speaking locals will tell you: 'We'll find our own way to our own Arab form of democracy in our own time.'

In socio-economic terms, the place is a curious mix, with the Dubai Nationals a mostly ridiculously wealthy, well-educated minority in their own land, outnumbered by exploited 'guest workers' and expatriate businessmen and professionals. The population breakdown is bizarre, but when you've got heaps of money why not get somebody else to do the work? The result of this psychological undercurrent is that, of Dubai's total population of around 1,029,000 only about 20 per cent or so are actually Emiratis. The remaining 80 per cent or so are other Arabs, Asians (mainly Indian/Subcontinent) and expat Europeans. One of the most glaring ramifications of this employment disparity is that only 2 per cent of workers in private business are Dubai-born.

The other 98 per cent are foreign immigrant workers. Think about that for a moment. They're pretty startling statistics. There's plenty of talk about 'emiratising' the workforce — code for relying less on expat workers and putting more of the local population to work. Good luck!

Despite being touted as an open economy with one of the world's highest per capita incomes, and almost manic recent entrepreneurial activity, including the IT and high-tech sectors, Dubai's extravagant wealth has created its own unique and paradoxical problems. Unemployment among the nationals has created a serious problem with negative social and behavioural ramifications: people with lots of non-productive time on their hands. The disparaging accusation that most Emiratis are 'oil-rich spoilt brats' is oft repeated.

It's certainly the case that wandering through any of Dubai City's proliferating retail malls is like being in a credit-card-wielding consumer paradise. The adult theme park analogy is both real and apt. In fact, an uncharitable label you could justifiably slap on the wealth-heavy locals — although there are some who are not all that flush with heaps of expendable cash — might be a variation on the old line: 'When the going gets easy, the Dubai Nationals go shopping.' It has to be said that, as Arab-Muslims go past, playing with their expensive worry beads, they do look a bit spoilt! You won't see many Palestinians strolling through shopping malls in Gaza or Nablus playing with their worry beads. For a start, there are no shopping malls in Gaza or Nablus. And the worry beads there are definitely not precious stones.

Like all societies, Muslims range over the full socio-economic spectrum, from the filthy rich to the just plain filthy. The lifestyle disparity is so enormous it's little wonder that radical Islamists such as Hamas and other extremists like them are able to stir feelings of frustration and anger among, for instance, Palestinian youth. It's these feelings of antagonism and vengeance that quickly and easily become the homicidal feelings of suicide bombers. Places like Gaza, with their sickening poverty and dire sense of pointlessness, have become fertile recruitment fields for extremist Muslim provocateurs.

On this 'hopelessness' syndrome, I saw an interview on American PBS television in which a Turkish commentator, far from being an Islamic apologist let alone a mouthpiece for Islamic extremists, had this to say, not so much *to* the current holders of world power as *about* them. 'If you want to run the world,' he said, 'you must understand the anger and frustration of those who do not benefit from the way you are running it.' That's a neat working definition of the iniquitous side of globalisation, a negative side of that economic ideology that Bill Clinton, for one, has acknowledged.

Palestinians clearly fall into the category of those who do not benefit from the way the world is currently being run, and so do the three billion people around the globe living on less than two dollars a day. On the other hand, even though not all of them live like sheikhs, you could never say that Dubai Emiratis are caught in the global poverty trap. Could that be why there is no visible terrorist threat in Dubai, why it is one of the safest and most West-friendly nations in the Gulf and Middle East area? Could it also be why so many have come to the conclusion that Arab-Muslim poverty is as much a root cause of the threat of a 'war of the worlds' as oil, land or even religion are ever going to be?

Corporate Islam — A New Cityscape

For all their ostentation and self-satisfaction, the privileged burghers of Dubai and some other Gulf communities just don't fit the misguided international perception of Muslims as poor, uneducated and lacking enterprise. That idea, it has to be said, has probably always been something of a misconception in terms of the bulk of Muslims anywhere. Like all Western communities, Muslim communities have their slackers, their spivs, their freeloaders and their unemployables. But Muslims, even in the direst of circumstances — destitute Palestinians and Afghan refugees being prime examples — usually display exceptional initiative and business acumen.

To anyone who's spent time in Muslim communities, the contrast between desperate Middle Eastern places like Arab refugee towns and villages on the one hand and the outrageous glamour and privilege of Dubai on the other, is magnesium-white and glaring. While the Israelis are bulldozing Palestinian homes in Hebron, in Dubai international construction consortiums are also bulldozing Arab land — to put up still more commercial monuments that some Islamic scholars argue have precious little to do with the heart and soul of Islam.

Even to the casual visitor, the contrasts, perhaps the contradictions, in the Islamic society of Dubai are starkly evident in the cityscape from your high-rise hotel. The slender spires of classic mosques have been joined on an ever-growing modern skyline by luxury office blocks and upmarket international accommodation.

Dubious Dubai, no longer dependent on oil, turns out to be a slightly mad melange of mega-industry and moderate Islam. For a religious society that on Qur'anic grounds spurns the ostentatious display of wealth, somehow Dubai Nationals can justify the culture of the Crescent doing business with the culture of the Corporation, of trade following tradition, of the Hajj employing high-tech facilities. Muslims moving with the times is one thing, but where's the cut-off point? I know that the Prophet was a businessman himself, but would he condone them praying for profit? The fact is that Muhammed had a lot to say about how Muslims should handle money, including things like tax and interest rates. In spite of or because of this, many of his devout followers in Dubai have become unlikely magnates. Nevertheless, despite the God versus Mammon battle being waged on every front in the Emirate, they insist they remain steadfast Muslims.

The New Islam — Shopping Around for a Compromise?

Without even trying all that hard, you discover the Dubai subdivision of the Islamic world is a seriously out-of-the-ordinary place.

The brand-new pseudo-Italianate Mercato shopping mall at ritzy Jumeira Beach, for instance, is totally over the top. The Starbucks coffee stop, brazenly American, is as it always is anywhere in the world, beautifully located and presented, but as usual the black liquid stuff in the oversized mugs is coffee in name only. By contrast, the passing local parade is quite something — and extremely well-heeled. Actually, every bit of them looks well, not just the heels. The hordes of consciously dressed-to-kill, Westernised women are striking. Women in strict Muslim attire — the *abaya*, the floor-length black cloak; the *shela*, the traditional black scarf; and the stiff linen face-mask, the *burka* — are extremely scarce. In this part of town, the cover-all society is more a cover-girl society. In an hour or so of deliberate people-watching, only one woman with her head covered was to be seen.

Instead, there was the odd naughty navel, lashings of exposed cleavage, skin-tight jeans gasping for body breath, close-fitting tops, dangerously high stilettos and gold jewellery by the carat-load. The men? They might have been completely outnumbered by the *Vogue* magazine look-alikes of the other gender but there was no way they were going to be outdone in the sartorial stakes. They'd also worked hard at their elegantly casual 'look' — designer polo shirts, button-down collars, chinos and smart business suits. Among this post-sunset throng, the Ramadan fasting was over until dawn tomorrow and the 'fast-livers', not the fasters, were on the town, at least at the Mall.

After all, we were in Jumeira, the dress circle district of this quite recently opulent city. Strutting your Western-style stuff is a relatively new thing. But you'd have to say that only Dubai would hold an annual month-long Shopping Festival — something, if the comment is not too offensive, like Ramadan in reverse. The younger locals were born to shop but the festival, first held in 1996, attracts outsiders, the more-money-than-sense class from all over the globe. They pack the city's luxury hotels and trawl the malls for things they don't really need but can't resist — all duty-free, low-price bargains as upmarket purchases go. To them, Dubai is a commercial centre, a shoppers' paradise — hardly the classic impression of an Islamic state. Then again, who ever said that Dubai was a classic Islamic state; it's more like a state of Islam, a very different state of Islam.

Commerce? What else? Other than their traditional pastimes of falconry, camel-racing, more recently horse-racing and the world game, soccer, sport was never exactly prominent in the Emirati-Muslim mentality — or, for that matter, the Arab-Muslim mentality generally. Living up to its bold business-oriented reputation, Dubai has recently gone out of its way to establish itself as the sporting capital of the Gulf region. It appears to have succeeded. The Dubai Emiratis, almost pathologically open to ideas and opportunity, currently host a wide cross-section of world-class sporting events, matches and competitions. But don't go looking for a quote from the Qur'an to back up this post-oil innovation. Then again, the Prophet Muhammed was a self-funded businessman in ancient Mecca and Medina before he saw a different sort of opportunity, and became God's messenger.

For Muslims, business and religion have never been an uncomfortable mix, and the 'thoroughly modern' Muslims of the Gulf are as businesslike and entrepreneurial as their non-Muslim counterparts.

Ramadan — The Clayton's Fast?

Why do they do it? What is it with this Ramadan? Is it that Muslims are into masochism? Is it, as they will tell you, about religious commitment, about proving to Allah that they really do believe what they say five times a day, that he is the one true God? Or is it maybe more a psychological thing, proving a point about personal self-control?

Many non-Muslims know that it's got to do with fasting and giving up things once a year for about a month. But for Muslims themselves it's about a lot more than fasting, it's a particularly special religious period. And yes, they do deliberately deprive themselves of things culinary and carnal. But essentially, they say, they need the deprivation of fasting during Ramadan so that for at least a specific period they have no distractions from their all-important Islamic faith. By fasting they spend less time on the usual day-to-day concerns and preoccupations of the flesh.

To a Westerner, it's a bit like giving up cigarettes, going on a diet, swearing off the booze and becoming voluntarily celibate — all at the same time! But in a more strictly Muslim religious sense, it's a time of worship, a conscious reaffirmation of their belief in Allah. It's a period of sustained, almost yoga-like contemplation. Stopping and having a bit of a think about things, we might say. Recharging the spiritual batteries. Taking stock. Setting aside a period to put 'things' — family, relationships, work, whatever — into perspective. The Qur'an itself puts it, as it usually does, simply but emphatically. 'You who believe!' it says, consciously leaving out those of us who don't. 'Fasting is prescribed for you as it was prescribed for those before you, so you can gain more spiritual awareness.'

That said, to pull it off, Ramadan obviously demands real commitment. Without it, all the good that Muslims believe can come from the fast can easily be blown. Telling fibs, bad-mouthing people, talking behind their backs, making false promises, greed or covetousness are regarded by Muslims as offensive at the best of times. But to be guilty of these hugely frowned-upon sins, is particularly wrong during Ramadan. They are as off-limits as off-limits can be. Together or separately, they can destroy all the benefits Muslims claim flow from fasting and the physical deprivation they force themselves to bear. It's a bit like a Catholic going to a priest to confess to beating his wife or to a psychologist to find out why, and then going home and beating her because she had the temerity to ask where her hubby had been after work. Not an exact analogy, but you probably get the point.

The procedure is simple with this, the fourth of the Five Pillars of Islam. Alarm clock or no, get out of bed well before first light. Normal ablutions out of the way, take a snack-type meal, the *sahoor*, in silence. It's not called breakfast, because you're not breaking a fast — you're about to begin one.

Now you say the first of the five regular prayers for the day, read a chapter or two — they're not all that long — from the Qur'an, and you're ready to face the day. But what a day! As Yahiya Emerick, the American Muslim writer on Islam I mentioned before, explains it: 'During the daylight hours you must abstain from all food, liquids, inhaled substances, sexual activity and nutritionally related medicine or any non-essential oral medicine.' Ramadan is a time for Muslims to confirm their faith; I can think of a few Westerners who'd need lots of faith to fast on that scale.

Dawn — a Black and White Issue?

To the non-Muslim, Ramadan is a curiously contradictory thing. During the working days of that Islamic month, you can find yourself dealing with bleary-eyed and drowsy Muslims. If you didn't know better, you'd say they were a trifle hung-over. Given the teetotalling side of Islam, of course that's out of the question. So why do many of them look a bit worse for wear, as we non-Muslim partakers of alcoholic beverages might put it? Easy. They were up eating, drinking heaps of sweet tea and cardamom coffee, doing business and socialising into the wee small hours. This goes on nightly after sunset when the Iftar meal is eaten. Iftar meaning break-fast after feeling peckish most of the day.

For the entire month of Ramadan, you don't hear Muslims complaining publicly but their minds must be preoccupied with a crucial practical question: When is it actually dawn and when is it dusk? In other words, when must you begin to fast and when can you stop? To make Ramadan life a little more manageable, these times are printed in the daily press. But the editors must be non-Muslims — they don't make the list as obvious as they might. In fact, it's often tucked away in an obscure corner, maybe jammed between a carpet-sale ad and 'Maids to Order', a very Dubai special offer. Strange, given that the Ramadan and prayer timings are probably at least as important to daily Muslim life in Dubai and elsewhere as the TV guides or even the all-important international stock reports.

But what if you can't get your hands on a newspaper and you're flying blind on the precise fasting period? Unless you're an expert on these things, the rules for when the sun has actually risen and when it sets are not so clear, no 'black and white' matter. It's a genuinely fine line, as it were.

In that often quite poetic and lyrical Islamic fashion, they'll tell you that dawn has arrived when it is light enough for you to tell the difference between a black piece of thread and a white piece of thread. Apparently, military types have used this method for ages to define 'first light'.

At the other end of the day, the reverse applies.

The Fast You Have When You're Not Having a Fast

A Western medico who's been practising in the Emirates for some years gave me an intriguing take on Ramadan. 'All they're doing is swapping night for day,' he said. 'By fasting from dawn until dusk, they're really just moving the hands on the body clock. They don't really suffer. Instead of not eating and drinking between when they normally go to bed and when they wake up, they don't eat or drink during the day. Then they make up for that by eating during Iftar in the evening. Give or take a few extra hours here and there, there's not a lot of difference. They get a bit toey during the day, but generally speaking — seeing that they start fasting at a pretty early age — over the years of repetition they get used to the fasting and work out their own psychological ways of handling it.'

'What about going twelve hours without water?' I asked. 'That can't be good healthwise.'

'No, it's not. That's probably a bigger concern than the lack of food. To be honest, if the whole thing's supposed to be about personal sacrifice bringing spiritual benefit, then the "no liquids" edict takes a far greater commitment.'

Ramadan is not an unconditional obligation for all Muslims, as Abdallah explained in his Crash Course in Islam. If you haven't reached puberty you don't have to fast. If you're sick or not considered healthy enough you are excluded, as are the permanently ill or incapacitated, or elderly folk too weak to get around, or individuals quaintly described as 'mentally challenged'. Women in menstruation, in labour or post-natal are also exempted. Travellers are given flexibility as well. And there are some other exceptions. If you slip up and miss a day's fasting, you can put it on the religious tab, as it were, and make up the time later.

Letting Off Muslim Steam

In the West we hear a lot about Muslims, Ramadan and fasting. What we don't hear much about are Iftar and the festival of Eid, the anything-but-fasting that goes on at the end of Ramadan.

When you're living and working with Muslims, you probably hear more about Iftar and Eid than you hear about the big one, Ramadan. There's a before, a during and an after the fast. The locals talk almost as much about the times when they are not fasting as the times when they are! And why not? Muslims might be Muslims, but they're also human beings. Not a bad thing to remind ourselves at those times when deeper and dangerous differences divide us.

But when Ramadan finally draws to a close after a month of self-deprivation, the party really begins. Eid — *Eid ul Fitr* in full Arabic — is really something. It's basically a celebration that goes on for three days. *Eid ul Fitr* means literally the Festival of the Fast Breaking. Without any doubt, it is one of the two most popular holidays in Islam. And why shouldn't it be? People can finally get back to normal after thirty days of depriving themselves of some of life's more obvious pleasures. Ramadan finally coming to an end sparks palpable feelings of accomplishment and relief. Suddenly freed from dawn-to-dusk fasting, Muslims party. And I mean party! For three days, after the obligatory prayers and sermons at the mosque, they get together with family and friends to eat, not drink, and, in their own way, be merry. The food is special celebratory Eid food and there's a fair bit of Eid gift-giving. It's Eid time, folks! Travel agencies and airlines offer special Eid holiday packages. The fairy lights come out, the decorations go up — and all this, by coincidence, their very own festive season, occurs three weeks before the Christian Christmas. Chronological irony or what?

A Long Islamic Lunch

My Eid was an all-male affair. Arriving at the vast, walled compound of 'VIP' Eisa Al Serkal and his extended family on the Deira side of Dubai's famous Creek was nothing short of daunting. As I pulled up outside, my cab looked just a bit

ordinary alongside the Mercedes and Range Rover Deluxes
with their waiting chauffeurs. Even through the huge gates, I
could see the house was super-palatial. It looked like an Arab
sheikh's residence because it was built like an Arab sheikh's
residence. It wasn't what you might call a 'storybook' palace,
but it was a palace nonetheless, an Arabian palace — colossal,
architecturally extravagant, ornate but not without taste; the
gardens immaculate, the lawns and edges clipped and trimmed to
perfection, the paths and walkways marble or at least polished,
marble-like stone.

Smart casual would be OK, I'd been assured. But on the spot,
surrounded by a dozen or so milling Emirati guys chatting away
in their spotless white *dishdasha* robes, I was beginning to feel a
smidgen out of place. Then things began to improve. A tall
Emirati, probably in his late thirties, approached with his hand
extended. 'I am Abdulmenom,' he said, smiling warmly through
his Arab hirsuteness, 'Abdallah's brother. Welcome!'

How could he tell it was me, the Australian journalist? Did I
look different?

'Come,' he said, motioning towards a large domed building at
the other end of the garden away from the house. 'The women are
in the big house with my mother. The men are here in my father's
majlis.' Boys at one end of the compound, girls at the other ... not
only was I at the right address, it was also the right country!
Abdulmenom whisked me across the marble courtyard, past the
giant stone Chinese guardian lions, up the marble stairs, through
the marble foyer — shoes being left at the door — and into the
majlis with its marble floor resplendent with magnificent thick
carpets, the like of which a carpet-nut can only dream of! All the
stuff of exotic tales from old Arabia? But no enticing music, no
perfumed bellydancers. This was commercially progressive but still
religiously conservative Islam.

When we entered Eisa Al Serkal's *majlis*, there were already twenty or so men in the circular room, seated on plush divans under the unbelievably beautiful stained-glass dome of the ceiling. With Abdulmenom, I followed a few other men in and observed the protocol. One by one they approached their elegantly greying host seated prominently opposite the door. He stood to greet them, clasping hands, they kissed on both cheeks and then on the tip of the nose, even some momentarily intimate nose-to-nose touching. The nose part of it I'd never seen before. They then moved off around the room, greeting all the other guests in the same cordial fashion. I thought I could tell relatives from family friends by the more overt displays of affection afforded to some.

There were kids present also, boys as young as five or six, and the adults flooded them with attention and affection. Later in the day, after lunch, I noticed Abdulmenom discreetly pass one little guy, a nephew apparently, a fistful of dollars. Later again, I saw the boy stuffing what looked like several hundred dirhams — about two dollars each — in a leather wallet.

When my turn came, Eisa stood to greet me too, but in my case a handshake was enough. And not a hint of 'Who are you and what are you doing here in my home?' Only later did I hear that after I'd gone he'd asked what I did. I also discovered that it's 'open house' at his residence every day, not just at Eid. Sometimes twenty or thirty people — family members, friends, business acquaintances, divorcees (for some obscure reason) and the like — are present at lunch. Meals on a VIP as distinct from Meals on Wheels!

Anyway, on this day, as an invited guest, I got to sit on the divan next to our host. He'd been to Australia and we talked about where he'd been and where I lived. I could tell he wasn't at all sure why I was there in his private *majlis*, but that didn't make him any less charming. Our polite conversation about anything that came into our heads was interspersed with his almost constant greeting and farewelling of guests. Clearly, some were family or at least extended family; others had popped in just to pay their Eid respects, either personal or business. Earlier, Abdulmenom had mentioned that the Al Serkal family had accumulated their vast wealth from oil and more recently from property management and what he called the 'service industry'. Meanwhile, the colourful crowd of locals in the *majlis* kept changing. As one of them thoughtfully explained, it was 'all very Eid'.

But after a while, fifty-odd 'stayers' were unobtrusively guided to a slender, hall-like area where we were to have lunch. After the obligatory washing of hands, in a bathroom with only eight separate handbasins, we moved into the dining hall where lashings of food had been spread on a huge 'tablecloth' on the floor. Cushions were arranged around it and the guests were invited to sit on the floor; yours truly opposite Eisa himself, apparently a privilege.

Lunch? It was more like a cross between a gourmet picnic and a beggars' banquet — platters and platters of just about everything that the Middle East and Gulf cuisines can offer: including assorted savoury pastries, the traditional selection of Lebanese appetisers known as *mezze*, the ubiquitous chickpea, lemon juice and crushed garlic *hummus*, rice, meat, chicken exotically spiced with cloves, tumeric, cardamom and saffron, *harees* — a special dish for Ramadan and Eid — meat and wheat seasoned with dried limes, slowly pot-boiled over charcoal for something like six hours, mashed and turned into a kind of meat porridge that the locals devour by the truckload, but definitely an acquired taste for blow-ins, *arayes* — spiced mincemeat fried inside Arabic bread, *kibbe* — fried balls of ground meat mixed with pine nuts.

Needless to say, no pork. For Muslims, all pig meat is *haram*, forbidden, the pig being considered unclean. All other meat that is eaten by Muslims has to be *halal*, killed according to Islamic religious law — basically the animal's throat has to be cut and the blood drained off. Ironically, the Muslims' *halal* requirement is not as rigorous as the *kosher* standards of their arch-religious rivals, the Jews, but it's pretty close to it. Essentially, a Muslim can eat anything that is not forbidden, which makes good sense if you know what is forbidden.

The entire meal — starters, mains, dessert and fruit — was consumed using only the right hand. If you don't know why, then you should! Ask a friend, but do so discreetly. Even though by the end of the lunch, I'd become much more adept at eating with just one hand, Eisa was concerned that his Australian guest had not eaten enough. I explained that I had eaten with the Bedouin in southern Jordan, with guerilla fighters in Mauritania in northern Africa, and occasionally elsewhere in the Muslim world, but my experience at eating an entire meal with my right hand was not great. 'You should have used a knife and fork,' he said, smiling. 'We do have them, you know.' I assured him I was well satisfied and that, besides, I'd wanted to see if I could manage an entire meal with just the right hand, 'out of respect'. He got my diplomatic drift, and I hoped he hadn't noticed a couple of basic slip-ups I'd made.

A Pillar of Society

The Third Pillar, one of the Five Pillars of Islam, demands that anyone who can is committed to giving. *Zakat*, as it's called, is supposed to total 2.5 per cent of a Muslim's annual individual income and the principle is especially high on the agenda during Ramadan. Muslims, you soon notice, don't talk much about inequality. And in this well-heeled part of the world, Dubai, you're not likely to run into any who might describe themselves as socialists. Muslims generally appear to accept inequality as a fait accompli of life. In fact they consider one of the crucial tests of a true Muslim to be how he handles wealth if he's got it and how he handles poverty if he hasn't. But they go on about the 'burden of wealth'. Each year, Eisa Al Serkal, in order to relieve himself of some of his very large financial burden, contributes to deserving causes, either directly or via charities operated by the government and the local mosque, 2.5 per cent of his total income.

In Eisa's case, that amount might be almost enough to wipe out the national debt of a small Third World country!

Born to Rule, God Willing

Watching Eisa Al Serkal in action during Eid got me thinking that, while we in the West mightn't like the idea of tribalism and inherited leadership all that much, there's a logic of sorts in this ostensibly undemocratic way of life in desert regions. It's how ruling UAE families like the Al Serkals have survived and prospered. It's why Abdallah will probably succeed his father as the kingpin of the Al Serkal property empire and eventually have a huge say in how the Emirates are governed; why, in recent history at least, revolutions, coups and uprisings are quite rare in the Gulf.

If you think about it, in old Arabia it would have been impossible to survive in the desert alone. So families banded together to find water and to move their flocks to new grazing lands. Once a particular tribal group got enough resources they guarded them jealously, refusing to share them with outsiders. To become a member of a tribe — the right family, would be our equivalent, along with the right suburb, the right school, the right job, that sort of thing — you had to be born into it, and marrying outside the broad tribal bloodlines rarely occurred. Even today in the UAE, first-cousin marriages are often encouraged. Keep it in the family and all that!

All this emphasis on the tribal collective tended to mean that few if any strong individual leaders emerged. Tribal leadership meant someone becoming 'first among equals' in a kind of consensus-rule arrangement.

Before long, leading families emerged within the tribes and over the centuries traditions of leadership got passed down. Even now, a well-off, largely compliant Emirati population assumes that certain families will provide the country with leaders as they have in past generations. Then, when the previously nomadic tribes living the desert lifestyle settled down in the oases or on the coast, certain families began to accumulate wealth; and with this wealth their political, economic and social authority increased.

To the nomad Arab-Muslims, in the days before the oil boom, controlling the desert's priceless water meant power. Now business and money do. And research shows that the handful of wealthy families who took control of the newly established Gulf states early in the oil decades were the families whose earlier generations were the region's powerbrokers 200 years before. Then, as luck or Allah would have it, the oil windfall of the 1960s allowed them to hold on to their power and influence. The way government officials are appointed today reflects these old tribal connections. Members of the ruling families get the nod first, followed by families and individual Emiratis with whom the rulers have been traditionally connected.

If you want to apply the basic Muslim principle to all this, you could easily put up an argument that attributes the relative lack of democracy in Islam to Allah. Nothing happens, they say, unless he is willing — including, apparently, more democratic, less authoritarian governments in the Arab-Muslim world. *Insh'allah*, we have democracy; *insh'allah*, we don't. Does this approach apply also to war, poverty, injustice, racism or human rights?

It doesn't come with the same regularity as *insh'allah*, but *wasta* is another Arabic word you keep hearing. At first, it's hard to put your finger on exactly what it is and how it works. Then it hits you: *wasta* is the Arab equivalent of what we in the West call networking, cultivating the right people within the system. It's hardly an exclusively Arab approach to life but, in the region today, *wasta* — being able to get to the right powerful person and having your case heard — is about as close as they get to democracy.

Not everyone sees the future of the ruling families as secure. Some actually think the old, established, privileged 'firm' is in trouble. 'The system of government in the Gulf is archaic,' one long-term expat told me. 'For God knows how long, this place has been all about nepotism, inherited power and *wasta*. But the whole "first among equals" thing is in danger of collapsing.' Down the track — and it may not be too far off — something less tribal and more akin to the Western democracies could quite suddenly emerge. Young Emiratis are now better educated, many of them in the West. As well as that, the internet is opening them up to a whole new world.

On the way from Dubai's airport to the city, a large hoarding hovers over Sheikh Zayed Road. 'Dubai,' it announces,

'Crossroads of the New Economy.' The New Economy meets the New Islam? A bit wishful perhaps, even for unequivocally can-do Dubai ... but who knows?

Islam — the Talk of the Town!

The always offered, coarsely ground, cardamom-flavoured Arabic coffee and its acquired taste duly enjoyed, it was back to the *majlis*. Post-lunch, the conversation was far more relaxed. The interloping Australian journalist had expected a resounding silence when his book-in-progress on the vagaries of Islam was mentioned. But not so.

'Our religion is the talk of the town,' quipped young Sultan, the English-educated 22-year-old nephew of our host Eisa. 'Because of what's happening in the world right now, everybody is talking about Islam. Is that why you are writing your book?' Hopefully it will be an objective look at Islam that might help break down the mutual ignorance between the Muslim and non-Muslim worlds, I told him. 'One thing that's come out of September 11 is that people in the West are asking questions about Islam,' he said. 'That's a good thing. It has never happened before. Some of them now know more about our religion than me. You probably do!'

I asked Sultan what he thought was the ultimate cause of the problem. 'Palestine is what it's all about — but I have no other comment about that.' Why not? He shrugged. He could almost have added that he didn't know me well enough to go into it or trust me with his opinion on such a delicate subject.

The Palestinian problem is something of a poisoned chalice for many moderate Muslims in the region. On any number of occasions, we got the impression that they supported the Palestinian cause on fellow-Muslim principle — not because they agreed with the way the PLO, Hamas, Hezbollah and the suicide bombers go about fighting for it. Many seriously question Yasser Arafat's leadership, regarding him as part of the problem, not part of the solution. To a man — knowing what the women think is a little harder to ascertain — they certainly wanted to see the back of Saddam Hussein, Osama bin Laden and their ilk.

We were chatting prior to the outbreak of the war in Iraq. On the related subject of September 11, Sultan was open, even resolute. 'In every country, every city, every religion, there are good people and there are bad people. We have to show the West that we are not all like those guys who committed that crime on September 11. That was a crime against Islam — not just a crime against America.' That fertile comment is the nub of what moderate Islam feels about the predicament they are in as a result of radicalised Islam and fanatics operating in the name of their faith. Indeed, like young Sultan, they are angry and frustrated by it.

When you press well-off devout young Muslims like Sultan about the wild discrepancies in wealth in their Islamic world, many eventually fall back on *insh'allah*, 'God willing'. 'God willing, I will be rich. If God is not willing, I will not be rich. Do I have choice?' is often the reply you get. Ideologues they are not.

As I was leaving, I noticed, at a distance, two covered women in their *abayas* getting into a car inside the walls of the compound. I had not seen a woman since arriving two hours earlier. I presume they had been showing off their latest Eid fineries in the main building — to each other. That's what I'd been reliably told happened at these sorts of divided Emirati functions. I couldn't help but liken the whole thing to the Great Australian Barbie with its male and female camps — gender apartheid! But the Emirati men and the Australian guest were not standing around at their end of the garden sinking cans of beer. At least in Islam, there's never going to be any argument about who's sober enough to drive home!

As a parting shot, with crunch-time approaching on weapons inspection and the serious possibility of a US invasion of Iraq, I asked Sultan what he thought about this threat. 'Insh'allah, nothing will happen and we can all live in peace,' he said. You have no choice but to get used to this sort of platitude when you're mixing with Arab-Muslims. But, for the sake of Sultan's generation and my two sons in Australia, I hoped this particular insh'allah would turn out to be a prediction as well.

But There are Other Eids

Away from the palatial Al Serkal compound, there was another Eid, in fact any number of other Eids, much simpler but just as festive and friendly. From the sheikhs down, Eid is an opportunity to spend 'quality time' with rellies and friends. It's pretty much non-stop socialising. They go on holidays, travel abroad, go off-road into the desert to picnic and barbeque. Generally, they are hellbent on having what we in the West might call a good time. Sound familiar as December activity goes?

Jasmin Jaffer, a Westernised Muslim, was visiting Dubai from Britain. 'We try to get back in touch with Arabic food,' she told the *Gulf News*. 'We'll explore quite a few restaurants in town and go deep into the local kitchen.' Jasmin's brother, Abdussattar, had lived in Dubai for more than twenty years and planned to take his visiting relatives to some 'cultural spots' — the popular Wild Wadi water park outside Dubai, the Islamic Museum a short drive up the coast in more traditional Sharjah, the Iranian carpet souk in Abu Dhabi and out into the desert and mountains — always with an eye on the food delicacies. 'It's the right time for having fun together,' he said. 'Eid is important.'

While many families enjoy the magnificent sun, sand and sea of the Gulf region during the Eid holiday break, others stick to the more obviously Islamic and Arabic traditions. Ibrahim Hasan, a UAE national, was doing his far more modest version of what I experienced at the Al Serkal residence. 'The first day of Eid is dedicated to all the relatives and friends in town. First, we cook traditional dishes and have a big meal at home. Then we start visiting friends and relatives and have food with them. We spend the whole day eating.' The Hasan family never travels abroad during Eid, preferring instead to go visiting in Dubai, nearby Sharjah or Abu Dhabi.

Aear Kizhuppillikarra is a Sri Lankan worker in the UAE. Don't you love Sri Lankan names? In the tongue-twister stakes, they're rivalled only by the names of Welsh railway stations. Anyway, Aear and his crowd, because of the near-perfect early winter weather of warm days and cool nights, spend a lot of Eid outdoors. He told the *News*: 'We are planning to go to Fun City [a theme park] on one of the days but we haven't decided on any program yet. Eid is like that. The most important thing is to relax and meet people.'

Peter Diago is an expat Indian who's a security guard at one of Dubai's commercial skyscrapers. 'My dear ones are in Bombay but I can't help that. I will work all three days of the Eid holidays.' Peter is a Christian but considers the Eid festival as important as Christmas, worth being celebrated by the entire community, Muslim and non-Muslim. 'I believe we all have the same God and should celebrate these religious feasts together. I make no difference between Christians and non-Christians. I believe a religious celebration is for everyone.'

Many Emiratis shared this idea. Maha Varaei, a Brit who's been resident in Dubai for eight years, commented: 'I don't make any distinction between religious celebrations. I like to enjoy them all. What I like about the UAE is this multicultural environment in which you can have friends of different nationalities and even religions. The intercultural exchange is very educational.'

Educational? We all have a lot to learn about how wrong the non-Muslim world's media-led stereotypes of Islam can be. The only thing that's 'threatening' about the vast majority of Muslims is their normality, their rationality and their reasonableness.

You've Got to Hand it to the Women!

Just before the Eid celebrations, beauty salons in the UAE are packed with eager customers, and they're not just getting their hair and nails done. Many of them are there to have henna — that colour additive you find in many Western shampoos and hair dyes — applied to their feet and the palms of their hands in artistically imaginative patterns. Some salons have around 300 henna-seeking customers a day just before Eid, at a minimum of Dh250 each. That's over A$100.

'The henna artists sit patiently for hours on end, filling hands and feet with intricate designs to the tastes of their clients,' Gulf News journalist Shadiah Abdullah says. 'The patterns range from simple flowers or butterflies for little girls to complex geometrical shapes for the elders. The adult shapes vary from the lacy vines of India and Pakistan to the floral Arab designs, to the bold African geometric patterns. The colours vary from the Sudani henna that's deep black to the more popular dark brown.'

It's hardly accidental that the henna habit has its origins in this part of the world. Henna is made from the leaves of a desert shrub. The leaves are dried, then crushed to make a powder that's sifted to make it superfine. Mixed with water, the powder is made into a paste, with added colour coming from extra ingredients like tea, lemon juice and, extraordinarily enough, petrol and oil! Each salon has its own closely guarded formula. The paste is put into a cone-shaped plastic container a bit like a cake decorator and squeezed out onto the waiting hands and feet.

Why relate this colourful Eid story about beauty salons? Maybe to make the point that not all Muslims, including the women, can be typecast as dour, dowdy and cheerless. Anything but in the Gulf! Wouldn't it be wrong to lump all Christians into the same basket as those sombre sects at the fundamentalist end of the broad spectrum of Christendom? Get my point?

The Package Pilgrimage

The Emirate of Abu Dhabi, more than four-fifths of the total area of the UAE, is not only the largest Emirate among the seven Gulf states but it also has the most oil and is politically the most powerful. Sheikh Zyad bin Sultan al Nahyai, the ruler of Abu Dhabi, is also the president of the entire UAE. You see posters and gigantic billboards with his picture on them everywhere.

Abu Dhabi, the umbrella capital of the Emirates, they say, has seen more growth in the past 20 to 30 years than any other town or city on Earth — mainly because it started from practically nothing. In the mid-1960s old Abu Dhabi was just 'a little huddle of houses between the fort and the sea', according to Shirley Kay, a prolific writer on the Gulf region. The rest, as you might say, is not only history but very recent history. Abu Dhabi is now a thoroughly cosmopolitan city with well-laid out streets, six-laned highways, towering office blocks and green gardens and parks, making it almost unrecognisable from the fishing and pearling village it originally was. As is usual in the Gulf these days, the picturesque wooden dhows are nothing more than a reminder of a very different past.

But Abu Dhabi 2003 is still very Muslim — modern Muslim, but Muslim nonetheless. In fact, Shirley Kay says this is the distinguishing feature between Abu Dhabi and just about any other modern Arab city, including Dubai. Firmly establishing its Muslim credentials are the mosques dotted conveniently throughout both the town centre and the suburbs. 'From any street corner,' Kay notes, 'a number of minarets can be counted.' And lit up for Eid, Abu Dhabi's mosques are not just numerous, they're spectacular.

Modern Islam has joined the UAE's massive property boom. A new Abu Dhabi mosque, under construction near the city's busy international airport, is colossal. When completed, they say, it will be second only to the mosque in Mecca, the largest in the world. It will take thousands of worshippers. Meanwhile, every day and every night, thousands of Muslims could be accused of worshipping the nasty Western value of consumerism. As in Dubai — aptly nicknamed 'Do Buy' — is this a demonstration of modern Islam's dualism or maybe just a spot of confusion about where their religion is headed? After all, as a Muslim friend of mine once pointed out, the Islamic teaching says: 'But commit no excess, for Allah loveth not those given to excess.'

At the showy Marina Mall on the bursting city's foreshore, modern Islam revealed itself yet again in its increasingly

Western, increasingly commercial guise. 'A Symbol of Giving This Ramadan' was the bold heading on the hoarding prominently displayed at the top of the escalator. 'Enter into the spirit of giving this Ramadan. Use our special Ramadan charity bags to donate your old clothes to the less fortunate.' Very Western wording, I thought, but a nice Ramadan touch? Then this: 'Spend a total of Dh200 for a chance to win Dh50 000 weekly in mail vouchers and package trips to Mecca.'

My tiny Western mind lurched. Spend the equivalent of A$85 in the Mall and win a fully paid pilgrimage to the Muslim holy place? Bait-selling the Hajj to turn a dirham? Now that's what I call two worlds colliding.

The Hajj in Living Colour

But why should we be surprised by this brash new commercialised Islam?

For some years now the BBC, CNN and others have been broadcasting live coverage of the Hajj, essence of the Fifth Pillar of Islam, from Mecca. And it probably rates hugely. Muslims own television sets and there are well over a billion people around the world for whom Mecca and the Hajj are the focal points of their Islamic existence. When my friend Hassan told me that his wife — he has only one — and two of his daughters lived in Mecca across the Empty Quarter in Saudi Arabia, it was with real pride. 'It is the birthplace of the Prophet, the Muslim holy place,' he said.

There are places, of course, that other religions single out as holy sites: the Wailing Wall in Jerusalem for the Jews, Bethlehem for Christians, St Peter's Basilica in Rome for Catholics in particular, Westminster Abbey for Anglicans, and the many holy places of the Buddhists, Hindus, Sikhs and other religions. But, as religious events go, for sheer magnitude the annual Hajj pilgrimage to Mecca by millions of Muslims, both men and women, is in a class of its own. No one disputes that the week-long event is the largest annual religious gathering in the world. Attended solely by Islamic believers and closed to non-Muslims — except, these days, on TV — it takes place at a different time each year but always in the twelfth month of the Islamic lunar calendar. Travelling from every nation on the face of the Earth and using whatever form of transportation is available or affordable, the wealthy, the anything but wealthy, merchants, intellectuals, simple working folk, they come. Terrorists — who knows?

Yahiya Emerick says: 'They come to worship God, to renew their faith, to honour God's last Prophet and to look at the meaning of life in a land where all conventional luxuries and worldly distractions are absent. It is a journey that all sane adult Muslims must undertake at least once in their lives if they can afford it and are physically able.'

It's a ritual, he says, the roots of which go right back to the Prophet Abraham — Ibrahim in Arabic. 'By choosing an austere desert region for pilgrimage, Muslims believe, God also wanted to show us that the world is really an illusion of sorts and that we are merely travellers here, so we shouldn't get too comfortable.' Ah, human weakness! Most of the Muslims I saw in the UAE looked pretty comfortable to me.

The focal point of the Hajj is the Ka'aba, the strange cube-shaped building in the centre of Mecca's Great Mosque, the one you see Muslim pilgrims filing around in their tens of thousands between the seventh and tenth days of the holy month. In one corner of the Ka'aba is the revered Black Stone, a meteorite (apparently about the size of a soccer ball) used by the Prophet Abraham in his original shrine. The pilgrims point to it and, if they can get close enough to it, they kiss the Black Stone during their circumambulation of the Ka'aba.

As you'd expect, there are restrictions. No sex, please, we're pilgrims. No shaving, no nailbiting, no colognes or scented oils, no killing or hunting of living things, no fighting, abusing, arguing or causing a public fuss. Bathe but no smelly soap. As Muhammed put it: 'Whoever performs the pilgrimage for Allah's sake and avoids intimate relations and does not fight with anyone or abuses anyone, he or she will return home like the day his mother gave birth to him.'

Intriguingly, men and women follow the same rituals at the same time while they're undertaking the Hajj. They go through the whole process in mixed groups — something you won't see at home at your local mosque. They even pray together. It's simply a matter of practical logistics — there are millions of them making their pilgrimage. So is the Hajj a potentially liberating experience for Muslim women? It could well be. 'Everyone, regardless of colour, race, status, education, economic level or gender comes together and is treated as an equal,' says Yahiya Emerick, who maintains there's nothing quite like being there. 'Everyone stands shoulder to shoulder, together, and no one receives preferential treatment — whether king, president, farmer or locksmith.'

Deserts, Dates and Oases

Deserts, dates, oases and camels are probably the most obvious things that spring to mind when the Gulf is mentioned. They come together — like icebergs, igloos, eskimos and polar bears in a slightly cooler part of the globe to the distant north.

Deserts make up most of the UAE's 80 000 square kilometres of aridly rugged terrain, the great waves of dunes perpetually changing their deceptively serene curvatures as they move noiselessly across the peninsula from the Gulf coast. There are deserts and deserts, of course, but all of them have that elusive natural beauty and the mystical feelings of seemingly limitless space, uniquely big skies and tangible aloneness. You don't have to be an Arab to fall in love with these dry sandy expanses, their rocky outcrops or their welcome oases.

Take the Empty Quarter, a vast, largely unpopulated area of Saudi Arabia south of the UAE, with one of those truly unreal names to lure the incorrigible traveller. Saudi, the land of the Muslim hardliner, is still pretty much a no-go zone for most non-Muslims, particularly inquisitive Western writers poking about among the blood and guts of the quasi-closed religious culture. So the Empty Quarter — like journalist-unfriendly Saudi itself — has to remain on the wish list of places to be visited down the track.

The Arabian desert used to be the home of the Bedouin, much like the ones we met in southern Jordan, living in their unmistakable black goat's-hair tents and grazing their sheep, goats and camels. These days in the UAE, sadly in many ways, there are only a few nomadic *bedu* living in the desert. For better or worse, the wealth factor has hit them like everyone else in the seven former sheikhdoms. Over the past 30 years or so, usually government assisted, they've stopped roaming the sands and moved into modern housing in the towns and villages on the edge of the desert or in the oases.

If deserts are typified by arid ground and the apparent lack of water, oases are at the other end of the Arabian geographic spectrum. We think of them as naturally occurring lush green spots out in the desert, with clusters of crowded date palms, a few Bedouin tents and precious water. But actually they are man-made. Surprisingly, in irregular locations in the 80 per cent of the Arabian peninsula that is desert, there are considerable supplies of underground water. More often than not, these water sources are close to the foot of mountains or even of sand dunes. When it does rain in these areas — which is seldom — the rainwater rushes down the slopes and into the wadis, the old dry riverbeds you see everywhere in the region. Once the rainwater passes along the wadis and onto the desert plains, it sinks deep into the sand, where it is held.

Over many centuries Arabian desert dwellers evolved a way of harnessing or at least exploiting this water, getting to it and moving it to areas they then developed into what we now know as oases. So the smart locals always knew where water was. They used an ingenious system of underground tunnels and aboveground channels known as *falaj*, a word with almost a spiritual ring to it in desert lands. They dug down to the water table and, miraculously, managed to get the water up from its source to an oasis.

These days it's a lot easier. Deep well shafts are still sunk into the sands where water is to be found, but it's amazing how much easier it is to get it up to the surface with the assistance of electric or fuel-driven pumps. But the old channel system, the *falaj*, still directs the water to where it's needed. However, the lush parks, gardens and trees along the UAE's exceptional roads use desalinated water pumped from the Gulf and transported through thousands of kilometres of plastic and rubber piping.

It's not just in the mind of a non-Arab outsider that deserts, oases and dates go so inextricably together. To people in Arab countries they're also inseparable. Desert oases now have other fruit and even vegetables growing in them, but date palms still dominate. The palms desperately need the underground water the oases supply. At Al Ain, an inland city in which I spent some time, the word was that there had been palm groves in the local oases for close to 5000 years, providing food and sustenance from way back.

As diets go, the desert-hardy date has always been crucial to the Arabs. There are dozens of different date varieties, all stuffed with sugar, and probably because of this they've been pretty much a staple food for the Bedouin and others for centuries. But the 70 per cent sugar content makes the wisdom of downing too many of them questionable. The sugar is also why dates, dried or sun-ripened, are edible for much longer than other fruits.

The palm is not just a food-provider. It has all sorts of other uses. As an ancient Arab put it: 'We shade ourselves with it; we eat its fruit; we feed our animals from its seeds; we make pots and mats with its leaves; we build ceilings and columns from its trunk; and we use it as a fuel.'

'Not only has it been a staple food for desert dwellers,' a Muslim acquaintance told me, 'it is well documented that the date has also done its thing for medicinal purposes. For instance, it was used as the primary ingredient to kill worms, to cure sneezing and to make a potion to accelerate hair growth. And mixed with cinnamon and milk, they say, it can be a pretty useful aphrodisiac.'

And it gets curiouser. My acquaintance said that legend has it that an owner of a date orchard in Basra in southern Iraq — a location with no geopolitical implications in this mythical tale — once had a dispute with his favourite date palm. The cranky owner told the palm: 'I will not water you.'

'I don't care,' replied the peeved palm.

'I will not fertilise you,' the owner went on.

'I don't care,' said the palm again.

'Nor will I prune you,' the owner continued.

Once again the palm's reply was: 'I don't care.'

At this, the owner became angry and threatened never to visit the tree again.

'No, please!' cried the palm. 'That would kill me!'

So the date palm, the 'bride of the orchard', could bear the harshest environment but couldn't imagine life without her owner. The moral of the story? The Arab and the date palm rely on each other for survival.

But date palms were revered by ancient Egyptians and later by Christians and Jews as well as Muslims. In fact, the religious traditions of the date, both the tree and the fruit, cross all the usual boundaries. Christians use palm leaves on Palm Sunday. Jews use them to help celebrate their Feast of the Tabernacle. And in the Muslims' Qur'an the date gets at least twenty mentions. Muhammed himself referred to dates more than once. 'A house with a date palm will never go hungry.' They're better *in situ*, by the way!

An Eye for a Camel's Eye

This is a story from the Emirate of Abu Dhabi about a doctor, a camel and the law — or how the astute can get around the notorious Sharia Law!

Dr B, a consultant urologist, is driving on the highway out of town. A camel wanders across the desert in characteristically mindless fashion and walks on to the road in front of Dr B's car, a rugged off-roader complete with a bull bar. He slams into the camel, but the animal isn't killed and the damage to the car is manageable. All very uneventful — but not according to Sharia Law, the ultimate non-religious Islamic authority.

Camels have been in the Emirates and in Arabia for thousands of years. The desert being the desert and camels so well suited to its dry, inhospitable character, they probably will be for many years to come. They roam free, but are loved and well cared for by their owners. The Arabs race them and good racing camels can cost thousands. They also come in for the occasional battering on the roads. It's not a good idea to hit one. It can be very expensive.

As the story goes, the Sharia Court rules that Dr B must pay the owner of the camel a sum equivalent to its market value, some thousands of dirhams. Although the camel should never have been allowed to stray onto the highway, and you'd think that the owner should accept responsibility for the damage to Dr B's vehicle, this is not to be.

This is the Gulf. This is the Sharia Court, the one that boggles so many Western legal minds. Dr B has to reimburse the owner. He duly does so and then, clever and clear-thinking, invokes some rights of his own. He asks for the camel. The owner is no longer interested in the injured beast and so Dr B gets it. And one sorry-looking dromedary it is. The poor creature is retired to a lean-to in the garden of Dr B's villa. With the aid of one of the local sheikh's camel vets, slowly the animal is nursed back to health.

Along the way, the camel becomes noticeably fatter. Dr B realises this extra weight is not the result of eating lashings of lucerne, leftover salad and the odd apple. A quick examination reveals that the camel is pregnant. A few months later, the happy event takes place in the back garden and Dr B now has not one, but two camels. The camel calf grows into a mean-looking prime bull.

Dr B sells both animals and makes a handsome profit. An eye for an eye — but not normally the way Sharia Law would interpret things.

Roadside Religion

It was just after dusk and my friend Hassan, like all drivers in the UAE, was belting along at a mild 150 kph. He was driving me out to the desert in Abu Dhabi to meet a mate of his. Suddenly he slowed and pulled off the road. 'It is my time to pray,' he told me. Hassan knew exactly in which direction to face to pray towards Mecca, essential geography for a staunch Muslim. Out of the car, he alternated between meditating, standing up, bending over and then kneeling, his head touching the ground. He repeated this ritual for several minutes, brushed the dust from his forehead and pure white *dishdasha* — how do they keep the robe so clean? — and returned to the car.

As he drove, we talked. No, he didn't mind me photographing him at prayer. He knew that, as a non-Muslim, I found it interesting. And Allah wouldn't mind because I was trying to find out about Islam. I asked him about praying at the roadside. 'Don't you have to wash before praying? Isn't that an Islamic requirement?' Yes, he said, but when you're travelling, Allah understands. So when you know you're likely to be travelling at prayer time, you wash before starting your journey, especially after using the toilet. You should also clear yourself of any excess gastric juices or stomach gas. This is the reason Muslims are not keen on too much onion or garlic in their food.

And then Hassan offered, unprompted, an awkward personal aspect of pre-prayer cleansing. He must, he explained, wash thoroughly after 'sleeping with a lady — if you are Muslim, only your wife'. Or wives, I speculated. Some outspoken Muslim women I met, by the way, rationalised the 'four wives factor'. They suggested it was Muhammed and God's way of accepting — and, writing it into Islamic law — that men have 'greater sexual needs than women'. For this reason, many Muslim women, it could be said, have a totally different attitude towards monogamy. Some will even compare Muslim men being able to take four wives — whom they're obliged to treat equally in every respect — with unfaithful Western husbands. I wondered aloud about which was preferable: knowing about your husband's other one, two or three wives or knowing that he was lying about having affairs? And what about Western divorce rates, including Christian and Jewish marriage breakdowns, Muslims will ask you. Don't they make a mockery of self-righteous non-Muslim notions of Muslim women being mere chattels, playthings of their husbands?

Hassan said he wouldn't know about this. He only had one wife. He asked me about my family and how many children I had. Two boys, 16 and 13. No girls. Was Mr George aware that, before Islam, the Arabs used to kill their daughters at a young age as a means of population control? Yes, I had heard that. 'I do not understand,' Hassan said, shaking his head. 'But the Prophet stopped this terrible thing. Before Islam, the Arabs lived just like animals.'

Is Anyone Really Born in Timbuktu?

Timbuktu in Mali has always seemed like one of those romantic names that's more a figment of our geographical imagination than a real place. But my friend Hassan was born there, deep in the Sahara Desert of north-west Africa. His wife and two of his daughters live in Mecca. Why Mecca? 'Why not?' he replied with an ironic touch I was going to get used to hearing. 'It is where the Prophet was born.' Silly me.

Before being sponsored to live and work in the UAE by the benevolent scrillionaire Al Serkal family, Hassan had lived in a colourful array of countries: Libya, Tunisia, Morocco, Algeria, Mauritania, Nigeria, Niger, the Ivory Coast, Senegal, Ghana, Benin, Togo, Saudi Arabia, and Mali, of course, where he was born.

In his stumbling but understandable English, he told almost incredible tales, real-life adventures like living in the Sahara for three months tending to a herd of 300 camels, wearing the same clothes the whole time, sleeping in a ditch in the sand dug with his hands and subsisting on camel milk, for which, amazingly, he has not lost his taste. He had other epic stories of working in the salt mines of Mali and driving alone with next to no money across thousands of kilometres of northern Africa to reach the Gulf, surviving on little more than his considerable wits.

'How important was Islam to you through all of that? In fact, how important is it to you now?' I asked. 'Full important Islam, Mr George,' he said, never taking his eyes off the road, always wise in the Emirates. 'I am living Islam. But I never see 100 per cent straight Muslims, not proper Muslims. Not all Muslims good, Mr George. You must separate Islam and Muslims. For me, there is one message, one letter in the Qur'an, not one message from God for me and one for someone else. God gave same message to everyone, same business. Islam tells me, take this message and talk it to everyone. If they take it — OK. If they don't take it, no problem. *Insh'allah.*'

The Milk of Muslim Kindness

Outside our vehicle it was almost pitch-black. Hassan suddenly pointed off to our left and muttered: 'My friend. Over there is my friend's place.' Off in the distance I could just make out what looked like a torch being waved up and down. 'My friend,' Hassan repeated, smiling. We bounced off the surfaced road and made our way along a potholed track gouged into the desert sand. After a few minutes the torch light got brighter and we were able to make out a wire fence and a narrow metal gate.

Inside the gate a robed and turbaned figure waited — Hassan's friend Ibrahim, the camel man. Behind him stood a simple hut of wood and iron. Ibrahim was a camel-herder from Mauritania in north-west Africa where Hassan himself had also lived.

As we walked across the sand in the thin beam of light towards Ibrahim's crude but tidy home, there was something wonderfully out of the ordinary about being there — in the dead of night, a long way from anywhere, with two Arabs and 300 camels!

Camels might have an intrinsic utilitarian role in desert Arab life, but do they have any religious significance? The Bedouin refer to them as *ata Allah*, which means, simply enough, 'gift of God'. I'm sure that Ibrahim, our host for the night, saw them that way. He was the simplest of Muslims, leading a solitary life with his camel herd and his God. 'He feels close to God out here,' Hassan told me, as Ibrahim made sweet tea while we drank fresh camel's milk from a large bowl. Camel's milk is super-rich — much thicker and creamier than cow's milk, but extremely pleasant. They also say it's healthier and more nutritious than normal milk.

Ibrahim poured the hot tea with its obligatory heaps of sugar from small glass to small glass, he then produced rice with saffron, spices and dried meat that we ate cold from the platter. Finger food, of course. No refrigeration, which explained the dried meat, camel, I think. We were out in the middle of the desert so Ibrahim's generous meal was just a little gritty with sand. The foreign guest made appropriately appreciative noises but didn't really eat a lot. Nevertheless, we dined like nomad lords, by candlelight, on Ibrahim's well-worn carpets. Cleaned up, they would have been worth a small fortune back home.

It was late and the eyelids were drooping. Ibrahim moved to another part of the hut with his herder's equipment of ropes and fencing material. Hassan washed his hands, feet and neck and face from a bowl of water, preparation for his late-night prayers, the final ones for the day. For several minutes, he prostrated himself, sang his rituals and prayed out loud in the direction of Mecca. I'd never been so close to a Muslim at prayer. At first it felt a trifle voyeuristic, but then more like a privilege. I got the impression that Hassan, a religiously devout but culturally moderate Muslim, wanted his non-Muslim Australian friend to share his prayer experience. I guess he wanted me to know him as a Muslim. Seeing him practising his faith, in such close proximity, there was no doubt that I was with a true Muslim.

Conversation with a Convert

Back in Dubai, I went looking for someone to talk to about basic Muslim beliefs. I found him at the Islamic Learning Centre's Hospitality Tent at the Mercato Mall. A Ramadan Hospitality Tent? How can you bestow hospitality during a

A younger yours truly, reporting for *60 Minutes*, with an old Islamic leader, Iran's prodigal son, Ayatollah Khomeini, in Tehran during what the author calls 'Gulf War I' — the one *between* Muslims, not against them.

After Desert Storm. The half-friendly, half-frightened stare from this Kurdish refugee on the Iran–Iraq frontier was unforgettable.

Through the Damascus Gate and behind the walls of Old Jerusalem, 'the battle for God', as religious writer Karen Armstrong puts it so pithily, goes on between Christians, Jews and Muslims — not necessarily with guns and explosives.

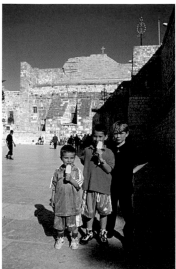

Top Left The author and his son Serge outside the mind-blowing Treasury building in 'the rose-red city half as old as Time', Petra. When Muslims and Jews can again marvel at it together — as they did a few short years ago — peace in the Middle East could be on the way.

Top Right Paddle-pops in Manger Square, Bethlehem. A short few months later, Palestinian fighters took refuge in the Church of the Nativity, pictured behind Serge and his mates. Bethlehem was under siege and like people all around the world, Serge saw the siege on television back home in Australia. He was pretty upset.

Left Bedding down with Bedouins in their goat-hair tents in Wadi Rum, southern Jordan. No interior photos were possible. The women from the nomadic Muslim family were inside.

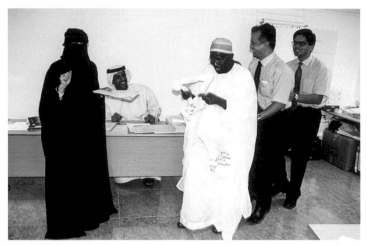

Confused about what being a Muslim really means — or even how they look? These tourism students in Dubai are clothed differently, but they are all Muslims. Allah's devotees are as easy, or as difficult, to categorise and label as Asians — the Tibetan monk vs a Filipino Catholic — or even us Westerners.

The author 'refreshing' in the desert near Al Ain, Abu Dhabi. This precious oasis water doesn't just happen, by the way. Over the centuries, ingenious Arabs have put in a lot of work to get it to those date palms and keep it there.

The author on a domestic spending spree in the central souk in Al Ain, Abu Dhabi. This is as close as a non-husband male is likely to get to seeing behind that distinctive Omani face cover. At first it feels strange to talk to women covered by it — but you get used to it. Their dress becomes part of who and what they are, certainly not a barrier to communication.

Our Tasmanian friends, the Angles, and their Muslim friends, Majid and his family, relaxing together. They all call Muscat, the Omani capital, home.

A boys' night out deep in the Abu Dhabi desert. Plenty of this sort of male bonding goes on when the boy–girl dating game just doesn't happen.

The *shisha* — you have to try it, don't you? It was hard going for a non-Muslim, non-smoker — lots of coughing and spluttering preceded the inhaling. A bit like Bill Clinton! It was apple-flavoured, in case you were wondering!

Top You can see why they call it the 'Wall of Death'! God willing, you won't die; God willing, you will! And that's about as Islamic as you can get — placing your life in God's hands.

Insh'allah — a religious philosophy in one word.

Left In the United Arab Emirates, you keep seeing the two Islams — the traditional and the modern, the old and the new — even at the Wall of Death. This teenage sport — quad-bike sandhill bashing — is as common on the sandy suburban street corners as skateboard parks are in our neighbourhoods.

Top Kirsty the photo-journalist isn't a Western hairdressers' kind of gal — but she had a ball at one of Dubai's many Henna Salons. It's very 'hands on'.

Left We told you they don't all 'cover'. But Dubai national Hessa, shows that the *hijab* can be sophisticated and fashionable. Arab-Muslims dour and dowdy? You've got to be joking!

صالون فلورا للسيدات
FLORA LADIES SALON

Two devout Gulf Muslims, old and young, readying themselves for Friday prayers. Normally, Muslim kids are not introduced to the prayer ritual until they're a bit older than this guy. Call it religious brainwashing, if you like, but how different is it from sending non-Muslim kids off to Sunday School?

For Muslims, cleanliness is definitely paramount. All mosques provide pre-prayer washing facilities. At the 'Open Doors Open Minds' mosque the author was allowed to wash the feet, hands, face and neck even though he didn't pray. Pretending for a moment you're a Muslim is one thing, being sacrilegious is another.

The mosque's director, Abdallah prays while the author watches. He had no objection to my being there, or the photo. 'Islam should have nothing to hide,' he said.

Half-way home and driver, Hassan, stops for this roadside ritual — evening prayers beside one of the freeways in the UAE. Allah, Hassan assured me, understands the pressures on busy Muslim travellers.

The Muslim and non-Muslim worlds in microcosm! Hassan described himself to me as 'a simple Muslim from Timbuktu'. 'George Bush is not a straight Christian — but many Muslims are also not straight Muslims,' he told me in one of our many chats about them and us.

A very basic Arab-Muslim meal, always shared from the floor, always on a platter, always with rice, always eaten with the right hand only! And how about that mobile phone? Told you Islam was changing.

Socioeconomics, meaning oil wealth, aside, the idea is the same at Abdallah's house where this lavish Iftar evening meal is typical of the culturally super-hospitable Arabs. Abdallah's dad, Eisa bin Nasser Al Serkal turns on an Iftar meal daily for sometimes hundreds of people — friends or people in need or away from their home, like I was. During Ramadan, that's zakat, a 'religiously compulsory charity' and one of the Five Pillars of Islam.

The author hard at it on location in a thriving oasis town near the borders of Oman and Saudi Arabia. Modern Arab architecture can be terrific — simple but elegant. Beats the hell out of your suburban double-garage brick veneer.

Mosques mushroom in the Islamic world. Some are unimaginably costly artistic showpieces like the Sultan's new one in Muscat.

The two Saeeds: the proud golfer and the traditional Arab-Muslim — in fact, the computer literate Arab-Muslim golfer never off the dreaded mobile!

Left An irresistible shot! — And the 'Arabic taste' did make a positive gastronomic difference to the product!

Below Says it all really — Muslims and the modern world together in a shopping mall. Surely that's not the so-called 'clash of civilisations', more like a meeting of the minds.

An Emirati local and the startlingly recognisable Burj Al Arab hotel in Dubai —
traditional and hardly traditional Islam. Muslims — looking forward to the past?

To an outsider, our Omani Muslim friend Khalfan Esry appears to live in two starkly different worlds. But he would argue there is only one — the world of his Islamic culture, tradition and religion, the cornerstone — in fact, the entire set of building blocks — of his existence.

As devout as Muslims can be, Khalfan is an engineer with a Gulf petroleum corporation, a former 'Islamic DJ' and an IT nut! Here he is explaining the Five Pillars of Islam on his self-generated website. These days, in most parts of the Islamic world, you can get electronic Qurans with the capacity and software to search, translate and index their entire faith — even a palm PC! Backward barbarians?

Abdallah's petrol-blue Porsche transported us to prayers at the Open Mosque in Dubai. I know we normally associate Arab-Muslims with camels and goat-hair tents, but Abdallah moves between the two Islamic worlds with consummate ease. The greater the movement between the moderate Muslim and moderate non-Muslim worlds, the greater the potential irrelevance of the homicidal maniacs calling themselves 'holy warriors', that we call terrorists!

Top Saeed Al Marjiby, another of our 'moderate Muslim' interviewees, is a member of the Majlis a'Shura, the quasi-democratic parliament in the Sultanate of Oman. His hope is that his kids — Zahra, Bushra, Sundas and Ahmed — will live in a less 'quasi' and more 'real' democracy. Saeed has one of the smartest minds I have locked political horns with anywhere in the world!

Below left Just as on the ball was lawyer Majid Al Toky. A committed moderate forever finding things to laugh about, Majid was nevertheless scathing about the American role in the Muslim world. 'As long as you're playing ball, playing the US game, you're a good boy,' he told Kirsty as she photographed him and his family. 'But if you disagree, then you're a terrorist!'

Below right Don't let the bare feet fool you! Sadek Sulaiman, a former Omani Ambassador to the US, was another profound moderate who was also — just profound. 'The Americans don't need criticism, they need reassurance. A strong person is not always a secure person,' he told me in Muscat. 'In the time immediately after 9/11, it was like somebody had hit them and it's still hurting — a lot!'

This Bedu woman had to ask her husband for permission for Kirst to photograph her at a roadside stall. But, as we speak, education is free and booming in the moderate Islamic world — certainly in the Gulf. So much so, there's a good chance her sons will live in a Muslim religio-culture where women won't have to ask for permission to do anything. Indeed, many have already reached that stage.

Muslim fast? 'We only man the tent after sunset, in other words, after Iftar, the evening break in the fast,' the religiously entrepreneurial young Khaleem told me. 'It's a deliberately relaxed environment where we serve coffee and dates to all our visitors and converse in English.'

So, as a Muslim convert, what was Khaleem's position on the three-way split on God? Whose God was it anyway?

As Khaleem saw it, Christians and Jews have both 'construed' God's message incorrectly. They've got a few basics very wrong. For instance, when Christians say Jesus was the Son of God, they've 'misconstrued' things.

How come Muslims are apparently so tolerant of the Jewish and Christian religions, I asked.

'Because Jews and Christians also believe in God, the same God that Muslims believe in — but that we call Allah.'

'But they don't appear to feel the same way about you and your faith. They don't seem to be that tolerant. They think you're wrong. They don't seem to regard their God and your Allah as one and the same and despite centuries of debate, that doesn't look like it's about to change. Is that the core of the tension between the three of you — more than oil, more than land, more than race or identity, more than war and all the rest?'

'For us, Islam is everything — religion, culture and life, all of them a gift from God,' Khaleem replied.

I commented that it was interesting that his Learning Centre had set up its hospitality tent in the shopping mall, right in front of a Western-style supermarket.

'This is our humble contribution to try and inform non-Muslims about Islam and the holy month,' Khaleem smiled, obviously referring to the many expats living in Dubai. 'We deliberately chose Iftar, when people have ended their fast for the day, as the time to do it. Have you eaten?'

I had, at lunch time, I told him. I wasn't fasting but had been thinking I might try — sort of pretending I was a Muslim. What did he think?

'You should fast,' he said, 'just for the physical experience, not a religious one.' He grinned. 'You can't pretend to be a Muslim. You either become a Muslim or you don't.'

Would it be disrespectful for me to pretend? He nodded. So much for that bright idea!

As the shoppers in the Dubai mall streamed past, Khaleem told me that converting to Islam was merely a matter of committing yourself to the idea that there is one God, Allah, and then following that religious commitment, believing the Qur'an to be the word of God delivered by the Prophet Muhammed. It sounded straightforward, but I couldn't help wondering if it really was.

Did he believe Christians and Jews had the same commitment?

'No, not really,' he said. 'Certainly not like we do in our five daily prayers. Not like we do by fasting for a month every year. We're not saying there are no Christians and Jews who claim to live by the will of God, but I doubt there are any who would fast for a month every year to prove it! Do you?'

I was sure there had to be some out there somewhere. But no, I said, I don't know of any personally.

It sounded like it was time to balance the books a little, at least in political terms. I pointed out that there were people 'out there' calling themselves Muslims who hijack planes and blow up buildings, killing innocent people. There are others who strap explosives to their bodies, take their own lives and knowingly murder Jewish men, women and children. Are they Muslims? I asked.

Khaleem looked down for a moment, thought about the

question and replied. 'Yes, they are Muslims,' he said. 'But they are wrong Muslims, bad Muslims.'

Outside the tent, the enthusiastic Emirati shoppers seemed more interested in ordering another Starbucks cappuccino than this religious war of the worlds.

No real Arabic cardamom coffee in the Mercato Mall, by the way. Another sign? But from whose God?

The Messenger — Not the Son of Allah

In Islam, conversations turn easily to religion. It's a real point of difference, I believe, between the Muslim faith and Judaism and Christianity. It's not that Muslims are necessarily more devout, it's just that Islam — the subjugation of everything in life to God, as they put it — is more intimately and constantly on their minds.

Muslims, even modern ones like my friend Abdallah, will claim that Muhammed was 'the complete human being'. They don't claim he was God, and definitely not the Son of God, but a flesh-and-blood human. Muhammed, Abdallah reiterated at his home during our Iftar meal, was 'the Messenger of God'. He was an ordinary man who at the age of about 40 retreated to a cave near Mecca, 'to think'. As he was meditating, he was visited by the Archangel Gabriel, who delivered the Word of God to him. Apparently, this recitation went on until Muhammed's death 22 years later.

Muhammed was a successful businessman for his times, the late sixth and early seventh centuries. But he was also illiterate.

They say he passed on Gabriel's revelations to his followers, who committed them to memory and later wrote them down on palm leaves, stones or any other material that came to hand. Islam began with Muhammed's memorised words. Even today, there's no disputing that the Qur'an is the most 'memorised' book in the world. Some Muslims have committed the entire thing — more than 400 pages in one English edition — to memory.

Interestingly, 1371 years after Muhammed's death, Muslims still hold all the early Hebrew prophets in high reverence — including Moses and Jesus, as baffling as this might be to Jews and Christians.

Oil and Troubled Waters

Thousands of years ago, the mountainous parts of the Gulf had enough minerals to make the region prosperous even then. But oil, the most valuable, almost priceless, natural resource ever discovered there, as English writer Shirley Kay put it, was 'the gift neither of the desert nor of the mountains, but of the sea'.

Kay's explanation is clear and helpful. 'In the shallow seas of the Gulf, small marine plants and creatures, mostly plankton it is thought, died and accumulated millions of years ago on the seabed,' she says in her 1993 book, *Land of the Emirates*. 'They were buried under silt and suffered a "sea change" to become the precious black liquid we know today as oil. This flowed under pressure through cracks and pores in the rock layer until it came to a dead end. There the oil might accumulate, perhaps under a rock dome which could hold enough of it to be worth extracting today.'

Super-lucrative oil, gases as well, energy sources in themselves, are now the great little earner of petro-dollars for what have become known as the oil states.

And it's all happened so quickly. Oil was discovered offshore in the Sheikhdom of Abu Dhabi, part of the latter-day United Arab Emirates, in 1959 — less than fifty years ago. But, as Kay and others point out, those years have been the most dynamic the area has known. The entire Arab-Muslim region has been changed more by the discovery of oil than by any other event since the coming of Islam. Kays adds: 'It's almost impossible now to envisage the country before 1960. All the roads, all but one hospital, all but two or three of the schools have been built since then. Photographs taken before that time seem to be of a different world. Only occasionally is some outstanding feature such as the Abu Dhabi fort or Dubai's creek still recognisable.'

Interestingly, some local observers point out that the region's oil wealth, while it has had an unfortunate, even damaging, impact on Muslim habits and tradition, has actually reinforced the religious basis of Emirate society. Islam came to the region from Mecca and Medina in what is now Saudi Arabia shortly after the Prophet Muhammed's death. It's been the root system of life for people living on the shores of the Gulf ever since — for close to fourteen centuries. But in a hugely ironic twist the oil-related development of the past half-century has resulted in the construction of hundreds of fantastic new mosques. These days, in any of the cities of the Emirates and further afield in the Gulf, it's said that no one has to walk further than half a kilometre to the nearest mosque. Exploring coastal places like Dubai, Sharjah and Abu Dhabi, and even inland Al Ain, this certainly appears to be true. And, along with the proliferation of mosques, improved literacy has meant that young Muslims are able to study their religion properly rather than rote-learn it from the Qur'an, which was all they could do in the past.

Again ironically, it also appears that greater religious tolerance has been another by-product of the modernity that's come to the Gulf. According to Shirley Kay, people living the Emirates brand of Islam are 'sufficiently confident and sure of their own faith to be tolerant of the beliefs and customs of other people'. Nonetheless, Emirati Muslims, like Muslims anywhere, are adamant that theirs is 'the one true faith'. Have no doubt, as they see it, Muhammed filled in the gaps left by the Old Testament prophets and even by Christ. The rest of us, whatever we believe or don't believe, have no choice as Judgement Day approaches but to follow Muhammed's message as conveyed in the Qur'an.

That said, Muslims in the Gulf, and most other Islamic places, are not evangelical in the same way that fundamentalist Christians can be, overbearingly and self-righteously. Others can believe what they like, but Muslims are convinced that they are right. But they're hardly alone in the religious arrogance stakes! What is it about religiously based explanations for life, Muslim or non-Muslim, that leaves no room for doubt?

On the very day I jotted down the preceding lines, sitting at a coffee shop in Al Ain in the Abu Dhabi desert, back at home in Australia, a wealthy, cricket-loving, Howard-voting, Christian-Arab Australian was refused permission to build a mosque in outer suburban Sydney for his Muslim clients. Hundreds of wealthy and not-so-wealthy, cricket-loving, Howard-voting, Christian non-Arab Australians had successfully opposed such an 'outrageous' plan.

Why? Answer that one and we are on the way to diluting the ignorance and prejudice barrier — and not just in the suburbs of

Australia. Meanwhile, the gross overreaction to the idea of a new mosque in their suburb from allegedly tolerant, egalitarian Australians was, to say the least, pretty disturbing.

Who knows, having a mosque around the corner or in the next suburb, attended by moderate Muslims, could be a start to learning to live with them comfortably, despite their and our quirky beliefs about this or that.

Open Doors, Open Minds

The fact is that wherever they live in the world, not just in Australia, very few non-Muslims ever get to go inside a mosque. In many places they couldn't even if they wanted to, because they aren't welcome without, that is, swearing prior allegiance to Allah. That's why Abdallah bin Eisa Al Serkal's Open Doors, Open Minds project at the Jumeirah Mosque in Bastakia, Dubai, is so different. You don't have to be a Muslim to go inside, at certain times and on certain days. In my experience, the place is unique in the Muslim world, a real breakthrough. 'We see it as an educational cultural centre, an opportunity to build a bridge across the gap between Islam and the non-Muslim world,' the affable Abdallah will tell you. All you have to do is ask. In Abdallah's eyes, the fact that Muslims and non-Muslims are different doesn't mean we can't be friends. We can disagree on things, but we can still be friends, he says.

His Open Mosque at Jumeira is the key to the work of the Sheikh Mohammed Centre for Cultural Understanding, a bold move in which Abdallah is the driving force. He's been the director of the centre since it was established, with the UAE government's imprimatur, in 1995. The fact that it is located at

Jumeira is not accidental: that's where many if not most of Dubai's extensive expat community live.

But Abdallah isn't all earnest do-gooder; his modest vehicle — a petrol-blue latest model two-seater Porsche with rich ochre upholstery and wood-panelled dash — somehow helped epitomise the hybrid nature of the UAE. Capitalism, culture and religion live comfortably together in this place.

Sharia Law — or Lore?

What's all this stuff about a Muslim way of life? Is there such a thing? You'd better believe there is, because it's not going to go away. Whether they live in the privileged wealth and splendour of glitzy Dubai or in the battered homes and perpetual strife of Palestinian refugee camps like Jenin in the Occupied Territories, for almost a quarter of the world's population there's definitely a Muslim way of life. Some of it is almost indistinguishable from our own Western existence. Other bits of it are hugely different. Some of the differences though are pretty mild; at the opposite end of the spectrum, others, not without reason, get tagged as 'barbaric' or uncivilised.

The word 'Sharia' comes from an Arabic term that translates as 'clear path'. It's based both on the Qur'an itself and the sayings of Muhammed conveyed in what's known to Muslims as the Hadith. But is it part of the Islamic religion? That's not exactly clear.

Over nearly 1400 years of Islam, Sharia Law has come to be regarded by non-Muslims as the only correct way for Muslim believers to behave on a daily basis. It certainly covers not just religion but politics, society, business, domesticity and even the most private parts of life — the things my friend Abdallah quaintly calls 'the husband and wife thing'.

Think, for a moment, about the extent to which the Bible, the Christian word of God, has influenced British and other law over the centuries. By the same token, are the Ten Commandments religious or cultural laws — or just common sense? Throughout Muslim history Shariah Law has been something of a legal and religious minefield, interpreted differently by different Muslims at different times. The two main sects, the Sunnis and the Shi'ites, have their similar but separate versions of it. The difference is in the detail, not the principle. Oddly enough, these two Muslim groupings came about as a result of a petty feud after Muhammed's death, not because they had any serious differences of opinion over their newly established Qur'an.

To many, both Muslim and non-Muslim, the Qur'an and its application in Sharia Law appear to be at odds. Religious extremists like the Taliban, who imposed their brutally rigorous form of Sharia in Afghanistan, are a classic example. Were they really behaving in accordance with the central teachings of the Prophet? My moderate Muslim friends were adamant the Taliban were not real Muslims, but 'fundies' who took Islam at ridiculous face value.

There's plenty in the all-important plank in Islam that Muslims call Sharia Law that is unfair, unjust, unequal, nasty, inhuman, even just plain nutty! But think about it, we Westerners often don't know what our laws really are until we break one of them or someone uses one against us. So how many of us are really in a position to compare the laws that govern our daily lives with the ones Muslims use as their behavioural ruler?

Death on the Highway

You've only got to see Emiratis driving to know that they believe as much in an afterlife Paradise as they do in this one. *Insh'allah*, God willing, most of them will probably survive long enough to enjoy this earthly life for a while. But Allah must be taking care of them on the roads, as they believe he does, because they take precious little care themselves. Muslims drive like bats out of Hell — or rather, bats trying to get into Heaven!

In Dubai one evening, quite by chance I found myself in the company of a different kind of driver. The Australian motor racing icon Peter Brock was in town to share his considerable expertise with a bunch of locals about to embark on the construction of an international motor racing circuit. After dinner, Brock invited some of us to go with him to a car fit-out business just off Dubai's main artery, Sheikh Zayed Road, a public strip that could itself easily double as an elongated straight for a motor race.

Multi-laned in both directions, Sheikh Zayed Road provides the locals with the opportunity to drive, swerve, overtake and exit at breakneck speeds, at all hours of the day and night. This seemed so particularly during Ramadan when, after the day's fast, Emiratis party until well after midnight. There are no pedestrian overpasses or underpasses, and dozens of Dubai Nationals are killed each year trying to get from one side of the highway to the other. In fact, the Emirates has one of the highest road fatality rates in the world, not bad for a country just emerging from the 'ship of the desert' era.

Anyway, at this place that Peter Brock took us there were about a dozen very flash, very sporty, very powerful vehicles in various stages of undress. Peter explained that they were being 'knocked down' and rebuilt to include every conceivable vehicular extra. You know by now that money is never an object to most Dubain nationals, but here were extraordinary vehicles already worth over 100 000 dollars having as much again spent on them to rev them up even further! The state-of-the-art garage was owned and run by the son of a member of a ruling UAE family, we were quietly informed. It was staffed by migrant workers from the Indian subcontinent. That made sense. In fact, given the nature of contemporary Dubai society, it was typical — wealthy Arab-Muslims enjoying themselves while far from wealthy Asian-Muslims did the work.

Even with his expertise, indeed probably *because* of his expertise, Peter was as gobsmacked as the rest of us. Running his knowing eye over these turbocharged, wired-for-sound rich boys' toys, Peter, out of earshot of the locals, whispered: 'These things aren't vehicles, they're bloody weapons. If they drive them the way you could after the remake, if they don't kill themselves, they'll certainly kill somebody else! These cars are great for the racing track, not a bloody road.'

I was contemplating this episode a few days later, still during Ramadan, travelling from Dubai to Al Ain, an hour and a half by road to the south, near the border with Oman. The dicing-with-death Emirati style of driving was in evidence again on the magnificent new six-lane highway — drivers changing lanes at will without warning, not using indicators, cutting in front of us, 'owning' the road with no obvious concern for their own welfare or that of others. What were they thinking? *Were* they thinking? It was late afternoon and maybe they were hellbent on getting to Al Ain for Iftar, racing to get home for a snack to put an end to the hunger pangs of the fast.

'Driving here is not for the obsessive-compulsive,' said my expat doctor friend, Charl. 'Traffic lanes are merely to remind

you that you're on a road. And indicator lights are just annoying
things that Western drivers use. Both the Emiratis and Muslim
workers from the subcontinent think, if Allah wants me to crash,
so be it. Of course, if they do crash, the recriminations are pretty
radical. Once we had members of two tribes fight each other in
the Emergency Room while we were busy resuscitating a car
crash victim. A man from one tribe had crashed his car into a car
from another tribe. Because of the melee the resuscitation
attempt had to be called off, and the victim died. But the fight
carried on.'

Wall of Death

On the outskirts of Al Ain, during one of my visits there,
we turned off the highway from Dubai and drove into the
gorgeous pre-sunset pink of the desert dunes. We were looking
for a guy who trained falcons there. A short distance from the
main road, at the base of a ridge of high dunes, we found him,
not just training his falcons but also teaching his younger
brothers how to train the birds. Falconry, for those unfamiliar
with it, is a traditional Arab method of hunting in the
Emirates and Oman. Over the centuries the Arabs, particularly
Bedouin nomads, have trained these sleek, fast-flying birds of
prey, very much like hawks in appearance, to chase down and
catch desert bustards and pigeons. Falconry is not practised
much as a way of getting food; it's more a social pastime.
Seeing them at it, it's also obviously a way to keep up their
proud Arab traditions.

We watched them with their protective arm-guards, enticing
young falcons to fly off the keeper's forearm and catch recently

killed pigeons tied to a rope twirled like a lasso in midflight. As we watched, entranced by this old desert custom, a new desert custom burst on to the scene. Suddenly, dozens of local teenagers arrived noisily at the same spot on expensive quad-bikes. For the next two hours, while there was light enough in the sky, they rode the rowdy contraptions at breakneck speeds, sometimes with a pillion rider, up and down the near vertical face of the dunes.

'What are they trying to do, commit suicide?' I asked my companions. 'Can't be,' came the reply. 'Suicide is against Islamic Law.' But getting bloody close to it obviously isn't!

The Dualism of Life

You could say that for many Muslims, not just the crazy quad-riders, there's literally a fine line between life and death. As we keep saying, it all comes down to *insh'allah*.'

An Australian, Steve Margolis, is professor of family medicine at the respected UAE teaching university in Al Ain. Steve and the author spent a day hanging out at some of his adopted district's many interesting spots. We took in the dusty camel souk on the outskirts of town, revelled in the crowded, noisy produce and bric-a-brac souk in Al Ain's centre, and drove the few kilometres to the Economic Free Zone in the neighbouring Sultanate of Oman. On the way, we stopped and gawped at part of what is to become an astonishing 500 kilometre long, five-metre high razor-wire fence forming an official barrier between the two Gulf states; it's designed to stop the flow of illegal immigrants into the UAE. We bought gifts of Arab perfumes made to ancient recipes and spices in the Omani market town of

Buraimi. We eyed off the refurbished rifles and traditional daggers also on sale there, remnants of old Islam. Back in Al Ain, that other, equally enthralling Islam, the ultra-modern Islam was waiting: Western-style shopping malls with their ATM machines, escalators, piped music, designer gear, exotic lingerie boutiques, electronic goods stores, slick coffee shops and retail outlets strictly for the Emirati oil-rich, including veiled women shopping for their 'designer abayas'.

In a few hours, we'd seen two worlds. Steve, in the Emirate of Abu Dhabi for four years, has made a study of what he called the 'dualism of Emirati Islamic life', the apparent contradictions and double standards that typify Islam. This dualism is definitely not confined to the way Muslims drive, he told me. It can have odd effects on behaviour — like the woman he tried to treat who was in the throes of an epileptic fit in the hospital waiting room. 'She was more intent on keeping her head covered and the veil over her face than being treated,' Steve recalled. Or the extremely distressed mother whose child was rescued, almost drowned, from the bottom of an Al Ain hotel swimming pool. 'She refused mouth-to-mouth from a Western doctor at the scene. She wanted to wait until a Muslim doctor could be called to her dying child. There was none around. Resuscitation did not take place and the child could not be revived. A sad but true story.

But if their attitude towards life is curious, most Westerners would find their attitude towards death even stranger, fatalistic maybe. 'For instance, there's no Good Samaritan law here,' Steve told me. 'So if you see an accident — and there are plenty of them every day — you have to curb your natural, let alone your professional, instinct to go to the aid of the victims. Apart from any other reason ... you could end up in trouble with both the police and the religious authorities if you did. There are actually cases of doctors going to the aid of dying crash victims — even dying casualty patients in hospitals — and being charged with culpability, even responsibility, because the person ultimately died. The doctor tried to help; the patient died. Therefore, it's the doctor's fault that they died.'

The 'eye for an eye' factor also comes into play. Most of these things can be settled, either through the Sharia Court or privately, by the payment of 'blood money'; there's apparently a sliding scale of reparation. But you have to ask just how different this is in practical effect from our application of common law to accident culpability cases and the damages claims that go with them. This is not a justification of Arab-Muslim 'blood money': it is merely to wonder whether there's a parallel of sorts in Western law. The law be an ass, wherever it's practised. As Steve put it: 'You become very aware of the contradictions in life here, but you also find yourself thinking about the contradictions at home, the ones you take for granted and don't regard as contradictions.'

Double Standards or Double Talk?

They are not alone in having them, but some Islamic double standards are intriguing.

Many Muslims secretly drink alcohol even though it's forbidden under Sharia Law and the penalties can be severe. In Al Ain, you can see expensive, Arab-owned, four-wheel-drive vans and sedans parked outside the expat-only liquor stores waiting to collect supplies of imported beer, wine and spirits ordered by phone, probably a mobile. On the other hand, Muslims would *never* eat pork. Pork is *haram*, forbidden by religious law, the pig being considered unclean. But, like the liquor stores, there are special shops and sections in supermarkets selling pork to non-Muslims. Do we regard the availability of these pieces of forbidden Islamic fruit as a double standard or as an admirable tolerance of other beliefs, customs and eating habits? That said, if you're absolutely desperate for a greasy pork treat, the Hilton Hotel in Al Ain serves bacon and eggs as part of its Western breakfast.

These contradictions-cum-flexibility abound. There's no insistence on non-Muslims abiding by strict Muslim dress code, as liberal as this is becoming in parts of the Islamic world. But in far more stringently Islamic places, like Saudi Arabia across the Empty Quarter, things are still much harsher. And so are the penalties for breaches of the law. Tolerant the Saudis are not.

Intrusive Western innovations like satellite TV, including its more raunchy content, and FM radio, almost impossible to curtail, are part of a slow cultural liberation process. Strangely, governments and religious authorities both encourage the use of the internet, but the Web is censored. Paradoxically, an aptly named US company, Watchdog, provides a proxy ISD server to enable the blocking of stuff offensive to Islam. 'But any Emirati teenager can crack it,' one local assured me.

If you think Islam is a pretty basic, earthy sort of religion that was born out in the desert sands and stayed there, think again! In the Al Ain shopping mall, for instance, one of the most up-to-date retail complexes you're going to find anywhere in the world, there's a shop called the Jumbo Super Store, a one-stop affair offering the latest model consumer electronics, electrical household appliances, the complete range of computers and IT products, office equipment, the obligatory mobiles and even satellite phones. And the ubiquitous Starbucks, of course! They are the latter-day McDonald's.

'Just looking' in the Jumbo Super Store, I came upon an item for 'the Muslim who has everything'. Prominently displayed and promoted as a Ramadan special, it was billed as 'the world's first digital Qur'an', a pocket-size guide to Islam you can tuck into your *dishdasha* or *abaya* that will tell you, among other things, those five vital prayer times each day.

But it gets better! The portable electronic-age Muslim's little toy features not just a cover-to-cover recitation of the Qur'an but also forty Hadith, the 'best of' Muhammed's sayings, as well as a complete guide to the annual Hajj, automatic wake-up calls for dawn prayers, plus a one-touch translation of the Muslim holy book into any number of languages. You almost had to buy one.

Booze — is it Worth the Trouble?

'Did you know that 27 per cent of all deaths in the UAE are caused by cardiac failure and the next highest — 17 per cent — are from road accidents?' My informant was another expat doctor resident in the UAE for years. He followed up this disturbing statistic with a tongue-in-cheek quip: 'They drive like bloody maniacs. Thank God they don't drink.' Crude? Religiously insensitive? Knowing the bloke, I can vouch that he is neither.

The 'booze issue' in Islam is a big one for both Muslims and Westerners. In the West, alcohol has become a part of everyday living. Its pleasures are measurable; the social negatives that flow from it by the keg obvious everywhere you look. But to buy alcoholic beverages in an Islamic country is not easy. In all of them, other than in specially partitioned sections of five-star hotels, you have to be issued with a licence before you can get your hands on the stuff, let alone your lips around a glass. In some places, you actually have to declare yourself an alcoholic to get permission to buy and drink alcohol!

After you've got your coveted licence and tracked down a not-so-immediately-obvious local 'booze shop', you have to ask yourself whether it's worth the hassle. That old crack about 'really needing a drink' definitely applies to getting one anywhere in the Muslim world. Islam is notorious for not only forbidding its followers to consume any and all forms of alcoholic beverages, but also for making it extremely difficult for non-Muslims to get hold of it. Wine, beer and spirits are off limits as distinct from off-licence. You come away with the distinct impression that Muslims would prefer you didn't drink while you were in their country.

In Al Ain in Abu Dhabi, there were two booze shops: one at the back of an obscure building, the other tucked away via a service entrance of the Hilton Hotel.

Why the excessive objection? The Qur'an does have a definitive word or two to say about it. 'If they ask you about drinking and gambling, tell them: "There is both harm and benefit in them, but the harm is greater than the benefit."' I think that's a 'no'. When you quiz Muslims about alcohol, they often sound like well-meaning Western social workers. They point out that the evidence against alcohol is indisputable wherever you look for it — in families, communities or entire nations in those parts of the world where it is freely available. It's hard to argue.

Muslims might not drink, but they do smoke. In Al Ain, they call them 'smoking shops', not inappropriate given that's what Emirati men do there — smoke. By smoke, of course, we mean the *shisha*, the hubbly-bubbly. But, where there's smoke, there's no booze, you could say!

A Failed Suicide Attempt

A sorry tale is told in Abu Dhabi of an immigrant Pakistani worker who'd lost his job and wasn't able to send money home to his needy family in Karachi. In his desperation and shame, he decided that suicide was the only acceptable course of action for a hopeless failure like himself. To this end, he threw himself in front of a car driven, as it turned out, by an unsuspecting English expat. The Pakistani was seriously injured but he didn't die. His suicide attempt had failed. Nevertheless, Sharia Law being what it can be, the hapless driver was thrown into jail. Witnesses to the incident testified that the man had indeed deliberately thrown himself in front of the Englishman's car. Subsequently the driver was released, but the Pakistani who'd failed to commit suicide demanded Dh150 000 in 'blood money' from him — and got it!

Silly cultural anachronisms can obviously become sad human anomalies. Had our desperate Pakistani succeeded in killing himself by jumping in front of the car, he would have gone straight to Hell. Suicide is unequivocally against Islamic Law. Instead, because he failed, he picked up a cool A$75 000 — not heaven on earth, but a good start.

Whenever I See Her Face

A favourite pastime for a young Emirati bloke enjoying all the leisure time that goes with being a well-off young Emirati bloke is to use his mobile phone to talk for hours every day to his girlfriend. That may appear unremarkable, but the use of the term 'girlfriend' is loaded for a start. Most relationships, at least in devout Muslim families, are arranged: dating is out. A betrothed couple can be in the same room if a parent is present, but in other circumstances they're not allowed to be seen to talk to each other. Enter the mighty mobile, the potential destroyer of cultures, Islamic or otherwise! Indeed, you might even facetiously suggest the tiny terrors are part of a gigantic non-Muslim plot to erode the traditional Muslim way of life!

When one of Steve Margolis's students mentioned talking at great length to his girlfriend on his mobile phone, Steve asked how this could be. Weren't these things strictly controlled? 'Yes, normally they are,' the student told him. 'But who knows who you're talking to on a mobile unless you're silly enough to tell them?' Steven then asked him how he felt about the girl, given the arranged-marriage system. 'Oh, it's not a problem,' the young man said. 'I've talked to her so much on the mobile, I know everything there is to know about her. It's just that I don't know what she looks like. I've never seen her face.'

Doing the Western comparison, yet again, I guess we could say that we certainly know what he or she looks like when our eyes meet across a crowded room, but beyond that, we keep our fingers crossed and hope for the best. How often do we discover that physical attraction is not enough — only when it's too late?

The Arithmetical Question of Polygamy

Whatever else it is, Islam is an extremely practical religion. In fact, Muslims everywhere, from Dubai to Lakemba, from Gaza to Islamabad, will tell you with conviction that it can answer any and all human problems. As well as the 'real meaning of life' issues, it offers its devout believers answers to day-to-day questions. Which job should I take? How do I make a profit? How to be happy? Who should I marry? How should I treat my spouse? Do I divorce my wife if she is barren? Sex during menstruation is not on, but what about sex with someone of the same gender? On this last tricky matter, unlike in other religions, the jury, the Qur'an, has been out and is back: 'For ye practise your lusts on men in preference to women, ye are indeed a people transgressing beyond bounds.' Homosexuality? Out of bounds — despite widespread Western suggestions to the contrary!

Purity, cleanliness, diet, clothing, adornment, sport, amusements, intoxicants, gambling, family life, parenting, kids, social life, economics, politics, international affairs, science and technology and, as you might readily expect, spiritual life all get a run in either the Qur'an, the Hadith or one or other of the many other Islamic texts.

But it's polygamy that's captured the non-Muslim imagination. 'What is the Western fascination with the "four wives" thing in Islam?' a two-wife friend from the Gulf asked, before showing me the relevant reference in the Qur'an, just to make it official. Here's what he showed me, but a warning — you could end up a trifle disappointed: 'If ye fear that ye shall not be able to deal justly with the orphans, marry women of your choice — two or three or four. But if ye fear that ye shall not be able to deal justly with them, then marry only one. That will be more suitable to prevent you from doing injustice.' Not quite what you expected?

So Islam allows 'restricted polygamy', as they put it, meaning conditional polygamy. 'You see,' my Emirati mate explained, 'a Muslim man is allowed to marry more than one woman if he is prepared and capable of dealing equally with each of his wives.'

Having learned of this 'restricted polygamy', polygamy with considerable financial and other conditions, it might also come as a shock to find that the typical Muslim marital practice is monogamy, one man married to one woman. In the Islamic world, so odd and off-centre to many Westerners, polygamy is actually the exception, not the rule.

The situations in Islam where polygamy is permissible are really quite mundane; they certainly have very little to do with male sexual gluttony or tame female acceptance of it. A barren woman (the Muslim description), and the resulting childless marriage is a permissible reason; a chronically ill wife another; society having more women than men (e.g. because of many war widows) is often a reason. And there's this: 'If a woman is happy for her husband to marry another woman and the second woman also agrees, why should anyone else object?' as another Muslim acquaintance rhetorically asked me. The answer would have taken a lot longer than the question.

Muslims are eager to make the point that unofficial polygamy they say, is carried on in Europe and America as well. The difference, they say, is that Western men are under no legal obligation to their mistresses, however many they have, or to the children if any result. The Muslim husband, on the other hand, has to meet the additional legal and financial commitments to his second, third and fourth wives and their children. 'Western men have lots of wives,' my Emirati friend said, smiling. 'You just call them mistresses. Whose system is preferable? You tell me.'

Interestingly, Muslims who can string a few words together in English seldom fail to come up with a Western counterpart of a questioned Islamic practice — be it polygamy or some other aspect of their culture — at which we look askance.

Human Rights and Human Instincts

In my Namibian-born, South African friend Charl's clever words, women are the only Arabs who wear trousers. The trousers are often black, but whatever their colour, they are usually beautifully embroidered leggings that extend down to the ankles. Over this, they wear a dress with long sleeves, with the same embroidery as the leggings. Covering the dress is the *abaya*, the famous or infamous — depending on your point of view — cloak that covers the head and extends all the way down to the ankles. When they're at home the *abaya* is removed, but underneath it the head is often covered by a second cloth in the same material, usually synthetic and hot to wear. They must really suffer during the hot desert summer months. 'Whenever you put your stethoscope on a female patient's back, you sympathise with her as it touches the hot, clammy skin,' Charl told me.

Muslim women are expected to at least wear a head scarf, when they're in the presence of men other than their husband or their relatives. This is why Western women wearing a scarf over their head is appreciated by Muslims 'as an outward sign of respect for their ways'.

Depending on where you are, various women — all of them in rural Al Ain, only some in cosmopolitan places like Dubai — will have a veil, the *burka*, covering their face, though with the passage of time and the liberalising of some Beduoin traditions, this seems more and more a practice adhered to, mainly by older women. Some ultra-conservative women, often the wives of ultra-conservative men, wear black cloth gloves.

Doctors, Charl told me, are included among the men who are not allowed to see a woman's face. At dinner one night in Al Ain, a young doctor told of the contortions he and his patient had to go through to enable him to examine her ears without removing her head scarf. Another mentioned a patient who cut a hole in her *abaya* rather than take it off. Others told of women on the operating table, minus every bit of clothing, naked, except for the *burka*!

Strange? Maybe not. Compare that with Catholic nuns who cover their bodies with the habit and leave their faces exposed! There are Muslim women, particularly younger ones, who describe the wearing of the *abaya* or the *burka* as just that — a habit.

So is it the case that it's a sexual issue, this Islamic men's insistence on covering their wives? Is it really to keep the women from being objects of lust and desire in the eyes of other men? If it's the face that's being jealously guarded rather than the body, could it be that we are misjudging Arab men, even underestimating their motivation? After all, even in Western society, the initial point of attraction for members of the opposite sex is usually the face, and then maybe the mind and even later the body. At least, that's the order of events for many people. Some, we know, will try and first convince us that the point of attraction was the mind! Pull the other one!

Charl's explanation was that Islam seems to see men as habitual lechers. All women are so physically alluring that men tend to judge women exclusively by their looks. As a consequence of this fatal attraction, the possibility of besotted men sexually accosting women is very real. So as not to deliberately restrict their freedom but to protect them from lecherous, degrading attention, Islam 'asks' its women to cover their hair and to wear loose-fitting clothes.

But these standards vary from place to place. In Saudi Arabia, things are very strict. Even Western women must cover up almost entirely. But Charl's wife, Rosalie, who has studied and written about the status of women in the Emirates, says that many young UAE women these days are taking tentative steps towards a Western style of dress. 'All the Western women's magazines are available for sale in the shops, although they're heavily censored with a black felt-tipped pen,' she says. And what do the young women wear under their black *abayas*? Calvin Klein jeans and beautiful lacy underwear, and they all prefer the latest in high-heeled shoes.

In Saudi Arabia across the border, all women — Westerners included — are required by Sharia Law to cover up. 'A few months ago,' said Charl, 'I was in Riyadh. Here in the UAE, Western women all dress conservatively when they go out for the evening. In Saudi, they have to wear the *abaya*, which covers not only their heads but the rest of their bodies as well. Arriving at a party that evening in the private compound of an American company, my eyes almost popped out of my head. Not even in South Africa had I seen women so revealingly dressed — or undressed! Once the *abayas* came off, not much female flesh was left uncovered by the minute evening dresses!'

For Muslim men, too, there's an identifiable dress code. It forbids tight clothes: the area from the knees to the navel must be covered (so no short shorts) and some sort of headgear is considered proper — as is a beard.

And cop this! In the Arab world, it's the norm to colour your hair or beard 'if age starts its bleaching process', as the youthful Charl cheekily puts it. 'In fact, the men all have very neatly trimmed hair and beards which are attended to at the hundreds of barbershops all over the city.' Yasser Arafat, with his highly recognisable designer stubble, is definitely not the only Arab-

Muslim male in the region with this characteristic look. Facial hair is regarded as manly, although sensibly, a lack of it is never seen as unmanly. From a Western point of view, though, as Charl noted, Arab men seem preoccupied with their physical appearance. They will quite openly stand in front of a shop window to adjust their *ghutrah*, their draped headpiece. And for nationals in the flagrantly rich UAE, almost without exception these days, the latest in mobile phones, Rolex watches and Mercedes Benz key rings are everyday fashion accessories!

Still on the Muslim fashion front, ponder this from the *Sydney Morning Herald* under the very clever headline 'Thrill of the Chaste': 'Don't, by your attitude and movements, exhibit your body, especially if you have a physique which turns heads. Don't dress in a manner which attracts attention to your body. Avoid all traps which have obviously erotic intentions that could lead to irreparable physical and moral damage. Avoid morally dangerous places and beware of friends of questionable morals, especially during summer!'

A classic pronouncement from an Islamic cleric you would have thought? Sorry! It actually came from Italian Catholic moral theologian, one Father Antonio Rungia. The good Father issued his warning to people who are young, beautiful, have a great body and are forever trying to resist a barrage of sexual advances, as the *Sydney Morning Herald* put it. Apparently, Father Rungia's self-help book, *A User's Guide to Chastity*, was prompted by a call by the Pope for greater chastity among Catholic youth. The surprising similarities between Islam and other religions — if you bother to look — are myriad; some can be subtle, but still similar. On assignment in Kuwait five years after 'Desert Storm' or Gulf War II, call it what you will, the author met a Kuwaiti contact, a US-trained engineer with an international oil company in the Gulf, in one of those massive new shopping malls that have mushroomed in the region over the past decade or so. I had just noticed in one of the mall's arcades, a women's lingerie store displaying undergarments, as 'exotic' as anything you'll see in the West. I must have looked a bit rattled. My Kuwaiti friend, a devout Muslim, smiled and asked: 'What's up? You look like you've just seen a ghost.' 'Not a ghost,' I replied, 'just that lingerie shop over there.' 'Oh, that!' my friend laughed. 'You're a bit surprised? What do you think they wear under their *abayas*?'

What ensued was an intriguing 'cross-cultural' conversation. My Kuwaiti friend, who'd had spent several years at uni in the United States and had mixed a lot with non-Muslim Americans, asked if I'd ever been present at a home anywhere in the West when a teenager or young woman came from her room to go on a date or to a party or the beach. Yes, I had. Had I ever heard a father say to his daughter, maybe dressed in tight jeans, skimpy top or some other revealing clothing: 'Where do you think you're going dressed like that? Go back and put some clothes on!' Yes, of course, I had. Most of us in the West probably had. 'Well, the difference here for us Muslims is that we just make it official. We don't have to make a fuss every time.'

The Muslim Woman's Place — in the House or the Mosque?

During one of my visits to the Open Mosque at Jumeira Beach, I talked with Abdallah and a female colleague of his, known to her English-speaking friends as Ju Ju, about the place of women in Islam. I pointed out that most non-Muslims have a problem with the Muslim attitude towards women, and asked why, for instance, women don't pray together with men in the mosque. This is a record of our discussion.

ABDALLAH and a female colleague, JU JU.

Abdallah: Actually, the women can come to the mosque and they can pray and perform the same prayers. They can worship and pray in the same way. It's just that they have been given the same reward in the religion by praying at home. They get the same reward from God if they pray at home without coming to the mosque.

George Negus: But why don't they come to the mosque?

A: That's obviously understandable, because they have more duties at home — the wife looking after the family, looking after the husband, the maids, school, whatever. But if she is — what do you call it in the West? — a 'superwoman' and can attend to all these things and still come five times every day to the mosque to pray, that's up to her. But she gets the same reward by praying at home.

GN: Fair enough, but why don't I see at least some women coming here?

A: See that door there? In every mosque, that door leads to the women's section. In every mosque here in the UAE and Gulf countries, you would have a women's section. You won't have it in places like the older mosques in Turkey or Egypt. In the holy mosque in Mecca, where the Ka'aba is, women would just pray on one side.

GN: Why not together?

A: Let me explain. Come to my right and you [to a bystander listening] on my left. Closer, a little bit closer, please. That's it. Now, assuming this is the direction of the prayer, if we are praying we'd all be like this — in a tight group prayer. The imam would be leading.

GN: Can you explain the imam?

A: Imam is a word in Arabic which means a leader, someone who would step ahead and lead the prayer. Usually we would pick someone as imam who has more knowledge of religion, a married person, or someone who knows more of the Qur'an. Those are the priorities. It doesn't have to do with the shorter moustache or the longer beard. It's the knowledge. We believe, by the way, that the beard drinks from the prayer, which is why so many devout Muslims are bearded.

So when we are praying we stand very close to each other, almost shoulder to shoulder, and feet touching. We are close to each other, not leaving any gap for the Devil — and I don't mean the Devil with the red horns in the comics. We mean the Devil that we human beings use to create the differences between us.

GN: So the differences between us are the Devil in us?

A: That's the Devil. I'm rich and he's poor. He's white and I'm black. I'm a pure Arab and he's not. I'm from the royal family in Pakistan and he's not. All these differences should disappear. We were created the same way and we will end up the same way.

GN: And how is that? How will we end up?

A: One day, we will stand in front of the Creator on Judgement Day. And while you're thinking of these things, while you're appreciating your Creator, both men and women need concentration.

GN: But what has this got to do with men and women not praying together?

A: This. I don't think a man would really have that concentration if a nice woman's skin is touching his arm — especially if that arm's naked. And the only time women would pray on their own side would be when there was about a three-metre gap between them and the men. Then the women's group would be praying on their own, close to each other, feeling comfortable, not being disturbed by a man in close and between them. It just wouldn't be comfortable for women to be praying close to men.

GN: Another obvious question. Why do women have to cover their heads in the mosque?

Graciously — and grabbing the opportunity to make the point that modern Muslim women, at least in the Emirates, can speak for themselves — Abdallah turned to his colleague at the mosque and said that he would let the lady answer that question.

George Negus: Why the scarf?

Ju Ju: You want to talk about the scarf? It's probably one of the topics people like to talk about in Western countries. Maybe it's not understood by a large majority of non-Muslims why we Muslim women are covering.

GN: It's certainly one of the great curiosities for non-Muslims, that's for sure!

JJ: Well, if you think about it, it's present in many other religions. For instance, in Christianity, if you walk into a church and see a picture of Mary, the mother of Jesus, the lady will be wearing something on her hair. You watch historical movies, where you have respected ladies of the past, they are also always covering their hair. It is not a distinctly Muslim thing. It's very much perceived as respect in just about every religion, with the Jews in Jerusalem, the Hindus in India and people in other places.

GN: So why do many non-Muslims see it as part of Islam's overall subjugation of women?

JJ: One might wonder why it's perceived as denigration. Maybe some people may fear that, as Muslim women, we are hiding when we are covering, that we are not on the same level as men. But in fact — and you may be surprised by the large majority of ladies covering — Muslim females are covering out of choice. They're really happy about it.

GN: Happy to be told they must cover themselves? Really?

JJ: This is one part that you may not know, George. It's true that it is an obligation in Islam to wear it, but it's not the priority. You can be a really nice person even if you're not wearing a cover. What is really important is exactly what you do, what you do through your life, your achievement.

GN: Do Muslim women here in the UAE wear the *hijab*, the cover, by choice — or because they feel their religion says they must?

JJ: It's true that some Muslim ladies may be covering but don't know what they are actually doing. This piece of material cannot make you a good person. Basically, it's just the highest level of practising one's faith. If it's out of choice, out of respect, that we should do this, we're not offending anyone when we are covering.

GN: No obligation?

JJ: None really. It's just our Islamic public dress code. If you think about it, it's just like you, I hope, would feel quite embarrassed to leave your home without trousers, you know. You walk around at home the way you want, but when you go to a public place you wear trousers — not because you are ashamed about your legs, but because you like to show you have a certain dress code. In the same way, because of their faith and convictions, Muslim women just add this little piece of cloth. They are women with the same heart and personality, not offending anyone by covering. It's just a simple part of their religion that is very much respected in our society.

GN: A case of religion and culture becoming one and the same via a public dress code? How much of it is to do with being Arab rather than being Muslim?

JJ: Coverage is much more out of culture than religion here in the UAE. The large majority of ladies may cover their face but it's out of choice. It's part of the culture, part of the mentality. I know that sometimes it's a little difficult to understand because we live in a very different society to the West, you know the way you appear in public. Where you come from, people may wear micro-skirts or long coats or have green hair or whatever and people don't look at you strangely, because this is the mentality. It's true, some Muslim women may cover their face out of shyness and because they feel more comfortable. It's difficult to understand, but some Muslim ladies don't like to even eat or laugh in front of a man. That's their mentality and, again, they're not offending anyone by that.

GN: Few in the West would realise it goes that far.

JJ: In some countries, especially here in the Arab world, in the Gulf, the way you appear in public is very important. Both men and women with the same mentality are going to public places covered, not, let's say, because they are being shy. They want to blend in and not have any bad reflection on their family. This is a very strong value we have.

GN: And, as you say, men 'cover' too to some extent?

JJ: Men have almost as much covering as ladies, except for their necks. You see, Abdallah is wearing a *kandora* with long sleeves. He also has something on his head. Men could, Islamically, wear half-sleeves or a shorter *kandora* or even shorter pants, but they don't because it's part of the mentality.

GN: But why more cover for women?

JJ: It's not that women are bad and men are good. It's just their mentality and culture. As I say, it's not an obligation for a woman to cover her face in Islam. Some may choose to do so because it's related to the culture — and we like that.

GN: No religious obligation or male force?

JJ: There is still a misconception about covering the female body in Islam. Some people say it's because we're under a man's influence — a father, a brother or a husband. But I know so many Muslim ladies who cover out of choice, in fact very few who would not cover both their hair and face. It is true that in some isolated cases they will have to. Like, for instance, in Saudi Arabia, it's a rule. Everyone there has to cover. Some Saudi females would be happy with this obligation and some others not. But if you go to Islamic countries, you realise there is no obligation from the government. Many Muslim women are covering and do they look miserable?

GN: In some places — like Saudi Arabia or Afghanistan — how could you tell if they were miserable or not? You can't see their faces.

JJ: If you approached them in Afghanistan, they will tell you, with the head, it's part of their life and they like to do so. It's the same with the face really.

GN: In Afghanistan surely not, given the excesses of the Taliban?

JJ: I know that in some countries — like Afghanistan — they had to and they were not happy about it. But maybe it was not so much the veil, but the way of life, the whole concept. This is found in Islam sometimes. The way the Taliban forced people to live was wrong. But, really, elsewhere mostly the way you want to cover in public is up to you.

GN: Are these things changing though? Say, here in the Emirates?

JJ: Some women may wear the veil for some years and then remove it. But again, it can't make you a good person just because you wear this piece of material on your hair. It's a way of practising a religion — and not just Islam as I said before. It was very much present in Western countries not so long ago. My grandmother was Swiss. She used to cover to go to a Catholic church and I'm sure your grandmothers did too. It's just not the way of life now. People don't feel it's useful any more, they don't understand that sort of thing any more. But if you go to South America even now, women would never enter a church without covering their hair. In the same way that Christians are probably covering out of respect, we are covering. It's just that it's much more a part of our daily life.

GN: Leaving aside the head scarf and the veil, many in the West — and not just feminists — are highly concerned about the status of women generally in Islamic society. Can you blame them?

JJ: That's a tricky question, the question about segregation. It seems that in many parts of the world women are segregated and especially, maybe, in some Islamic countries. So what is the real situation? What exactly is the place of a woman in Islam? Here again we have to separate the culture and the religion.

GN: But whether it's a matter of culture or religion, how can you justify it?

JJ: It's not like you think, that a Muslim women cannot do anything without a man. This is not a must in Islam. A lot of

Muslim ladies may not be married or may have lost their husbands and they have a very desirable life. It's again a matter of mentality and culture. But if you go to Saudi Arabia, for instance, or to some other Islamic countries, you would be quite shocked if you come from another culture. You will not understand what is really going on.

The thing is that, in general, Islamic women are not segregated. It may be perceived as such because in some cultures females, let's say, are put a little aside from the society.

GN: To put it mildly!

JJ: This is a reality, but not just in some Islamic countries. My parents are Spanish. Ever since I was quite young, when I used to go to Spain, I realised that a boy and a girl there are not the same. If you look at history, you realise that in many ways women have been denigrated and put down by minorities, but significant minorities, of males. They don't have to be Muslims or be in Islamic countries for that. Women have suffered throughout history. This is well known. Even in the time of the Renaissance, for instance, in France, the Church would say that women were just creatures of Hellfire, that they would never enter Paradise. But I'm sure Christianity does not support this kind of idea. It was just a group of men who thought that women were there to tend men.

GN: So you are saying this denigration of women is not a uniquely Islamic problem?

JJ: It happens all over the world, not just the Islamic world, that some people have weird ideas. We know that women have been suffering now and in the past. The reality is that an Islamic woman has rights, just like an Islamic man has his rights. All the duties are the same — the prayer, the fast etc. It would be really stupid to think that because you were born with different organs there's not any way you're going to have a place in Paradise. Islam encourages both sexes, aware of the differences, to work together and to reach harmony. It's true that in some Muslim countries you will see denigration, things that are not really fair — but not just in Islamic countries. It happens all over the world.

Beyond the Veil — Feminism?

Originally from Holland, Rosalie has been living in the Middle East for ten years, the last seven of them in the UAE. Talk to her about the plight of Muslim women and she gets straight to the point. 'Most fundamentalist Islamic societies,' she says, 'are far more sexist compared to other societies with different religions.' To the outside world her chosen temporary homeland, the thoroughly modern Emirates, seems to be the exception to this Muslim rule. It gives an appearance of having found a compromise between adherence to Islam and Westernisation. Emirati women have made more advances than women in most other Islamic states — but, in this tradition-bound part of the world, advances are always relative.

'The UAE is still very much a society ruled by a patriarchy,' Rosalie says. 'Despite appearances, in reality the UAE is full of contradictions. On the one hand, there appears to be hardly anything left of an Arabic culture and society when you look at the outward appearance of the country itself, with its ultra-modern buildings and its glitzy facades. On the other hand, the religion, social structure and functioning of not only the country but also the Emirati family are dominated by men. The situation clearly favours men, often deliberately discriminating against women and restricting them. It's emancipation on the one hand and restriction on the other.'

Before the discovery of oil close enough to fifty years ago, the UAE was pretty much a tribal society. The men travelled with their camels, went pearl diving or fished. They were the sole sources of income. 'Women stayed at home to look after the children and the agricultural livelihood of the family. But since then, much has changed,' Rosalie says.

Unlike so many in Islamic states, Emirati women get direct financial support from the top, including from the country's aging supreme ruler, the legendary Sheikh Zyad. The sheikh's wife, Sheikha Fatima Bint Mubarak, is the head of the UAE Women's Federation, a government-backed organisation that just wouldn't exist in most other Islamic countries. All over the region you keep hearing about the persuasive powers of apparently subservient women. So don't let the veil distract you. As Muslim women gain more freedom and therefore clout in Islam, the whole relationship with non-Muslims might also change.

The Constitution in the UAE states that 'social justice should apply to all', so Emirati women should be enjoying the same legal status, the same claim to titles, the same access to education and the same right to practise the professions as Emirati men. But, as Rosalie tells it, these admirable new laws and all the old sexist Islamic traditions and attitudes still clash.

Changing the habits of an entire culture makes most other monumental tasks look easy, but that's the UAE goal — to invite Muslim women out from behind the veil. 'Illiteracy is still high. Emirati women have to learn to use their leisure time to become literate. This way they will acquire knowledge about the modern world and become better equipped to raise their family's standard of living. On the one hand, they've been boosted by oil and, on the other, held back by hidebound Islamic values.'

As incredible as it may sound, before the 1970s, there were only two girls' schools in the whole seven Emirates. But overall, things are getting better, not worse. 'Emirati women have taken advantage of the new educational opportunities,' Rosalie says. 'By 1993, 98 per cent of UAE girls were attending at least primary or intermediate schools. At the secondary level, 70 per cent of Emirati girls have completed their education. Only a little over 60 per cent of the country's boys have done the same.'

Like others, Rosalie is convinced that literacy and education offer the only chance Emirati women have of gaining 'a personal identity'. But achieving this goal is still restricted by Islamic lore. 'The fact is,' she says, 'although most Arab fathers would like their daughters to be educated, any prospective working career will be shortlived, due to the old Islamic cultural tradition of arranging a marriage for their daughters at an early age. Women still complain of blatant discrimination and to avoid the flagrant sexism in the workplace, many educated women actually go out and become their own bosses rather than be held back by the bias against them.'

Despite the oil and new wealth, there are still Emirati men opposed to women having independence. In other words, their society is still male-dominated and patriarchal. 'Not only do fathers dominate their wives' and their daughters' lives, even male siblings influence the daily lives and the future of their mothers and sisters,' according to Rosalie. Ultimately, women are expected to adhere to the old Islamic cultural, religious and family traditions. A Muslim female more often than not automatically accepts the family's view of the world. She has been conditioned to accept that either her father, her husband or even her brothers will decide her future.

But, Rosalie says her experience is that Emirati women are questioning their restricted world. Divorce figures are reflecting a shift in their position. There's a higher divorce rate than before, and women are more likely to speak out and debate the issues at stake. Emirati women can hold government positions, but there are very few actually in them and there are still no female members in the Federal National Council.

There are grounds for serious optimism, but the worrying mix of religion and patriarchy still holds sway over the lives of most Muslim women. 'Islamic men remain the real barrier for Islamic women,' says Rosalie bluntly.

A Question of Subjugation

Whether it's the relatively benign veil — a fashion statement of choice for women in moderate Islamic countries, religious law in others — the barbarity of genital mutilation in Sudan, sanctioned pack rape in places like Bangladesh and Nigeria, or 'honour killings' in southern Asia and the Middle East, the maltreatment of women in Islam recurs and recurs.

For many, this has become Islam's supreme test, the thing that stops non-Muslims from tolerating the religion as a whole, a stumbling block for those striving to accept Islam for its human qualities.

Feminists and human rights activists throughout the Western world have been up in arms about it. They see it as an anomaly. How can Islam be a religion based on principles of love, equality and acceptance, and relegate women to the status of second-class human beings? Whatever human measure is used — Muslim, Jewish, Christian, Buddhist, humanist, atheist — it is difficult not to see Islam's treatment of women as flying in the face of not only human rights, but also the teachings of Muhammed himself. Wherever you find yourself in the Muslim world, it's close to impossible to get even progressives to talk openly about the more personal aspects of their lives and their relationships. But what's

so different about that? Isn't that also the case in any sort of
society? Unless, of course, it's that boring drunk in a bar in
Melbourne or Milwaukee telling you how his wife doesn't
understand him! So who do you turn to for reliable information,
as distinct from hearsay, if it's not the local expat doctor?

When Charl started at the hospital in Yemen, he was acutely
aware of the Islamic idiosyncrasies of both the people and the
place. But, as time passed, things had become 'blurred into life's
daily pattern'.

Nevertheless, Charl reached the view that female circumcision,
one of the most controversial of Islamic practices, was still
common in parts of the UAE. Not long before we spoke he'd seen
a small girl, eighteen months old, who had been circumcised in a
private clinic. 'Her father was an educated and very nice man,
obviously a VIP,' Charl told me. 'The best I could make out was
that the distal end of the clitoris had been amputated.'

According to Charl, there are three kinds of genital
mutilation. The first, sunna circumcision, entails the removal of
the prepuce or the tip of the clitoris. The second variation
involves the removal of the clitoris plus the adjacent labia. And
the third, the one that's provoked the most heated reaction in
the West, is infibulation, also known as pharaonic circumcision
— a more extensive mutilation still.

Despite this sort of story, female circumcision is 'absolutely
not endorsed in Islam,' according to Islamic writer Yahiya
Emerick in his *Complete Idiot's Guide to Understanding Islam*, a
book to be taken far more seriously than its title would suggest.
'It's a practice mainly found in isolated regions of Africa, and is
not sanctioned by Islam. It's a pre-Islamic cultural relic.'

There cannot, of course, be any condoning of genital
mutilation. While it goes on with the implicit endorsement of
some in the hierarchies of the Muslim world, we will keep

hearing the term 'barbaric' being used by those opposed to Islam itself.

Dishonourable Killing — but is it in the Name of Allah?

To the interloper, Islam can be a disturbingly secret place, frankness a rare commodity. Case in point, what is an 'honour killing' — and is it actually an Islamic practice? Usually, that unfortunate scenario begins with a woman bringing dishonour on her family by dating a man without her father's knowledge or permission or, even worse, being sexually promiscuous. The punishment is as drastic as punishment can get.

With civil law apparently powerless against this horrendous aberration of Islam, the daughter can be killed to protect the family's reputation. But as American Islamic writer Yahiya Emerick puts it: 'There is no sanction in Islam for such a horrible practice and Muslim scholars in those countries have issued fatwas against it. But people cling to culture more strongly than to religious dictates.'

It's a curly one. Where does religion end and culture begin? With things like so-called 'honour killings', moderate Muslims invariably point to their religion being distorted by cultural pressures. They deplore honour killings as strongly as any of its Western opponents. They are disheartened by the simplistic, often sensational way the Western media report the actions of extremists, tarring them with the same evil brush. How would Western Christian communities fare if we were to apply similarly selective criteria to their religious and cultural behaviour?

At the time of compiling this update, the author of the huge bestseller *Forbidden Love*, Norma Khouri — who had become something of a celebrity for her apparently authentic account of a so-called 'honour killing' in Jordan — was in the news. Shockingly, Khouri was accused of fabricating her quite salacious yarn about a Jordanian Muslim friend she claimed had been murdered by her father because of a relationship with a Catholic Christian.

Debate raged in Australia, the UK and elsewhere in the West where the ostensibly non-fictional book had been published; the dubious tale was removed from the shelves; an elusive Khouri scrambled to explain herself and gather proof of the authenticity of her story and headlines of a deliberate and outrageous 'literary hoax' boomed. Weeks later, Khouri had failed to convince either her critics or, more crucially, her publishers, that her book was fact rather than fiction.

Forbidden Love was branded a blatant 'literary hoax'. But the whole scandal was and is far more potent as a hoax, full stop. It amounts to a hoax against the Islamic faith and the hundreds of millions of its followers who would never condone, let alone carry out, so-called 'honour killings' in Jordan or anywhere else.

In the book's penultimate chapter Khouri called 'Afterword' — 'Afterthought' would have been more appropriate — she finally gets around to acknowledging the anti-Muslim misconception that she herself had aided and abetted. 'The most frequent, and mistaken, claim is that these murders are born of Islamic faith,' she says, 'when in fact the murders are a cultural hangover of tribal life that pre-dates both Islam and Christianity.'

Khouri herself notes that honour killings have their roots in the Hammurabi and Assyrian laws from 1200 BC, 'which declared a woman's chastity to be her family's property'. She adds: 'These laws evolved in an unforgiving desert and are common to all Arabs of the region, of whatever faith. These days, Christian women are just as likely to be killed as Muslim women for "dishonouring" their families.' Earlier, Khouri wrote that murder as a way of 'cleansing family honour' was most common in Jordan and among Palestinians. Most tellingly, she added that this is 'firmly rooted in ethnic Bedouin tradition, which is still pervasive as a desert sandstorm in even urbanised Arab families'.

This is the rub! In the context of the impact of her bestseller, for 190-odd pages Khouri, consciously or indeliberately, fostered popular negative attitudes towards Muslims as perpetrators of barbaric behaviour, atittudes rife in the aftermath of September 11. Her comments were almost certainly too little, too late. The damage had already been done. Tens of thousands of her factually innocent readers would have automatically linked the so-called 'honour killing' of Khouri's imaginary 'friend' Dalia with Muslims and the Islamic religion. Many would have concluded that honour killing was an Islamic thing.

The least that could be said about *Forbidden Love* — in its literary hey-day or in its current disgrace — is that it has done nothing good for relations between Muslims and non-Muslims. It was both the juicy, blood-curdling dinner party stuff of unsubstantiated legend and handy propaganda for anti-Muslim forces in the West.

Khouri's authorship and her sources of detailed information about Jordanian life have to be seriously questioned. Fact or fiction, from where did she get her basic information? There's nothing in her shadowy Chicago past or her recent Australian present to suggest anything vaguely resembling an academic or literary bent. The question of where she obtained her information has been completely ignored. If she spent only the first three years of her life in Muslim Jordan, what — or even who — prompted her outrageous storyline and apparent local knowledge? What was her motivation? Money, notoriety — or something else? She now claims to be a campaigner for women's rights in Jordan. But where is the history of feminist activism? This sceptic's grave doubt list is open-ended.

Khouri's alleged concoction was published soon after September 11. Juxtaposed, the two things very quickly gained a symbiotic connection. But we pragmatists don't believe in conspiracy theories, do we? But maybe — just maybe — there's much more to the *Forbidden Love* story than mere literary hoax. Stay tuned, as they say.

PART FIVE

CONVERSATIONS WITH MUSLIMS

The Islamic Conundrum

It distresses me that so many people seem to think the
next period of history will be a fight between your part of
the world and mine. It is true that we live elbow to elbow
with each other. It is also true that our elbows have
banged painfully together many times in the past. But,
almost 2000 years after the birth of your Jesus and more
than 1400 years after the birth of our Muhammed, let me
start by asking whether it really has to start all over again.

**Part of an imaginary dialogue between
Christian and Muslim religious leaders in
The Economist, Great Britain**

Oman — the Islamic Past, Present and Even Future?

'You've got to go to Oman,' Saeed, a young Emirati friend from Dubai, told me. 'It's only an hour's flight or a few hours' drive — but it's a world away. It's not new and flashy like this place. It's laid-back, far more traditional, a lot like old Arabia used to be.'

It's not only Arabs who make these sorts of comments. No matter who says it — locals or expats — it's an opinion that's proffered with enthusiasm. You get the impression that it's also offered with a sense of nostalgia, even melancholy. It has to be said that it was quite a while since this professional traveller had heard such universal commendation for a place. Anyone who's been to the Sultanate raves about this genuinely striking land, right on the proboscis of the *Jazirat-al-Arab*, the Arabian peninsula.

One particularly spellbound Gulf 'raver' put it this way: 'Oman is just amazing. Somehow it's what Arab Islam used to be like, what it's also like now, and what it could be like in the future. If one place can be living in the past, the present and the future simultaneously, then it's Oman.' How could that sort of intriguing spin be resisted? It can't, so we didn't try! As it turned out, Oman — a place they used to call 'the hermit of the Middle East'— let down neither this ensnared traveller nor itself.

How can I put it? The Sultanate of Oman is the Gulf, but it is definitely not the UAE. In fact, it's about as different from the likes of Dubai and Abu Dhabi as a modern Arab-Muslim nation can get and still be one of the so-called Gulf States. For starters, it's not disgustingly oil-rich like others in the region. It does have its oil supplies, albeit limited, but the wealth that's flowed from them is nothing like the nouveau riche ostentation of the over-the-top Emirates. Not only that, but Western encroachment over the decades has been slower. In fact, as travel writers Lou Callan and Gordon Robinson tell it, under the previous sultan, Said bin Taimur — suddenly, dramatically and bloodlessly deposed in 1970 by his estranged son, Qaboos bin Said Al-Said — 'The country was almost hermetically sealed off from the outside world. Said banned anything that smacked of Western influence. Even sunglasses were not allowed!' In fact, Said bin Taimur's great dread that the wicked materialistic ways of the West would inundate and corrupt the Omani people prompted him to impose all sorts of petty curbs on their behaviour. It was not only sunglasses that were forbidden; so too were Western clothes generally, and even playing soccer, dancing, singing, men moving from their district of birth and women leaving their villages were outlawed.

These sorts of loopy incursions against human rights and freedoms notwithstanding, 'charmingly backward' was the way one Omani described his beguiling country's quaint recent past. Thirty years ago, there were practically no sealed roads in Oman; a mere thousand or so vehicles — imported into the country with the express permission of the sultan; electricity only in the capital, Muscat, and the port of Muttrah; one hospital and three primary schools. Back then, many Omani kids got their only education from Qur'anic schools, where boys and girls were taught to read and recite Islamic texts in makeshift outdoor classrooms. Religious indoctrination? If you like, but if you're not sure ask the country's former colonial masters, the Brits. They're the ones who did bugger-all to provide education for the locals.

Whether or not the old Qur'an schools were the cause, today the Omanis are devoutly religious. Omanis were among the first Arabs to convert to Islam when it began to spread in all directions from Mecca and Medina 1400 years ago. But just when you thought you had a reasonable grasp on the Sunnis, the Shiites and the Wahhabis of the Muslim world, the vast majority of Omanis are followers of the Ibadhi teachings, a benign offshoot of the many early differences and power struggles that followed the Prophet's death.

Their religion is a bit like the Catholicism of the Italians — it's there every moment of the day, but it doesn't dominate their affairs. Omani Muslims struck me as devoted to, but not distracted by, Islam. There are only just over 2 million of them and they obviously like being Muslim. But that seemed as much a lifestyle choice as a religious commitment — to this interloper from Australia anyway. Certainly the four Omanis you will meet shortly were pragmatic about the relationship between life and religion, between being a Muslim and being modern. They appeared open to the idea that political, social, economic and even cultural change was possible in their magnificent little Arab backwater — without compromising the essentials of their Islamic faith.

Whatever else Omanis may choose to change down the track, the traditional dress will survive. Fortunately, you'd have to hope, the government appears to be using considerable friendly persuasion to encourage the employed members of the population to wear traditional garb to work. Omani attire is without doubt the most vivid and colourful in any of the Gulf

States. Not just out in the rural and desert areas, but even in the city, many men still wear the curved-blade dagger, the *khanjar*, on a belt around the waist. There are no veils as such for the women, but their face-covering masks are thoroughly original and make them look dangerously like they're wearing one of those Groucho Marx false-nose-and-glasses combinations! Then again, we couldn't find any reference in the Qur'an as to exactly how Islamic women should hide themselves from the leers of the opposite sex.

'A new dawn will rise for Oman and her people,' the new sultan, Qaboos, declared in 1970 when he took over from his dad. The old bloke had closeted himself away in the rugged southern coastal cliffs of the country for years and Oman had been pretty much rudderless. Now, rumours about the young, childless sultan possibly being Oman's lucky-last benevolent semi-despot are rife — as are the ones about his sexuality!

'The Kingdom of Frankincense' is one of Oman's more exotic tags, and it is indeed a veritable spice heaven. They're all there and almost as colourful as the women's shawls and *dishdashas* — cinnamon, tumeric, saffron — plus rarer little numbers like frankincense and myrrh, mainly used for burning, incense-like. Throughout the day and into the warm Gulf evenings, fabulous aromas waft through the alluring alleys and souks of old Muscat, bewitching and intoxicating the visitor. As you might have gathered by now, we'd go back there at the drop of an Omani's brimless, embroidered cap — the *kumma*.

There's a curious religious twist to the so-called Kingdom of Frankincense. Most of us, Christian or otherwise, know the Christmas story of the baby Jesus' birth in that celebrated manger in Bethlehem. It's a bit of a mess there right now after Israeli counterattacks to intifada sorties pulverised the old religious site, but it means a lot to a lot of people. The cheeky

Muslims of Oman will gleefully tell you of their role in the birth of Jesus — whom Muslims everywhere acknowledge as a great prophet, even if he wasn't, they say, the Son of God. Remember the Three Wise Men who followed the star to that modest manger in Bethlehem? Remember what they brought with them as gifts for Baby Jesus? Gold, frankincense and myrrh — from Oman!

But the gift that the author took away with him from an all-too-brief period in Oman was the openness of the Omani people. We came away convinced that dialogue with at least that part of the Islamic world was not just possible, but impossible to avoid. They want it. All we have to do is respond — without the usual predictable prejudices. I met and spoke with a fascinating array of Omanis. One described himself as a 'casual Muslim', another as a 'lapsed Muslim', and a third as a 'Muslim atheist'. Confused? Don't blame you. The 'lapsed Muslim', by the way, had an impressive knowledge of vintage wines, not that he necessarily drank any of them — well, not until he 'lapsed'!

To be honest, returning to the Gulf and Middle East in late 2002 at a time of scary international tension, with the dark storm clouds of war hanging over the region, it wouldn't have been at all surprising had the locals been tight-lipped, not keen on talking about much, let alone the obvious. Not only that, they live in lands and within cultures and systems where freedom of speech is a pretty doubtful commodity. In most of the Gulf States it's in short supply. But my exchanges with the Omanis were open, easygoing and informative — and never anything less than a delight.

You'd like to think Oman could be a template for the Islamic future. It's already an enthralling reminder of its past and a terrific advertisement for its present.

Operation Iraqi Freedom and the Muslim Backlash?

In mid-April 2003, coincidentally the time we made a return visit to the Gulf to re-interview some key Muslim opinion leaders, a revealing poll of Arab opinion was released. The poll surveyed more than 2000 Arab-Muslims in six nations traditionally friendly to the United States, including the likes of Saudi Arabia, Egypt, Jordan and Morocco.

Most of the Arabs polled were convinced that with Saddam gone, Iraqis would elect a Shiite government reflecting the Muslim majority in the country. This would give post-Saddam Iraq a religious regime similar to the one across the border to the east in Iran, its old Shiite enemy. Ironically, Iran was another member of George Bush's Axis of Evil. Exactly what this sort of 'new Iraq' will mean for American policy in the region, only time will tell, as the commentators say.

But what it does mean for Muslims is that they see a bigger, not a smaller role for Islamic law and the imams, the clerics, in Iraqi political life — democracy or no democracy. Despite George W's boast that the military defeat of Saddam would make the Middle East and the Gulf safer and more democratic, pointedly, less than 6 per cent of the Arab-Muslims polled believed that.

Jean Abi Nader, the managing director of the Arab–American Institute that sponsored the survey, agreed that given the opportunity, Iraqis would elect a government along the same religious lines as the one in Iran. This is a booming irony, given that Iran was the US enemy twenty years before Iraq — precisely because of the Islamic fundamentalism that flourished there under the locally revered Ayatollah Khomeini.

Abi Nader told Australian ABC Radio that if elections were to be held in Iraq before the end of 2003, the Iraqis would elect 'a fairly conservative Shia government, similar to the Khatami government in Iran'. Not exactly a development to make the Americans deliriously happy? 'No, I don't think so,' Abi Nader told his interviewer. 'Although the United States have liberated the country,' he said, 'the Iraqis feel that the US is still the primary reason we have instability in the Middle East region and the unresolved Palestinian–Israeli question.' Haven't we heard that before? Indeed, where the strained relations between the Muslim and non-Muslim worlds are concerned, we keep hearing it. It's the old cracked record or these days, the scratched CD!

There are other crucial issues that not just Abi Nader but other observers have raised in the aftermath of Operation Iraqi Freedom. How is the task of reconstructing Iraq going to proceed? How are the country's lucrative oil fields going to be managed? Which companies from what countries are going to be handed the reconstruction windfalls? Aren't the bin Laden family, estranged from renegade son, Osama, in the oil and construction industries? Now there's a possibliity. But, dubious jokes aside, as Abi Nader says: 'All these things will have an impact on how the Iraqis feel about the Americans.'

As ABC reporter Raphael Epstein suggested to Abi Nader, if the Iraqis were to elect a deeply religious Islamic government — as any Shiite government would be — it would be openly hostile to Israel. 'I think any Arab government elected in the current climate in any country is going to be opposed to Israel's actions in Palestine,' Abi Nader agreed.

And there was this chilling comment from Professor Shibley Telhami, the architect of this Arab survey: 'The vast majority of the public in the region believes that the Middle East is going to witness more terrorism, because people understand that militants are likely to use this as an instrument of mobilisation. That is going against the conventional wisdom in the United States, which says that this is going to put militants on the defensive and reduce terrorism.'

After Saddam — the Moderate View of the World from Islam

Later that month, April 2003, the four-week 'wonder war' in Iraq was, to all intents and purposes, over bar the proverbial shouting. But Muslims and non-Muslims around the world were still totally befuddled about the real motivation for the war, most of them as concerned as they ever were about what the chaos in Iraq might mean to the future of the Arab-Muslim region.

In this context, we returned to the Gulf, to our moderate Muslim friends, to find out what they, the majority in Islam, were thinking.

For the so-called Coalition of the Willing, including a US-compliant Howard government at home in Australia, 'liberating' Iraq was clearly the thing. But an angry and confused Islamic world was not convinced that the invasion of Iraq, and the turmoil that would and did follow, was the only way to rid the region and the world of Saddam. Why the invasion had occurred, let alone how it was conducted, was an issue that had burned deep into the heart of Islam.

Sure, serious problems had been solved, but others remained and even fresher ones had been created. Out of the ashes of innocent Iraqis and Islamic places like that devastated country's precious and irreplaceable antiquities museum, gigantic question marks still hung over the relationship between the Muslim and non-Muslim worlds.

In Israel, the loudly lauded US-backed 'Roadmap to Peace' was tentatively on the table in Israel, but no peaceful outcome was evenly dimly in sight. Indeed, hoping against hope was still the order of the day where the hard-core Palestinian–Israeli dilemma was concerned. Palestinian Muslims were still killing Jews and Jews were still killing Palestinian Muslims, State and non-State terrorism continued, and while that was the scenario the Muslim and non-Muslim worlds remained planets apart and at dangerous loggerheads. We explored the issues, both pre- and post-Iraq with some thoughtful Omani Muslims.

Democracy — What Democracy?

Saeed Marijibe is an extremely sophisticated Omani Muslim political animal. He was so enthusiastic at the idea of talking about Islamic politics that he drove from his home some kilometres away to collect the author from a service station in suburban Muscat. On the short journey to his home, Saeed took me to a vantage point above the city so we could enjoy a stunning view of the Sultanate of Oman's dramatic mountains and its rugged rocky coastal cliffs, an almost surreal coastline quite unlike any other the author had seen. Our brief bout of sightseeing out of the way, Saeed proudly took me to the tiny mosque his family had built for their neighbourhood on the outskirts of the capital.

Though Saeed lives and works in Muscat, he was born in the poor African nation of Tanzania. Affable Saeed's adolescent education was in Catholic mission schools in that country. In his early twenties, Saeed took off to Cairo, where he studied at the American University. In Cairo, he met and fell in love with an Omani girl who was also studying in the teeming Egyptian capital. 'I am from a completely different version of Islam,' he says, 'I am Muscati Muslim, an Ibadi, and she is Shiite. It's like Protestant and Catholic. They don't like each other, but we got married and are a really great family. We are very moderate. We pray five times a day like any other Muslim. We're just Muslim.'

'But maybe I'm not like the others,' he says with a wry grin. He goes to the mosque regularly but has many friends from different religions. 'If I was asked to choose which religion — after I have seen the others — I would go to Islam, for sure. I believe that Jews have a correct religion and that Moses was a true prophet. And Jesus and Christianity is a pure religion, a gift from God, like Judaism. Islam is the last religion. I believe all three are correct. When I read the Qur'an and compare things in the Bible, I think the Qur'an is correct. I like Jews and I like Christians. Even with Muslims, there are people I don't like.'

Saeed is an experienced, Omani government bureaucrat. He regards himself as a 'Muslim democrat', or at least an advocate of Muslim democracy. He was not afraid to speak his considerable mind.

SAEED: The Islamic Democrat

Saeed: We've started something. This coming year, all Omanis will have the right to vote, all Omanis from 21-years-old and up. Yes, we actually elect MPs. Is it effective? Somehow yes, but it is not a democracy.

George Negus: What would you describe it as?

S: I would say it is a Shurocracy.

GN: Shurocracy?

S: *Shur* in Arabic is consulting. It is not democracy the way you know it. Shurocracy is something very new. Arab people are starting to use it. We tell the government what we think it should do, but it is up to the government to do or not to do it. In the next election here in Oman — after three years maybe — we will have more facilities. But a parliament, it still has to be granted by the governor. The Sultan still has to say this is no, this is yes.

GN: You're right. That's certainly not democracy as we know it in the West.

S: Right now, we can say please can you do this and please can you do that. If he doesn't do it, we'll try again. So, this is not a democracy. It is, as I say, shurocracy — a consulting democracy.

GN: One of the big problems in the relationship between the West and the Islamic countries is the fact that you are not democracies as the West knows them.

S: Lack of democracy in the Arab-Muslim states is the main reason so many people are against their own government. But many of us feel that because we are not participating in our own decisions, this is the main reason people like Osama bin Laden have emerged and then left places like Saudi Arabia, in particular. If Osama had a following in his country, he could stand and say what he believes. He would not leave his Saudi palace and go to live in the mountains in Afghanistan. But the absence of freedom of speech meant that is what he did. You cannot criticise anything political in Saudi. We are Muslim, and we can criticise even God. I know it's not right, but people can criticise the prophets. But you cannot criticise the son of the leader of the country. This is the kind of freedom Muslim people want.

GN: Folk in the West would definitely find strange that you can criticise God and the prophets, but not the government.

S: Here in the region — not only Oman — a king or a leader can buy a Boeing 747 as a gift to his son. It will cost say 200, 300 million dollars but you cannot say anything. If you say anything, you are against the leader. What do you call this? It is his religion? He's a very good believer — that makes him the leader of our country, but we cannot criticise the leader.

GN: So why does this situation persist? How does it continue to be the case that democracy and freedom of speech have not become part of your way of life?

S: Because these governments, although some are doing a good job, but not in a democratic way, get power or support from the West — and we cannot change the West.

GN: So what are you saying? That it's the West's own fault that there is no democracy in the Arab-Muslim world?

S: Yeah! It's the West who support these leaders. It's the West who puts these leaders on their thrones.

GN: By this, you mean the royal family in Saudi Arabia, the Sultan here in Oman and the sheikhs in the United Arab Emirates?

S: Yeah, yeah! If they didn't have support from the United Kingdom and the United States, they wouldn't stay in power in those places for ten days.

GN: That's indeed a paradox.

S: This is the core of the whole problem. Why? The worst thing is that because these leaders exist the West will get anything they want from this area. We have oil. The West wants oil. It's the big playing chip. If oil goes up 10 per cent in price, the entire budget of the West collapses. But Saudi Arabia can put the price of oil down, even though that means they are losing money, even in the middle of a war in the area, just to make people in the West happy — even if citizens here in the Middle East and the Gulf suffer as a result.

GN: Someone said to me in Dubai that the West — and the United States in particular — because of their acceptance of the Saudi royal family and the lack of democracy in that country, actually created the terrorist phenomenon of Osama bin Laden. That appears to be your view too?

S: Sure. It's as simple as saying one and one is equal to two.

GN: So if you're right, why can't the West see that the problem they face is their own creation?

S: There are other considerations. George Bush and others cannot solve this problem just like that! They don't have royal decrees. There are people who have influence in the oil industry in the United States and they will not renew George Bush to be president next election. They have much influence over there, so our problems are not solved here in Arabia. Plus the Jewish lobby is a big influence, believe me.

GN: We certainly know that the Jewish lobby is powerful.

S: Even though Americans know what's right, they also know what they say is wrong. Somebody like Rumsfeld, Dick Cheney, even Bush; these people know what is right. Can you believe that they say Sharon is a man of peace? Do they want us to say you are right, Mr President? I cannot say that.

GN: Do you think there is any possibility that this deadlock, this impasse between the United States and the Arab-Muslim world — even the moderate, non-terrorist Muslim world — is likely to change?

S: It is going to change. We are seeing something happening now.

GN: The seeds of Arab democracy?

S: Small, but it should start like that. If it starts sharply like in Iran, we have problems. We know ourselves how we should act. Right now in Bahrain and Qatar they have some democracy which will look like Kuwait or something like that. But it's not enough. Even the Saudis think that democracy will come. We don't have democracy, but it is starting to sprout.

GN: But the logic of your argument seems to be that at the moment you don't have democracy because the West, the United States in particular, is quite happy to leave things the way they are?

S: Exactly. If we have democracy here, America would not be able to say dance and they dance. Stop dancing; they stop dancing. If we have democracy, Arab leaders will not say I want to make Washington happy. No, the electors here, they are the ones who should be made happy. Then I will not take any consideration from what others in Tel Aviv and Washington are saying. Every day Muslims are killed. American bombs kill them, even if Americans don't command it. Why do Arab leaders accept this? Because they want their bosses — those in Tel Aviv and Washington who put these leaders on their chairs — to be happy because they are, in effect, the electors. And right now, they are. But when the day comes and your citizens are those who put you in the chair, then you will take into account their considerations, then you will want them to be happy because you want to be elected next term.

GN: Is the anger that many Muslims feel ultimately to do with what they see as an unbalanced attitude towards the Arab–Israeli problem?

S: There are two reasons: injustice and the absence of democracy. And injustice is the way people in Washington look at us. There's no religious logic in the American position. Sometimes people don't like us because Muslim clerics say that the only religion is Islam. All the others, they can go to Hell. Those in Israel, they take this comment and put it in banner headlines. They know how to market it, those guys.

GN: On the other hand, your people have not learned how to market the positive aspects of Islam?

S: Believe me, I am a Muslim. I am a moderate Muslim. I believe that there are three main religions. But because I am Muslim, Islam is the real religion. Christianity is a pure religion and Judaism is the first religion. Without this Jewish religion, Islam does not exist. I believe all the prophets and when I pray five times every day in Arabic, I mention this. Why do people want me to do more than this? Christians, they mention only the last two prophets and Jews only the first one.

GN: You argue that Judaism and Christianity are narrow by comparison with Islam?

S: People don't want to move from other religions. They don't see good Muslim examples to follow. Now they think we are evil. We are not.

GN: I enjoy saying to my friends at home in Australia: 'I have lots of Muslim friends.' They usually reply: 'You have Muslims who are friends?' Why — because of this stereotype of the Muslim as a terrorist.

S: Unfortunately, that is the stereotype.

GN: That must be very frustrating for a moderate Muslim like yourself to have to live with, that so many people in the West think all Muslims are terrorists, or at least potential terrorists.

S: Well, other people help this image — like Saddam. He did make that mistake twelve years ago, but people have tried to reverse that mistake. He didn't do anything over the last ten years. But with the attacks on September 11, the American government had to do something to show that they won. But, understand me, they really didn't do anything. They took some parts of Kabul but the rest of Afghanistan is still under religious groups. But Americans didn't win. Did you notice they didn't celebrate, and you know the Americans, they love a celebration. Now George Bush cannot keep quiet. He wants to win anywhere. Because for many years, America didn't win. Even in Vietnam, they didn't win; even in Somalia, Lebanon. In many places, they didn't win. Now they have to win to show they are a super power. And they have media. They can tell everybody. Jews use their money.

GN: Saeed, we know the differences between the Muslim and non-Muslim worlds are partly to do with oil, but also to do with power and geopolitics and religion. But how much is to do with 'identity'? Maybe people in the West feel better about their own faults if they can point the finger at Muslims and say, 'But at least we're not as bad as they are.' Is it the way that Sharia Law is represented — amputations, floggings, occasional barbaric acts perpetrated in the name of Islam, the eye-for-an-eye aspect of the law?

S: Most of us say don't chop the hands off those who steal. You cannot punish this way, although it's written in the Book. You cannot go in a country like Saddam's Iraq where people are poor and cut their hand off when they steal. Nobody's doing this. But, at the same time, if you cut the hands off those who steal, then you would cut the hands off many of the members of the royal families in the Arab world.

GN: That's quite a statement!

S: But nobody would implement this, even if it was written.

GN: Muslims blame Jews, Jews blame Muslims, the West blames Saddam and bin Laden. How do we break this vicious circle?

S: Very simple — democracy.

GN: Democracy in the Muslim world?

S: Democracy first. Democracy will force justice, because that day no one will any longer come and say to Arab-Muslim leaders, to the sheikhs: 'Do this, do that.' Then people here in the Arab world will not care who thinks what in the West. Instead, they will say to the West: 'I will be elected next term if you want or you don't want.' That way the people here will force the Americans and Israel to talk to us, respect us. As things are now, nobody respects us.

GN: It's easy to say that Muslims need democracy, but how are you going to get it?

S: It should start in strong Arab-Muslim centres. But, you know, in Egypt, despite what they say, they have a kingdom. After they took out the king, we have another king and he wants his son to be a king — like Syria, like Iraq, like Yemen, like Libya. All these are presidents who receive their orders from America.

GN: What about Arafat? Surely he doesn't get his marching orders from America?

S: Arafat is another dictator. But now people blame Arafat because four or five years back, he refused the Camp David Accord thing.

GN: Big mistake?

S: When he refused, Baraq [then Israeli prime minister] agreed and then Sharon refused. Sharon went to the Al Asqa Mosque [in Jerusalem] with his five thousand people — and this was the start of the whole thing. Now, people are trying hard to forget that Sharon was the main refuser of peace.

GN: That was the start of this last intifada and all the killing that has gone on since?

S: Sharon refused Camp David, number one, a strong refusal. Arafat refused because he didn't want to be blamed. Arafat is a crook. All you have to do is give him a small country with a flag and a stamp with his photo on it, and he will agree. He cannot continue to exist. People say Arafat is building democracy in Palestine. Whose democracy? Why do you need him to have a democracy? He is a guerilla, fighting for his country, not a democrat. I have not heard of a guerilla being a democrat.

GN: Given Sharon's role and Arafat's role, will things change and maybe get closer to the justice and democracy you talk about if Sharon and Arafat were no longer on the scene?

S: Arafat will not be there in the coming years. He's very old. He's sick. He will die. But the electors in Israel are very disappointing. In Israel, they elect the one man who will stop peace.

GN: Never a dove?

S: They never go for somebody who is calling for peace.

GN: With or without Arafat, what do you think the Palestinians should do? It's so depressing, so 'eye-for-an-eye'.

S: What do you expect from the Palestinians when they see all these Jews in the street: give them a red nose — or what? Or if there is somebody who is completely devastated, whose two brothers have been killed? There is all this Western media about how some people have this culture of revenge. What is the difference — if they kill me with a bullet or if I put explosives on my body? Many people want to put about this attitude of 'See how they kill? They use their children as suicide bombers to go and kill.' What about Americans who go to Iraq? Don't they kill themselves? Some of them will be killed, but in a different way. Yes, they have these means, these modern weapons. So Palestinians killing themselves in the battle or in the streets of Israel — what's the difference? Forget about which political party — Labor or Likud — is in power in Israel; if the Palestinians are treated fairly, if battle is fair, we will see Israel in peace. We will all be in peace. We will not see another September 11. But people don't want to talk about this.

GN: You have to go to the source of the pain?

S: Yeah, but what they're doing there is like: I have a pain in my feet, but I put ointment on somewhere else. It will not cure things.

GN: Muslims don't believe the Americans are genuine? How could they believe in democracy, when they're ignoring the lack of democracy as the cause of this whole thing? Is that what you're saying?

S: Exactly! We cannot believe them. Yes, they keep changing their president every four years, but that is not what we want. The way they vote in the West, you cannot be president of the United States or even prime minister of Australia unless you are very rich.

GN: Certainly in America. In America, you just about have to be a millionaire to be a politician at all.

S: Even to be a member of Congress you've got to be a millionaire. Is what Americans have really a democracy?

GN: They would argue it's still better than anything in this Arab section of the globe.

S: I think there will be some sort of Arab democracy and I think it will start from Iraq.

GN: Are you saying that Iraq could be a blessing in disguise?

S: You could say that. Number one, the Americans don't want to spend money on Saudi oil. Number two, the Americans want to implement democracy. The Iraqis are very dedicated, very educated in the Arab world. But they are tired and don't want another butcher. It all depends on how America handles this war — if they handle it correctly and implement democracy in the heart of the Arab world, it will affect Iraq's neighbours. It will spread.

We should start from Iraq and it will spread to Saudi Arabia. Saudi Arabia, as you would know, is a very sensitive point. The Americans warned them to change their way of life. You cannot tell people how to change, but you can affect things from afar. You can support the opposition without them feeling that they're being pressured by the Americans, and they will change themselves, even in Saudi. You don't have to tell them.

GN: How long do you think that might take?

S: It depends on how the Americans do in Baghdad. If they are successful then Arab people in the region will think that's a good thing that's been done. The Iraqis now have a much better life, they will think. People in Egypt, even people in Libya, will think, 'Why not like Iraq? They're Arab like us, so why not do like them?'

GN: A situation that looks as terrible as Iraq, you say could be the key to unlock the whole Muslim problem?

S: Yes, for two reasons: oil and that starting point for Arab democracy. Oil and people power!

In a separate interview, Kirsty Cockburn asked Saeed whether he thought Islam, as a religion, was more generous towards other religions than they were towards his. 'True, very true,' was his instant and unequivocal response.

Kirsty Cockburn: But do you expect your children will explore different faiths?

Saeed: I will give them a chance to read about and understand people, other groups, other religions. If they just hear from somebody and copy that religion, I will stop them, tell them that is wrong. But it's their decision if they want to be in a particular religious group. Not everybody should wear clothes like mine, pray like me, act like me, sleep like me. Everybody has his own choice.

KC: Do your children wake every morning, with you, to pray?

S: Yes, they do. I go to the mosque. I don't go five times a day. I go sometimes — at least twice or three times. Ahmed, my son, goes if he want to go. I never force him. He goes with my daughters. They go and pray and we are all very happy after praying. We are happier because we've done what we should be doing as Muslims.

KC: How many Muslims would rise at 4.30 in the morning?

S: Many. It depends from house to house. To be frank, I cannot do it. My God knows that I cannot do it. There is no point in telling you that I'm doing it when in fact I'm not. I thank Him for creating me as a man, as a human being, enjoying this life. But I cannot work if I wake up at 4.30 and go to the mosque, pray, come back, sleep again and go to the office. That would not be for me. It would not be easy for me for the whole day. For me, that would be tough. On work days, I wake up one hour and a half before office time, take a shower, sit down and pray, pray deeply. It takes only two to three minutes.

KC: Do you pray on your own or with your colleagues?

S: On my own, in my office. I have a mat there.

KC: What do you think the future of Iraq and the Gulf and the Middle East is in the post-war circumstances?

S: Let's compare Iraq with Japan and Germany after World War II. When the West won over Japan and Germany it told them, 'You are defeated. You are not allowed to have weapons, army, this, this and this; don't do this, don't do that.' Since then, these two countries have concentrated all their effort in technology and education and today we have Japan a giant industrial country in the world, and even West Germany. How wonderful if this will be implemented in Iraq, a country with very educated people — more than the Japanese were educated in 1945, much more. Iraq has something like thirteen big universities. They have two rivers in the desert. They don't have to wait for rain for their agriculture. So they have a very good source of water, education and a very good history in many things. They have everything possible to make Iraq a very good country. But does America like to see Iraq like Japan and West Germany? I don't know. America is not a country you can depend on when they take a decision from here. It's the lobby behind it. Jews will be an influence in Iraq. I will not be surprised. I don't mean Jews, I mean the State of Israel. That's one side. Another side is whether Iraq will be a democracy, a pure democracy. I don't think America wants Iraq to be a democracy. They want to go somewhere further. Iraq is only the first stage. They think they have been bitten by Saudi's Osama bin Laden and these terrorists in New York — but they cannot create war with Saudi Arabia.

KC: What is it with the Saudis?

S: It was the Saudis who created this environment of hating America among the Arabs. But because the United States cannot stop Saudi doing this straight away, they have to find another enemy, invade him, win and then keep going until they arrive at their last destination, the Gulf. They want Arabs not to be religious; they want us to be just like others in the world — like Americans, like Japanese, like Canadians, like Australians with their life not based on religion. After that, they believe they would have peace, that they would not have another Osama bin Laden. So Iraq is just the first stage to impose democracy.

KC: What about the theory that the real American motive was geopolitical, to use the war against Saddam, Iraq and terrorism as the first cab off the rank to completely reshape the Middle East and the Gulf region in America's interests and image?

S: That's correct. What it's doing is trying to make the shape of America outside America, and support Israel. Americans support the terrorism of Sharon. Can the US president tell the Israeli government not to build more settlements? No. They cannot because any American leader has a right to criticise anybody in the world except two groups — Jews and homosexuals. These two groups affect their elections a lot. I told this to American officials in Washington during my last visit: 'You have the right to criticise anybody. You are a super power to the whole world, but you cannot criticise Jews in Washington! You'd be out of your office within three hours.' And homosexuals. Is that freedom? I don't think so.

KC: What reaction did you get in Washington when you said that?

S: They know this is the truth, but they just say, 'Oh, it might be right, but I don't know.' I told them: 'You don't have freedom in America, you have freedom in some things but not in everything. You don't have democracy because your president won with less than 50 per cent. The president is running a country where more than 50 per cent don't support him — or didn't support him in the election. Any king in the Arab world has more support than your president.'

KC: In your view, why is there so much resentment and anger towards the United States in the Middle East and Gulf regions?

S: America wants us to love them or they won't consider us at all. They supported Arab dictators even though they know those dictators don't have support among their own population. They support the State of Israel and they know this will make all Arabs angry. We are people. I can't remember once when America did anything in the interests of Arabs as citizens, but they are ready to support those who dictate to us; they are ready to do anything possible to make the Jewish state happy. For example, Iraqis hate America because America didn't do anything for them during the last fifteen years, nothing in their interests. No medicine, no this, no that. But Saddam would have more medicine in his house, more facilities than George Bush or Bill Clinton. But those who suffered are children.

It's difficult for people to like America. And again, all the weapons used against Arabs in Arab wars were either financed by Americans or sold by Americans. So after all this, they expect us to love them — difficult, very difficult! If in the near future — say, in two years' time — America will act correctly in Iraq, we are very quick to forget, very fast to forget if we see that America is doing the right thing.

KC: What is the right thing?

S: We don't see America doing anything so far in Iraq. They don't have any plan of any government, any tangible government. Tell me one thing, one thing which Saddam did in the last fifteen years against Americans, one thing within those years? Saddam didn't do anything. Saddam is not a good man at all, but the war against Saddam has no reason. If it is done to liberate Iraqis, there are many countries that need to be liberated also. Are the Americans going to liberate all these people as well?

KC: Where would you say needs to be liberated?

S: The entire Arab world. It's like a domino. If you do it in two, three, four countries, all the others will just fall. They will just follow. If the Americans have success in Baghdad, it will not be up to any President of America. Any staff from Foreign Affairs can just pick up the telephone and call Arab leaders, one by one. 'Implement democracy, okay? You have one minute.' Then call another one, and another one and it will be implemented. Where do they get their support from? Howard in Australia, where does he get his support from? From the people. But dictators here in the Arab-Muslim world, where do they get support from, where do they get the power? From the people? No, from the support they got from the West — otherwise they would not be there. So it is that you get a command from somebody you depend on, and if he tells you jump from here to here, they fly. They are very happy to do whatever they tell them. That is the relationship between Arab dictators and the West!

KC: So what will have to happen in Iraq for the Arab world to be convinced that the end justified the means?

S: First of all, they need to have a very strong government, not Saddam but strong like Saddam — but not supported by America — for one year and for a community group to write the Constitution. That Constitution should consider the culture and the way people of that country think and implement that within six months from now. Then have elections, and this interim government should not participate in the future government, but for just one year and then disappear. Now this Constitution, when they finish and implement it in two or three years, if it works, if it is a success in Iraq, then you take it and photocopy it and send it to other Arab countries. Just change the name of the country. You can implement this same Constitution in Egypt, in Saudi and in other Arab countries. This is justice. Give the people the right to write their own Constitution. In some countries, like Saudi Arabia, people don't have the right to do anything — except getting married to four women! They don't have the freedom to do anything else.

Here in Oman, this whole country will do some changes. We have an election coming up and we'll have a new parliament. We all think it will have some modification.

KC: In a democratic sense?

S: Yeah, we're just waiting. This year, 2003, we will move to the new parliamentary life in this country.

KC: What is it that Muslims can do to avoid more trouble? What can Muslims do to improve their side of things? Obviously more democracy and fewer authoritarian governments, but what about control over Islamic extremists — could the Muslim world as a whole be better at that?

S: Oman is not like Egypt. It is not like India. It is not like Iraq where people can go and work in the fields, agriculture and fisheries and the like. Oman is a country that has civil offices, about 100 000 working in the government. We have more than 700 000 students. This is the problem — where are we going to take all these people? You have to make them happy, otherwise you are in danger. Seven hundred thousand people in a country where you cannot send them into the field like Australia and give everybody 20 hectares, pay him some money to start his business, his life. You cannot do that here. All the people who work in the oil industry are not more than two to three thousand. But when you have millions, where are they going to work?

So this is the danger. It starts from here — to control people, to control who is to give them jobs and give them income. It is very difficult to control people — and the extremists are among these people. When young people are jobless, either they can become thieves because they want to eat, and a few will go to the mosque. Often they will support anything you don't like, just because you don't like it. They can go against you just because you are the government and 'I don't get anything from you'. So that's the nature of things. Where will this sort of person go? He will sit outside waiting for somebody to give him money. He doesn't get a job; he doesn't get enough education and so it's very hard to control extremists. You'll stop them if you give them a job, but where are the jobs?

KC: So there are economic challenges even in the oil-rich Gulf countries?

S: The challenges are huge. The government here did a lot of things in the last thirty years since the oil dollars came. But now, the big challenge is that many young poor are coming like rain. What are we going to do unless some foreign government helps Oman to create jobs, to create chances?

KC: Can you remain Muslim if the 'democratising' of the Arab world occurs? Won't that interfere with the influence of the Islamic religion?

S: Islam is a very simple religion. We can live with democracy. Islam, in fact, is already democracy. In the Qur'an, there's a thing called Shura and Shura actually means consulting. In politics that means democracy, Shura is democracy, the Islamic way of democracy. Here in Oman, we have the State Shura Council. I work there. In my job, I ask everybody in the Council, what is your feeling on this or this or that. I collect all their views and then I decide what to do. This is Shura. This is consulting. There are committees which meet every day — a committee for education, for law, for economics, for social affairs and there are many committee members. I work as a Director of Information. I support them with information they need, from Oman and from outside Oman. Whatever they need, it's my job to provide them with information.

So you see, Islam is already democracy. One of the main texts in the Qur'an is never to take anything by your own idea. You should — in fact, it's a command — ask others. God says: 'Ask them their ideas.' He didn't say ask them if you want; he commanded Muslims to consult. If you go to any Arab parliament, even the Saudi parliament, every parliament, they put this verse there, it's the first thing on top.

KC: So you're saying that the principle of democracy is already there in the Qur'an?

S: Yes, but the implementing is not. Some countries say, for instance, 'I can consult with you only in social affairs. I cannot ask you about defence matters; I cannot answer you in foreign policy matters.' But the Qur'an does not say: 'Ask them this one and don't ask them that one.' No, it's a command from God. It's not: 'If you want do this, and if you don't want do that.' It's a command — ask them, consult them.

KC: So there's no reason why democracy can't work with Islam?

S: No, none!

KC: Do you think, in terms of future relations between the Muslim and non-Muslim worlds, that the so-called Roadmap to Peace in the Middle East is going to work?

S: No, not at all. Next year you have an election in America and George Bush cannot repeat his father's trick when he squeezed Shamir, the Israeli prime minister in those days, saying: 'I will not give you a loan unless you do this and this and this.' Now, if junior George Bush says: 'Israel you should implement the Roadmap,' and they say 'No', it is no. If they say 'Yes', it is yes. It's up to Tel Aviv. It's not up to George Bush or anybody else. Sharon is not a person who wants to see Palestine there. He doesn't want it to be there. OK, we change Arafat and all the things that they say should be done. OK, now it's up to you, can you do this? Sharon will say 'No'. It's just lies and lies and lies. If you and George were living in this place, would you be happy to have Sharon as your neighbour here? I think not. He killed a lot; he killed kids.

Let me put it this way, yesterday when twelve Palestinians were killed in Gaza — among them children, very young children — nobody in Israel or America mentioned it.

KC: To what extent is this whole thing anti-Islam; how much is it religious?

S: It is not religious: it's just killing; it's politics. Bush is not acting as a Christian; Arafat is not acting as a Muslim; Sharon is not acting Jewish. They don't act except for their political interests. There is nothing religious in it. If I was Japanese or African or anybody else hearing about this, I would be angry because what is this, where is the justice, where's the fairness? It's not religious.

KC: The advisers to Bush are Jewish and right-wing Christians, but it's not about my religion is better than yours?

S: No. It is not because they're Jews. They are not acting from their Book. If they read the Bible, they would not do this, believe me. The Bible does not allow anybody to kill anybody else — nor does any other holy book. Even if you read about Hindus or Shintus or whatever religions they have in Japan or India, they would not allow you to kill anybody.

KC: Does the situation with Israel and the Occupied Territories remain the root cause of the Arab-Muslim hatred and antagonism towards the United States?

S: Yeah. If America's best interest is for a billion Muslims to love them, they must put pressure on Israel. 'Please, you are worsening our name. Please cool down. You cost us too high a political price. All Muslims, a billion Muslims, they hate us because of your actions.' But can the United States stop it? They are financing it. How can they stop it? Is it impossible for us Arabs to do it.

How About an Elected Sheikh?

We touched down in Muscat on a magnificently mild, sunny autumn morning. The Omani capital turned out to be thoroughly enthralling. It's far more traditional than the UAE capitals. Plus it's a Sultanate. Quite simply the country's ruled by a sultan — not the sort of place you'd expect to be able to discuss the thorny subject of Arab-Muslim democracy.

But less than an easy hour's flight from Dubai, Abu Dhabi and the freneticism of the UAE, it was a case of being dropped right into it. Immediately. My Muscat contacts — Australians who'd been living and working in Oman for seven years and loving every moment — had arranged an interview with Sheikh bin Afla, one of Oman and the Gulf's most prominent Islamic scholars.

The charming, English-articulate Sheikh Afla was about to head off overseas to a meeting of the European Islamic Dialogue, a think-tank formed to break down the barriers between the people of the Muslim and non-Muslim words. I spoke with him in his family's office building on the outskirts of the city.

SHEIKH BIN AFLA: The Scholarly Muslim

George Negus: Sheikh Afla, democracy — or rather, the alleged lack of it in the Islamic world — is a subject that critics of the Arab world in the West raise continually.

Afla: Especially now!

GN: You're not wrong. But it's understandable. Why aren't the Muslim nations democracies?

A: There is no simple reply to that. But before we talk about Arabs and Muslims becoming democracies, we have to ask the more basic question: 'What is democracy — anywhere?' And how do the various forms of democracy compare with what we in the Islamic world call *shur*, consultative democracy? It's possible that what we are developing here in our Sultanate of Oman could turn out to be a model for Arab democracy.

GN: Why Oman, of all places, as a model for Arab or Islamic democracy?

A: I've been involved in Omani politics now for the last twenty-five years, since the first mention of a Council of Officials, then an appointed council, and then moves to ensure elections. Here in Oman we have two parliamentary chambers

— one is the Upper House which is all appointed, while the other, the Lower House, is elected. I left the Lower House and now I am in the Upper House.

GN: So as an Omani Muslim, you've been both elected and appointed. Who elected you to the Lower House — the entire population?

A: Well, the election here is every three years. There have been changes since it started and they are still going on now. And this year, any Omani twenty-one years old — female or male — has the right to vote. Before that, the percentage was less.

GN: So you would argue that you are moving more and more towards your own form of democracy?

A: Yes, slowly.

GN: Right now, what do you feel about the world situation where — because of September 11, because of terrorism and Iraq, for all the wrong reasons — everybody in the Western world is talking about Islam? It's the 'talk of the town', as one young Emirati said to me in Dubai recently.

A: The issue here is twofold. One, we as Muslims are to be blamed for that and, more importantly, I think, the Western world, the world outside Islam, also has to be responsible. I gave a talk at Washington University, and afterwards one man stood up and said: 'You talked about Islam and you mentioned the right Islam. What surprises me is that what we know about Islam is not that, not the right Islam but the wrong Islam.'

GN: And that's the opposite impression to the one you would want people to have?

A: Exactly. He used the word 'intolerance'. He said, 'I have just read in the newspaper that a young boy in Afghanistan was beaten to death because he was playing football wearing shorts.' He gave other examples of intolerance in Iran and Algeria and said that to many in the non-Muslim West, this is what Islam is.

I said to him: 'Would you mind me asking you a question? What happened in the Oklahoma bombing — is that Christianity?'

Hardly. I will go even further. The assassination of Yitzhak Rabin in Jerusalem — is that Judaism? Is that what we call the religion from God? But there's even more. You remember the gas that was released in the Underground in Japan — is that Buddhism? I will reply on your behalf. I will tell you on behalf of Christianity, the Oklahoma bombing is not Christianity. The assassination of Rabin is not Judaism. The same thing with the gas attack in Japan. That is not Buddhism.

GN: But wouldn't you say these things are perversions of religion, not the religion itself?

A: For God's sake, don't take the actions and deeds of one Muslim and translate them and say, that is Islam. That is completely wrong. Unfortunately this is the view of the majority of non-Muslim people — and with all due respect in front of you, also, I think, the media.

GN: As a journalist, I agree the media have much to answer for.

A: The media in the West — indeed, the majority of people in the West — have not taken much interest in understanding what Islam is. On the other side, as Muslims, we have not portrayed totally what Islam is. That's also wrong. For example, I'm sure you know that we are not allowed to drink. Now that doesn't mean that when I drink, I *am* Islam, a Muslim. For that is not what Islam tells me.

There are things that unfortunately have been done and have been happening in the world. After September 11 occurred, it became worse. Some people have used this against Islam.

GN: It's true that because of the way the media treats these things, the actions of a few Muslim fanatics are used to judge the many.

A: Exactly, to judge the majority! Today, Islam is not a religion you can categorise as those who believe only in the Prophet Muhammed. That is not Islam. Our understanding, and what the holy Qur'an tells us, is that Islam is a religion of all the prophets who came before Muhammed. That is why if I, today, believe in Islam, I cannot believe that the Prophet Muhammed is the only prophet; I have to believe he is a prophet and so are those who came before him. I have to believe in Jesus Christ. I have to believe in Moses, in Abraham, Jacob. This is a very important issue that unfortunately non-Muslims don't understand.

GN: I'm not sure that most non-Muslim Westerners — whether they are Christians or otherwise — realise that the three faiths have the same origins.

A: Right. It is important that we talk together and understand all the religions. A famous French academic has written a book about the Bible, the Torah, the Qur'an and science. He made a comparison of all three faiths, the three holy books. To his surprise, he reached the conclusion — and I'm not saying this because I'm a Muslim, but because of his findings — that of these three books, the only book that doesn't have any conflict with modern science is the Qur'an.

GN: Do you believe that Christianity can't stack up against scientific scrutiny because Christians don't see Christ as a normal man? That they see him as the Son of God? Is that the basic discrepancy between the beliefs? Is that why many Muslims find Christianity unbelievable?

A: One thing, though, that we should understand and accept is that as Muslims we have to believe in the Bible. We have to also believe in the Jewish Torah. What we don't accept is that the Bible is the Bible that came from Jesus. It is not the Bible of Christ. It's had a lot of changes.

GN: Are you saying that it is not really the Gospel according to Christ?

A: That's right. But what I want to highlight is that we all believe in the same God. A Muslim must believe in all the prophets that we know — Jews, Christians and Muslims — and we must believe in all those holy books. What we don't accept is that those holy books are as they say they are.

GN: What's so different about the Qur'an?

A: The Qur'an has never changed. The Qur'an that was read during the Prophet's time is the same Qur'an we are reading today. That's one thing that is important to understand.

GN: What about the dreaded Sharia Law though? That's what many non-Muslims fear most. It's the Sharia Law that contains so much that non-Muslims regard as barbaric — amputations, beheadings, the treatment of women etc.

A: The springs of Sharia are two: the Qur'an and the Hadith, the other messages of the Prophet. If there's anything in the Qur'an that conflicts with the Hadith, you don't take the Hadith. If you read the Qur'an, it will give you exactly what a Muslim should be.

GN: But what about Sharia?

A: Unfortunately, both Muslims and non-Muslims reach conclusions that are not right. As Muslims, they have not followed the Qur'an. They don't look at the Qur'an. Instead, they look at the deeds of Muslims. To understand Islam, it's very important to read the Qur'an properly. Sharia Law is man's law, not the Prophet's law, not the Qur'an's law.

GN: I certainly know lots of people who call themselves Christians who've never read the Bible ...

A: And there are Muslims who do not follow the Qur'an — same thing.

GN: On another very basic note, can you explain *insh'allah* to me? Is it simply God's will, because it's difficult for a non-Muslim to understand that it could be God's will, for instance, that there is war in Iraq.

A: God has shown to us the correct ways and the wrong ways, but we are the ones doing the bad deeds. It is upon us to follow which way we want to follow. God is telling us if you follow the right path you will be in peace and harmony — not while you're here, but in the after-world.

GN: But *insh'allah*?

A: Now that's a long story. But to cut it short, *insh'allah* means the wish of God, by the will of God.

GN: So that means that if there is war, for Muslims that's God's will. And if there's no war, that's also God's will. How can that be? Isn't that having a bet each way, as we say in the West, in Australia?

A: That is not right. Exactly what *insh'allah* does *not* mean is 50–50. God willing, God will help you in fulfilling your promise, this is what *insh'allah* is.

GN: Let me try again — and this is a typical question from a Western journalist — but how could it be God's will to allow a war in this region? Everyone is frightened and fearful of war. When there is war, do you as a devout Muslim say: 'Oh, well — *insh'allah* — it's God's will?'

A: No, no! I wouldn't say war is God's will. What I am saying is that our acts, our deeds, what we are doing, they move us to do things that we ourselves don't like. God is *salam*, peace. In Islam, that is one of his names. You cannot expect that God would do something against his own will?

GN: So, you say that war is not God's will, but man's will?

A: Man's will! Yes. Because of those things that we ourselves have done. What do you call it in English — a test? It is a test from God.

GN: I think I understand. But what should our attitude be towards people like Osama bin Laden and Saddam? Do you regard Saddam Hussein as a Muslim? How can Al Qa'ida do what it is doing, in the name of Allah?

A: Well, first of all there are two different things here: Osama bin Laden, Saddam Hussein. If we look at Saddam Hussein, there are schools of thoughts in Islam. Just like in Christianity you have Protestants, you have Catholics, you have Orthodox and others. I would say you could call Saddam a Muslim — but does he follow Islam? That's another story.

You have people who are Muslims in name only. They have never done anything right as far as Islam is concerned. We call them 'Muslims of the tongue'.

GN: In English, people who give lip service.

A: Yes, lip service. These things that Saddam has done to his own people, to the religion — you can test him by looking at what the Qur'an says an individual should be. The Qur'an tells us also what a leader should be. Use that barometer and you will see Saddam is not a proper Muslim.

GN: What about bin Laden?

A: Same thing. The same question, the same way of examining, the same way of testing, you can also test bin Laden. What I will tell you is that you cannot use Islam, you cannot think that Islam is a vehicle to reach one's goals if those goals are not within the context and the approval of today's Islam. Islam is not a stagnant religion. Let those who understand Islam properly tell you what Islam is. Whether it's Saddam or bin Laden or anyone else, you cannot and should not do things that are acts that will keep your religion in the wrong place.

GN: Bin Laden would say, I imagine, that even though it's against Islamic law to kill innocents — like they did on September 11 — all of America is the enemy and therefore he can conduct a jihad against all Americans.

A: I'm a scholar, not a religious leader, but I will say that there is no understanding in Islam that you can kill innocents, whoever they are. But at the same time, the unfortunate thing in today's world is that we are seeing what is happening in Israel with the support of the Americans. That is something that would make the public in Islam go with whoever is crying out that they want business to be done against the United States. But even in time of war, we are not allowed to kill innocent people.

GN: Only combatants?

A: Correct! If Islam says you cannot kill a lady, an old man, you cannot even cut a tree, then how can you reach a conclusion that says you can kill innocent people?

GN: Is the Arab–Israeli conflict ultimately the most important issue for the Islamic world?

A: Yes. Muslims, we who understand this part of the world and the world itself, must understand that the conflict between the Arabs and the Israelis is a problem, a conflict that needs understanding, needs solutions. Unfortunately, what we have seen and what we still see is that people in the West have got — what do you call it — blinks?

GN: Blinkers.

A: Yes, blinkers on their eyes. They don't see what is right. We only see and hear what you in the media report. I mean, we see on the television how innocent people are being killed in Palestine. Only the day before yesterday, the tanks came and fifteen Arab houses were suddenly gone. By doing that and because of what the media shows and because today's world is one small village, extremists can easily get people behind them.

GN: If you could tell George Bush what he should be doing at the moment, what would you tell him?

A: Well, before telling him what to do, I think there are three things that George Bush should understand. He's talking of world peace and a world without terrorism. He should first define what terrorism is, who the terrorists are. Therefore, one thing I would like him to really say, in fairness, is exactly what it is that we are trying to fight. Let's define terrorism, and be fair in defining it. There may be some exceptions. But first of all, we need to do that — define it.

GN: What should we be doing about the Arab–Israeli conflict and the question of the Occupied Territories?

A: It's one of the most difficult issues. What can we do? For the last fifty years, the state of Israel has been supported by the West and by the United States in particular. Maybe Israel should never have been there, but now that it is why doesn't the world tell George W. Bush to read history. Let us look at the base issue for more than our generation. I will tell him this is an opportunity that you should take quickly. Do you want our younger brothers, our children and our grandchildren to have this heritage, this misunderstanding, this conflict? We have a great opportunity and the longer we leave it, unfortunately, the more difficult it will be. We should look beyond our own interests and our own generation.

GN: When I'm talking to Arab-Muslims, it always comes down to this — their claim that the Jewish lobby in America is the crux of the problem. It can't be that simple?

A: I agree. The Arab world is also to be blamed. But what surprises me is how people on both sides, mature people, people who today are supposed to really lead the world, don't sit and think carefully before taking action.

To me, knowledge is the most important thing that we need — Muslims and non-Muslims. The second thing is that each one of us — apart from religions, apart from communities, apart from countries, even as individuals, you and your wife, maybe you and your sons — are different. Every one of us has his own uniqueness.

GN: A religious version of peaceful co-existence? Is that what you're suggesting?

A: I should respect your religion. I should respect your uniqueness even though I may not agree that what you are doing is right. That, to me, is the best world. I wish that you people in the media would really use your technology so that humanity and the generations to come may live in peace and harmony and understanding, rather than this conflict and greed that is all over the world.

My partner, Kirsty Cockburn, armed with the author's contacts and a bundle of post-Iraq 2003 questions, flew into the Omani capital, Muscat, in May 2003 to check feelings in the Gulf following Operation Iraqi Liberation.

Kirsty met up with Afla and asked what he thought was the future of Iraq, the region and indeed relations between Islam and the West in the light of the Iraq War.

Afla: It would be wrong for me to say that what has happened in Iraq will not affect the Middle East and even the international way of things. I think that it's had its own effect in each and every part of the world, every corner.

What concerns me most is what is going to happen to Iraq and to the region if there is any other hidden US agenda. That's the worrying situation. It is not easy to just go and have a war to change a regime. That may be easy, but it is not easy to maintain that after the war. People need to see there is no double standard, that the so-called Coalition has taken that action because of humanity, because of human rights, not just do things because this is the way they think things should be in Iraq.

Kirsty Cockburn: Do you think there's an element of the US believing its way is right and that the rest of the world should be stamped like America?

A: Oman has said all along that we don't think the right way to reach solutions for the Iraqi problem is by using force.

KC: In other words, Saddam shouldn't have remained there, but that end does not necessarily justify the means?

A: What I'm saying is that we all agree that what we need is the good of the Iraqi people, the Iraqi public. Even the Americans say that. Everyone agrees that is what is needed. How we reach that conclusion, every one of us has his own idea. That is what worries me. Have we reached that? Have we given peace to the Iraqi people? We may have reached that now — maybe — but the repercussions, the consequences of reaching that peace in the way that we have, is there any side effect on the Iraqi people?

KC: Do you see terrorism being on the increase as a result of the war on terrorism?

A: The problem of terrorism is not only because of the Iraqi crisis. There are a lot of things in the world that are happening to cause it.

I met some people just before the Iraqi war, academics from the United States, and I said: 'For God's sake, we need to look at whatever we are doing before any action we take. We should not just look at the Iraqi thing. You need to do it in a wide spectrum. You have a problem in the Middle East, the Palestinian problem, that has not been solved.' That's why it's very difficult to reply about what is going to be the effect of the Iraqi crisis in terms of terrorism. We have a problem still in Afghanistan; we have a problem in North Korea; we have big problems in what will be the effect of globalisation — a very important issue we're unfortunately trying to ignore. We are living in a small village but we need to look at the mass.

KC: Could one of the pluses be a greater desire by the Western world to really understand the Islamic faith, to know more about the Arab world and the rest of the Islamic world than they have in the past?

A: This is a sword with two edges. Unfortunately, today's media has not been fair in giving a proper understanding of what is truly Islam. Probably the main reason for this is the Zionists have been controlling the United States media especially. But maybe a few academics and others who really want to understand what Islam is will now have a better idea. To that extent, it has probably played an important role.

KC: Do you see all this as a sort of religious war, a war of civilisations, of Islam versus George Bush's version of Christianity?

A: To answer this question is really very difficult. People from the United States keep saying that this has nothing to do with religion. Is it religion versus religion? Someone would say yes. Others would say no, that it has to do mainly with resources, with oil. Others will tell you it's got nothing to do with that, that it is solely because of the Jewish state. What Bush has said is that we are now seeing the Anglo-Saxons coming together — the United States, Britain and Australia — for the first time. Is that religion?

KC: How has the war affected the Islamic public's ability to form a view on all of these issues? Has it liberated Muslim people in terms of expressing their views?

A: Because of the wide range of what you can see, the media is a new force. Take the Arab channels. You just press a button and you get them in Australia. You get it everywhere. And we are getting more from the non-Muslim world. But it's how you digest these things, how you make a view, that's the point. No doubt, the Gulf crisis has given people more to understand — rightly or wrongly.

The Ongoing, Post-Iraq Problem: Islamic Resentment and the United States

Sadek Sulamain was Oman's Ambassador to the United States for almost four years. In his first overseas assignment with the Omani Foreign Ministry, Sadek was posted to Washington in 1973 and stayed until 1976. He went from the United States to Islamic Iran for a couple of years, returning home to Muscat for two years. He went back to the United States as his country's senior diplomat in that mission. He remains one of the Gulf's most experienced and thoughtful commentators on Arab–American relations and the role of Islam in the wider world. We chatted for two hours at a mutual friend's home in the Omani capital of Muscat.

SADEK SULAMAIN: Former Omani Ambassador
to the United States

George Negus: When non-Muslims talk about Islam, do you think that maybe they confuse the Islamic religion with Islamic culture?

Sadek: Yes. Islam is a young religion, comparatively. It is also a religion which has a very concrete history about it. Islam is different from other religions because its origins are so strong, well-documented and its spokesmen come across as real people.

GN: Real people — including the Prophet Muhammed himself.

S: Indeed, including the Prophet, not some metaphysical construction. We're talking here about a real individual.

GN: I get the impression that one of the things non-Muslims find hardest to believe about Islam is that Muhammed was an ordinary man. Because it's a religion and it was his life that led to the formation of one of the world's great religions, he had to be other than human. Maybe that's why — because the Christian belief, rightly or wrongly, is that Jesus was the Son of God — they wonder how somebody as significant as Muhammed could be an ordinary man.

S: That is the basic Islamic understanding. Muhammed was a human person. In fact, if you look in the Qur'an you will see that one of the accusations made against him is that he was so human people would say how could a Prophet be walking in the marketplace, eating food, doing the mundane things of daily living.

GN: And illiterate to boot?

S: And illiterate — but, mind you, he was illiterate only in terms of reading and writing rather than in terms of comprehension of the world. So one has to be careful with that word 'illiteracy', in that sense that in the Arabian environment in which he was born there was literacy of speech rather than writing. Back then, writing was very rare.

GN: You could say he was uneducated in the formal sense?

S: He was a man who declared himself a prophet at the age of forty. Before that, he was a normal person, yet a very reflective person who from his early beginnings talked cosmically of one place, one city, one tribe. It is amazing that the early Qur'anic verses are so universal. These are cosmic concepts. God is the God of all people.

S: How can a man coming out of such a limited environment think so broadly, taking humanity into his concerns? When we're talking about Islam, you are looking at a real human situation where an ordinary individual comes and takes on the world. What is it that makes a human being see what he is giving to the people, a man who has so much to say — and yet he says, 'These words are not mine.' What happens within a person that makes them do that? If that person were someone who were suspect in his speeches, you might say we have a charlatan here. But the story of this man Muhammed is one of being very truthful from his early years.

GN: There was no reason to doubt his veracity?

S: No reason at all. He was the most trustworthy person before he became a prophet. When a person says it is not him saying something, you are listening to a man who is connected in some way to something very, very big.

GN: One of the things that other religions find hard to grasp is when they discover that not only is Islam a much younger religion than Christianity or Judaism, but the three religions have the same roots.

S: Absolutely. But Islam is presented in the Qur'an itself as the culmination of the eternal message.

GN: Muhammed was not the only prophet, but the last prophet?

S: He is the last. And when you come to this point, why is it he is the last? Again here is something to look at. It is as if humanity henceforth will be on her own, that there have been enough prophets.

GN: Humanity being set loose?

S: Liberating the human mind. Having introduced the basic wisdom, now you are on your own. But no religion could ever satisfy you intellectually 100 per cent. People can become fanatics but the human mind has its own autonomy. There remain intellectual problems within Islam, like there are problems in the Christian and Jewish religions. What you have in Islam is not only the belief part, the message of the Prophet Muhammed, but a way of life over centuries.

GN: Can we talk about that — the difference between Islam as a religion and Islam as a way of life?

S: Well, when we talk about religion, we talk about the particularities of a religion. When we talk about faith, we talk about a universal nature of religion. You can be a man of faith even though you may not be a Muslim. Someone from a Chinese or a Japanese religion would say he is a man of faith. Faith is the inner state of mind in which we are rooted. It's almost like an existential thing, like without it we might not even be able to get up and do anything at all. I always think of that as being like clinical depression.

GN: Speaking of depression, as a Muslim how do you react when the Muslim many are being judged by the extremist few?

S: I can understand both sides. Fanatics can be born in any tradition and create conditions which produce extremists. They emerge all over the world. In the September 11 case, there are particular circumstances in which these people were involved. On the other hand, I also understand the insecurity that the other side, the United States, feels. Feeling like the victim of what happened that day is justifiable. Whether we like it or not, whether we want it or not, it's a natural thing for them to associate all Muslims with what happened, why you would become at least suspicious of Muslims. Wise people from all ages have always alerted us to this stereotyping, even in the Qur'an.

GN: As a Muslim who's lived among them, do you think the United States approach to this whole Muslim versus non-Muslim problem is the right one?

S: I can understand why our people would think they shouldn't be acting the way they are, but I can also understand why the Americans would be so scared of the world around them. The United States has invested a lot in this world. They have turned a whole continent into a great, unprecedented human society. They have many assets, many. There are many ways in which you can appreciate them. How people could come together to produce a Constitution which remains to this day the same. How can a Constitution survive from 4 million people, when it was written, to 280 million now — with all their diversity? If you look at it, there's hardly a thing on which they haven't had an impact. Technology, systems, science, organisations, all kinds of things. But now they realise that while they were doing all this, in the process they were stepping on other people's toes in so many ways. A great deal of resentment built up against them without their really being aware of it.

GN: You feel they were a bit shocked by that build-up of resentment?

S: They were shocked alright, and it was demonstrated in such a dramatic fashion.

GN: Why are they picking on us? What have we done wrong?

S: Absolutely. What have we done wrong? The Americans don't need criticism, they need reassurance. We've got to reassure them.

GN: But how do you go about reassuring somebody as powerful as they are?

S: A strong person is not always a secure person and people look at America as a strong nation and equate that with a sense of security — which is false.

GN: Despite their economic and military power and all their achievements?

S: The Americans need reassurance, then they might think things over, review things. But in the time immediately after 9/11, it was like someone had hit you and it's still hurting — a lot. Your first reaction is not to indulge in debate. Your first reaction would be to take the gun away and then say, 'Alright, let's see why this happened.' Americans have taken this attitude. Let's first neutralise the capacity to attack us — rather than work out why we were attacked.

GN: But many people believe the US contributed to that by their foreign policy, by their attitude towards Islam.

S: There are definitely American policies that have built resentment around the world.

GN: I get the feeling that there are Muslims who believe that the Americans don't take them seriously as people, not necessarily because they're Muslims but they just don't take people seriously who are not like them.

S: I would put the question the other way round. When we say, 'You don't take me seriously,' I have to ask myself why am I not being taken seriously? And ask them: 'Why aren't you taking me seriously?'

GN: Do you think there is an element of racism in the American attitude towards Muslims from this part of the world?

S: Americans are not against Islam. They are not against Arabs.

GN: That being the case, most people I've spoken to in the Islamic world believe the basic problem is the lack of balance in the American approach to the conflict between the Israelis and Palestinians.

S: No question, there is an imbalance. There is no question about the uneven-handedness, if you will. But, one has to look at why this is so? The burden always is to understand why the other person behaves the way he does towards you. If someone, for instance, feels they have no alternative but to terrorise — why is this? Our diplomats have made this argument to the Americans for many, many years. Why is it that you are favouring the Israelis so much, while your major interests are with us? We are your real partners.

GN: Oil alone would suggest that.

S: During the Cold War years of the 1950s and 1960s, people forget we were on the brink of devastation. Everything was looked at in the light of pluses and minuses with the great powers. The Israelis very cleverly knew that their future lay with America, so they offered themselves as a staunch ally. Meanwhile, of course, during those years, the Arab states were leaning to the other side. They were more into the socialist part of the world. Up till that point, there wasn't really a special US relationship with Israel. Israel was looking more at Britain and France to be there for them.

GN: So, you see a direct link between the Cold War and Israel's bonding with the United States?

S: What we Arabs found was that the relationship between Israel and America was cemented back then in a very clever way, not just strategically but also emotionally. Despite their differences as Jews and Christians, it was kind of religious. All the other things that would reinforce that basic relationship, they brought to it. Suddenly, we Arabs found ourselves waking up to the reality that Israel is not just a valued country, it's a strategic ally of the US, part of a forward strategy. And this relationship developed to the point where America would say: 'No matter what, I'm not giving up on this ally.' Even if Arab nations offer military bases and what not — as they have — that other relationship with the Israelis is there. The unevenness and the bias cannot be undone.

GN: On a less esoteric basis, what about the cold hard fact of the Jewish lobby in the US?

S: It's very strong. It's very efficient. It is, in fact, to my way of thinking, not really even consistent with the American ideal of a secular, diverse, humanist society.

GN: Why? Is it just money? Is it just the size of the contribution that they make to party political funds?

S: That's traditional, historical. Jewish money, how to make money. The money is part of it. But there is also the other part. Many influential Jews migrated from Eastern Europe to the United States. These were not just unknown commodities. Many of them were very prominent people in science, especially in science.

GN: They were incredibly valuable imports?

S: Very valuable imports. Then, of course, there was the legacy of World War II and the Holocaust. And there are the more recent events, the religious dimensions, the way these so-called evangelical Christians are framing global questions into the metaphysics of the Bible. That is very strange.

GN: If that imbalance that we're talking about in the Middle East conflict doesn't change, how the heck can we change the situation before there's a greater conflict?

S: This is not the end of history. We will be producing generations after that. But I do see deficiencies in Arab diplomacy, a great deal. I see patterns that are not very attractive.

GN: But in the meantime, it's crisis management we're dealing with here.

S: That's right — absolutely! One of the aggravating factors in the way we deal with the rest of the world is that we expect the worst — and we get it! What I am saying is that we have to deal with one another positively, rather than negatively. And that includes Arabs dealing with Americans.

GN: You can't accuse the Americans of being arrogant and then ...

S: And then say, 'Please be kind with me.' You just can't do that.

GN: Do you give any credence to the theory that this is all ultimately about geopolitics, that Saddam and Iraq are just the first brick in the wall?

S: If that's true then a conflict exists between two ways of life — Muslim and the non-Muslim — encroaching sometimes, accommodating each other the rest of the time.

GN: A question of identity?

S: Cultural identity on the one hand, and on the other a yearning for political reform. Both things are there and I'm seeing young Arab-Muslim political leaders coming up really trying to juggle the two in a way that would mean they retain the identity and also carry out the political reform thing, to the extent that the West would not intrude on their new political identity.

GN: So you could say that land, religion, tradition, oil, money are all important, but probably, in the long run, none of those things together or separately are as basic as identity.

S: Where Arab-Muslims are concerned, it is all about identity: more than religious identity — cultural identity. Oil, in a way, has had a corrosive effect on Arab life. You can look at it that way. The present political leaderships are also not looked at very well. They don't necessarily represent the Arab peoples. If you look at this part of the world, we have a fifth of the world here. For the entire Islamic scene, the Arabs are still the main repository of Islamic tradition. We still constitute the faithful culture within Islamic cultures.

GN: Even with people like the Indonesians?

S: Even with Indonesian Muslims. Islam is not a culture; Islam is a civilisation.

GN: You use the word 'civilisation'. But I can imagine what your reaction would be to the provocative Huntington thesis — nonsense, many say — about the so-called 'clash of civilisations'.

S: To tell you the truth, I didn't find it was nonsense. I read it when it was first written back in 1993. At the time, I said to myself that he must be looking at something maybe the other side aren't thinking. Huntington invited people to write their reactions and almost all of them were against what he was saying. But actually he wasn't saying that we should engage in a cultural or a civilisational war. What he was saying was that the way things are, that's where we're headed.

GN: And what do you think?

S: When people of different civilisations come together to conduct business, it is not easy. So referring to the Huntington thing, we should be aware there is a potential clash. We need to be alert and aware of it. Not that anyone wants it to happen. But if we are not aware of it, we could be asking for trouble.

GN: Acknowledge that solving the problem has a long way to go?

S: And be ready for it. When I was in the US, one of the remarks I would make was: 'Look how much time and effort I have invested in learning your language, in learning your history, in getting to know you as Americans . . .'

GN: And, how much time have you invested in learning mine?

S: Exactly. Now let's see what you've invested? They might reply that they haven't because they are the stronger side. And that is definitely the case, of course. Instead of people saying we're facing the possibility of a clash between our two civilisations, we should be defusing any of the factors that could lead to such a clash.

Remember, we are only one species. We come from the same evolutionary track and within us is something which makes us survive. One of the conditions of our survival is to avert wars and devastation. It seems right now that it is inevitable, but to my way of thinking, we are still evolving, growing. Humanity is young in the calendar of creation.

GN: So you believe we will survive the current tensions between the Muslim and non-Muslim worlds?

S: I trust the human mind. Think about the millions of people who are doing the right thing, not the wrong thing. You asked me about optimism. Yes, I am optimistic.

The 'Talk-Back King' of Muslim Radio

Muscat-based Sheikh Khalfan Al-Esry is the talk-back king of Omani radio. He has his own regular program on which he answers any-and-all questions from Muslims and non-Muslims in both English and Arabic about his beloved Islam — the religion, its values, its people, its politics, the lot.

But Khalfan wasn't always a devout Muslim. 'If I can go back fifteen years, I was finishing my engineering studies in the UK,' he says, 'and coming back here to this region, to Saudi in fact, I just came to an awareness of my own religion. I began reflecting on life, and I realised that as a society we Muslims tend not to be so appreciative of the gift that we have, the gift of Islam. The Qur'an itself is an example. It is so rich spiritually; it can bring so much happiness, tranquillity, peace in ourselves; it's so powerful. That is how it started — I'd go to pray in the evening after working hours.

And I'd just sit around at dinnertime with a couple of friends and chat about Islam when I finished work as an engineer in the desert.'

On one occasion, Khalfan made a presentation for both Muslims and non-Muslims at an Islamic event and that was a turning point. 'People began to approach me for information and it just went on and on and the audience became more. The next trend was that whenever the expat community working here had visitors coming from abroad to visit Oman or other Arab-Muslim lands — the American Embassy being an example — they would invite me to speak to them about the Omani culture and how strong its links are to Islam. So I became like an entertainer, free of charge, providing information about Islam.

Khalfan is sharp, witty, articulate and personable, but he obviously doesn't suffer fools all that well. After he'd taken me through his impressive laptop presentation explaining the vagaries of Islam — proving how presumptuous it is to assume that Muslims are a backyard lot who have not joined the new millennium's IT world — we chatted easily at the house of my recently acquired Omani lawyer-friend in suburban Muscat.

SHEIKH KHALFAN AL-ESRY:
The Communicative Muslim

George Negus: Khalfan, what do you think about the geopolitics of Islam at the moment? Everybody's now talking about Islam. Everybody's reading books about Islam. Everybody's asking questions about Islam. Everybody, it seems, is wanting to know about it. It's the talk of the town. What impact is this having on the Islamic world — including you folk here in the Sultanate of Oman?

Khalfan: You're right, we are the talk of the town, as you put it. What happened on September 11 was very unfortunate, but the way I see events, it could have been a blessing in disguise. Events have forced even Muslims to go back and ask themselves sincere questions. How much of Islam do I know — because now Islam is a target. It has hurt a bit. People have access to what I call a massive library — the internet. And you people putting their views who are not true about Islam, not representing the true Islam. But the platform for gaining real knowledge has suddenly arrived and, as you say, you non-Muslims are beginning to ask questions.

GN: Non-Muslims — not just in Australia where I come from but everywhere — are thirsty for first-hand knowledge of Muslims. That's why I want to talk to outspoken Muslims like your good self!

K: Yes, but I also think largely sentimental Muslims need to equip themselves with understanding of their own religion. Islam does not want you to follow it blindly. The first thing that is taught in Islam is knowledge. So you should go and open books, Islamic books, that try to teach Islam — how to pray and how to do things. The book of knowledge is the first book, the first chapter.

GN: Are you saying there are Muslims out there who don't really understand Islam themselves?

K: I know many Muslims who go and pray and I usually ask them: 'Why do you pray?' And they say, 'To worship God.' 'Do you know who is God, the one you're trying to worship?' I ask them. 'Yes, I know him,' they say. 'He's the Creator. He's the one giver who gives us everything.'

GN: How do you reply?

K: I say 'no' to the slogans. That's what you've been taught, but it's what you know, what you believe that matters.

GN: The same could probably be said of many Christians or Jews.

K: Did you know that half of the Omani population is still at school? More than half, actually, are under the age of twenty. So I say that many Muslims have taken Islam by tradition, by inheritance — not by personal belief.

GN: So September 11 was, in an awful way, a real 'wake-up call'?

K: Yeah! But in Islam, there are no stupid questions. There are no hard questions either. There's not even a blasphemous question — as long as it is being asked for the sake of gaining knowledge, not to debate, not to defame or try to underplay or criticise God. If it is for the sake of knowledge, it's very much encouraged. So please ask me any questions you like. The Prophet Muhammed himself probably asked the same questions to God. But if those questions were to be asked today, they would be considered blasphemous. For instance, the Prophet Abraham said to God: 'Show me how you resurrect the dead.' That basically questions one of the Five Pillars, the very foundation of Islam, the Hereafter, the Resurrection. If somebody comes now and asks the question doubting the Resurrection, that would be taken as blasphemous. But Abraham asked that question and was given an answer. So Muslims — or anybody else for that matter, including you, my friend — seeking knowledge for the sake of understanding are always encouraged.

GN: To get back to what you think about what's happening in the world at the moment between Muslims and non-Muslims, why do you believe it's a blessing in disguise?

K: In America right now I'm told that all Islamic centres are running flat out, with people asking questions. Books on Islam are basically running out of shelves. Book people are asking for support because they're running out of published information. It's expensive to distribute all this free of charge, so here in Oman, for instance, we're using emails and internet chat rooms and these discussion platforms to answer the questions being asked. It's mainly the general public that go to chat rooms and political forums and talk. You can hear what they are saying on the street.

GN: Speaking of politics, what do you think about George W Bush's Good versus Evil statement? How significant has that been in changing the whole debate from a relatively predictable, normal one about the two religions to a more vicious, even ridiculous, one? How did you react when, post-September 11, Bush claimed the attack occurred because Muslims, or at least Muslim extremists, envy the US, that they're jealous of American progress, that sort of stuff?

K: Using the words 'good' and 'evil' — there are definitions behind them. It's not who says it, it's the meaning of what is good and the meaning of what is evil. Today, if 'good' is coming from America, from the government, not the people, what about the evil taking place not far away in Israel? People are being killed there for no reason. What is happening there is even closer to apartheid, yet it is the Bush administration who is supporting that evil in Israel. Why does the US veto every time the whole world says Israel shall abide by UN resolutions? What is the goodness there? Carpet bombing using B–52 bombers to bomb innocent people, villagers? Why didn't they take Saddam out at that time when they came to war over Kuwait? What Saddam did to Iraq, including Kuwait, is not any different to what Israel did to Lebanon. The only reason Bush was using those words — and the whole world is following him — is because of American power, economic power, as well as its military might.

GN: He's stopped using that term. Why do you think he's been told not to say it?

K: He's been told because when he says it, within half-an-hour the words were being used everywhere. Also when he talked about a crusade against Islam, in no time those words were out in public — and some people accepted them as meaning all Muslims, not just terrorists.

GN: To me, it almost seems like the Cold War has disappeared, so the new war is 'Good versus Evil'. America and anybody associated with them are 'good', and the rest of the world, including the Muslim world in particular, are the potential baddies, the Red Indians — as if the whole world is one long Hollywood cowboy movie.

K: You can already see that. Islam is growing in numbers, in economy, in population, in migrating. Islam is gaining momentum and you have to stop it.

GN: How crucial to the resolution of the overall situation between Muslims and non-Muslims is the Israeli–Palestinian question? Can one be resolved without the other? Is that a microcosm of the whole problem?

K: All that is required is justice. All we Muslims are asking for is justice and human decency.

GN: But I guess what I was getting at was that if justice occurred in Palestine and Israel, wouldn't that be a sign that justice and fairness are possible anywhere? That's why I find myself calling it a microcosm. Everyone in this part of the world — the Arab-Muslim world — keeps coming back to it, even moderate Muslims. Bin Laden and Hussein, hated by moderates as they are, claim that they're doing it for the Palestinians.

K: I once read an article from an American who says — and he's an American supporting Israel — that what is happening in Israel is because of the Jewish law being American. His argument was that the Jews are taking America to destruction, all the wealth of America is spent in simply protecting a handful of Israeli Jews. Historical information confirms that the Qur'an says Jews never had independence, they were always under the protection of something or someone. In Arabia itself, they used to co-exist with Arabia, they were under the protection of Arabia, then the Romans, the British, at one time France, Germany, Spain — and now they are under the protection of America. So they can never be alone.

GN: But how can peaceful co-existence occur between the Muslim and non-Muslim worlds until that Middle East situation has been resolved — until there is a Palestinian state for instance?

K: It's not only a Palestinian state. You can go to India which was ruled by the Muslims for five hundred, six hundred years, and Muslims allowed others to practise in peace, yet they do not have rights in India today. So it's not just a question of a Palestinian state. It's justice for Muslims everywhere.

GN: Do you agree with the two-state solution?

K: Yes, but I think it goes beyond just Israel. What is happening in Israel — and we need to understand that there are two things: there is managing crisis and there is management by crisis. Currently, the world is preoccupied with crises to ensure that someone can manage them. But somebody is creating crisis after crisis in the world just simply to keep you preoccupied and focusing on what is good and what is right. Even if the Palestinian case is settled, I can guarantee you it won't stop there.

GN: There'll be another crisis somewhere else? George Bush's 'Axis of Evil'?

K: Yes, there's North Korea and there is Iran, but there's also Pakistan. There is Syria. There is Iraq. There is Yemen. There is Somalia. Whatever basically you need to keep the business of producing weapons and selling them at extortionate prices. We need to keep the world preoccupied with problems. If it is not a military problem, it is another problem. I have no love for America, no respect for America. What it's doing is just draining countries, nations. Whatever investment comes there is not for the sake of the country but for America. Keep them preoccupied with crisis.

GN: So how is that peaceful co-existence going to happen? Or is it just wishful thinking?

K: It's not wishful. It is probable. We'll just give a blueprint for mankind, that's not impossible.

GN: Does that mean the Islamisation of the world?

K: It doesn't have to be per se, but why should we be talking about a relationship between Islam and the rest of the world?

GN: Because everybody else is.

K: Yeah, yeah. But there are others who are fighting. There are Irish people fighting. That fight has been there for ages. It's also about relationships. You fight with your brother or you fight with your sister. These problems are there for others as well, not just Muslims. Terrorism is not only a problem for Muslims.

GN: Christian terrorism in Ireland, maybe?

K: That terrorism is associated with religion also.

GN: Timothy McVeigh [the Oklahoma City bomber] maybe could be considered as a Christian terrorist?

K: But you don't hear that word 'Christian' when they talk about what he did.

GN: No you don't. The people who bomb abortion clinics in America certainly call themselves devout Christians, but are they categorised as terrorists when they kill and maim in the name of their religion?

K: You don't hear the word 'terrorist' mentioned about them, do you? They're just madmen! The fact is that evil and good will continue to be.

GN: Whatever religion we are talking about?

K: Exactly! Historically, the first crime ever took place in the smallest community of mankind — back at the time of Adam and his wife, Eve. It was a homicide, a killing. So we should expect good and evil will continue, but to also have a blueprint, a law or a government that can introduce the peace we all desire.

GN: And you're convinced that that blueprint is available in Islam?

K: Take the crime rate. Take the alcoholism rate. Take the drug consumption rate, suicide rate, rape, abduction, usery laws, property, from any angle you like. You will find that it is the lowest in practising Muslim communities. An example. The black continent of Africa is infested with AIDS. Look at statistics on the west coast of Africa where most of the countries are Muslim, look at the AIDS figures there and compare them with central Africa where there are not Muslim countries. Look at the difference.

GN: Is your argument that a Muslim can handle any situation because they self-police whereas most non-Muslims don't self-police, they're not very good at self-control and self-discipline; they have to be controlled by laws, armies, corporations? They allow the outside world to control their behaviour?

K: Yes. Muslims fasting is one way of practising such control.

GN: To a non-Muslim, the Ramadan fast of one month sounds like a long time. I also worry about the dehydration factor. Health-wise, no eating and no smoking and no sex might be fine, but the no water bit is a big worry. I talked to a couple of

Western doctor friends of mine working here in the UAE about this and they said they worry about it too.

K: Yes, but back in Australia — your big land — usually if you have a long way to travel, I'll bet you fill up at the last petrol station to ensure that it takes you the full journey ... and if you fail to stop at that last station because you were too lazy, or you did not focus or whatever...

GN: You run out of petrol!

K: That is right — and the last station for a Muslim is just before sunrise, about an hour and a half, so I fill up.

GN: Really fill up, so not just the seven dates recommended in the Qur'an?

K: No! You really have a main meal. You talk of spiritual benefits, but there is a part to be healthy, getting rid of all the toxins. We are even told that the blood vessels, everything improves. And there's another benefit. A preparation for disaster — disaster can come at any time, a calamity can come at any time. As Muslims, we have learned to have that mental switch, to go without eating and drinking, or even missing that morning coffee. The morning coffee is the one that is amazing. On the first day of Ramadan, I go to work, even the urge is not there. I just continue working — nothing. You have that mindset.

GN: Khalfan, at the moment, what is your view of the world from Islam, from your Islam?

K: The way that I see the world from my Islamic view is a world yearning for peace, yearning for happiness, for tranquillity. People at the working level, at the normal level, want to live and enjoy whatever life that they have. But for one reason or another, they are given to taking advantage of others. The strong are taking advantage of the weak to the extent of exploitation. What I believe is that the only happiness is at a personal level, the family level, society level. It can only be once we know and are at peace with the Creator of this earth. Without Him, we continue to be unhappy.

GN: So when you look at the world from your position as a Muslim, that's what you find yourself concluding? You can link everything that's happening back to that basic belief in God?

K: Yes, but now what I say to Muslims is do not keep this treasure to yourself. The Qur'an is not property. We owe it to mankind. We are the inheritors of the prophets, holding the message. It was not meant for us to keep it to ourselves. We need to share it with the world. To non-Muslims, what I say is that this book is not a book of religion, it's not a book of worship, it is a blueprint for mankind. It's an encyclopaedia, a roadmap for eternal happiness as well as eternal bliss and salvation.

GN: What about the non-Muslims who say to you, 'That's fine, but I want to remain a Christian,' or 'I want to remain a Jew. I don't want to become a Muslim.' Do I have to become a Muslim to believe in God, in Allah?

K: What I say is that Jews believed in Moses — by force, I think. Christians believe in both Moses and Jesus. But we Muslims believe in Moses, Jesus and Allah. So we have hit the jackpot! This is hard for non-Muslims to accept, but a Muslim is also a good Christian. In other words, we are true followers of Jesus. We pray and follow the commandments of Jesus more than Christians. Think about it. Jesus didn't allow people to drink wine, or eat swine. As Muslims, we don't drink wine or eat swine. Jesus purified himself before he prayed, so do we. Jesus covered his face when he wanted to pray and we follow that too.

GN: Did he?

K: Yes. It's in the Bible. Also, Jesus says, 'Have no table in the Church, the place of worship,' and we don't have a table in the mosque. So basically, when a Christian tells me that they are a true believer in Jesus, so are we Muslims.

GN: What about Mary, who Christians believe to be the Mother of Jesus?

K: In the Qur'an, there is a chapter dedicated to Mary. We say, 'Behold and the angels say to Mary, in the month of arki, Allah has chosen thee for the heirarchy and purifies thee and raised you above all women.'

GN: So you believe in the immaculate birth of Jesus?

K: Definitely. It's mentioned in the Qur'an. I believe in it, the miraculous birth.

GN: So if you said to a Christian that to be a good Muslim you have to be a Christian, what do you say to the Jews?

K: To the Jews I say, I am a good Jew as well because I believe also in the Ten Commandments of Moses. Give me one commandment of Moses that Muslims refute? We are not refuting his message. We are not refuting his prophethood. We are not refuting his laws or his miracles. We respect him and follow him.

GN: So you believe yourself to be a Christian and a Jew as well as a Muslim?

K: A Christian and a Jew and a follower of all prophets.

GN: Why can you say that, but I don't know any Christians or Jews who could say the same thing about your Prophet Muhammed?

K: Because we have the authentic, the untouched, the unchanged divine law.

GN: Why do Christians appear to think that Islam has been there for ages — almost like an ancient cult — and then this bright new kid on the block called Christianity suddenly came along? There are a lot of Christians that don't even know that there's six hundred years difference between Jesus and Muhammed and that Islam has only been around for 1400 years.

K: Moses is mentioned sixty-nine times in the Qur'an.

GN: Sixty-nine for Moses — and Jesus?

K: Twenty-five for Jesus.

GN: And Muhammed?

K: Just five times.

GN: Sixty-nine for Moses and five for Muhammed? How come?

K: Because it's not about him. He is just telling the message. It's the message that has been given to him in Arabic by God, whereas the story of Jesus is about his miraculous birth and his miracles. Even when Mary was born is mentioned in the Qur'an.

GN: You have no problem whatsoever in saying what you said about Moses and Jesus, but Christians and Jews find it almost impossible to get the word Muhammed to come out of their mouths.

K: They cannot. But in the Bible, in the final decision Jesus gave to his disciples, he says you cannot understand everything I am about to say unto you, but when I depart, the comforter will come and he will do this and he will be like a Moses.

GN: My study of Christianity is long gone, but I would've thought Christians would say that meant what they believe to be the Holy Spirit, the comforter.

K: No problem. But we say that the only reason we have been selected to be better than anything else ...

GN: Isn't that a trifle arrogant?

K: I don't think so. It's because of the intellect, the application of logic and the beauty of Islam that it allows you to reason, to put reason to the glad tidings given in the Bible. Only that will bring you to one conclusion, to answer all of the unanswerable questions — including the ones from Christians.

GN: It's interesting, isn't it, how all religions — yours or anyone else's — believe that their truth is *the* truth? But why do you think you Muslims can't get Christians to accept the whole Muhammed messenger thing has happened? Moses — that's easy.

The Ten Commandments — yes, that's very important. Jesus — whatever they say he taught them, but they appear more interested in celebrating all the Christian festivals than talking about what Jesus taught.

K: That's true. We pray five times a day to show how much we believe in the Prophet's message.

GN: Most Christians — or at least people who call themselves Christians — if you asked them to quote one thing from the New Testament, most of them couldn't do it. They know when Easter is and when Christmas is, but they wouldn't have a clue about any of the things in the Gospels: their equivalent, I would have thought, of your Qur'an.

K: We believe that they have even got the date for Christmas wrong. It's meant to be celebrated in [the northern] summer.

GN: Some Christians prefer not to even accept that Muhammed existed. Do you think maybe that's because you Muslims say that Muhammed was nothing other than a normal man who was a messenger, whereas Jesus, Christians claim, was the Son of God and that's a miraculous, larger-than-life, spiritual experience. But how, they would say, could a guy like Muhammed who couldn't even read or write, go to a mountain to meditate and suddenly change the world? That's just not possible, they would argue. That's like saying ordinary people — like you or me — could be God's messenger.

K: Is it because people feel that once you open that door of accepting anything about Islam, you have to accept the lot?

GN: The whole question of Jesus being — or not being — the Son of God has to be crucial to the argument between Muslims and Christians.

K: What do you mean?

GN: Well, I had one of the strangest experiences of my life in the south of Iran, near the border. I covered both sides of the original Iran–Iraq conflict. I went first to Baghdad and Basra near the front, and a few months later to Tehran and Bostan in the southern marsh area. I found myself overnight in a hut with some Iranian fighters, naturally calling themselves mujahideen, holy warriors of the jihad. There was a mullah with them and we got talking after we'd had something to eat. I didn't know what the Australian producer I was with believed about anything, let alone religion. Anyway, the mullah asked me whether I believed that Jesus was the son of God. I told him: 'No, I don't.' He then asked me: 'What then do you believe Jesus was?' I replied that he was a prophet, in Western terms probably also a political stirrer, a troublemaker. Then the mullah asked what I thought Muhammed was. Also a prophet, I replied. And Moses? Same, a prophet. Suddenly, this other Australian interrupted.

K: What did he say?

GN: He said: 'What did you say about Jesus? Did you say that Jesus wasn't the Son of God?' I replied that I didn't say Jesus wasn't the Son of God; I said I didn't believe that Jesus was the Son of God. He just lost it completely. 'As a Christian,' he said, 'I am not going to sit here and listen to you defame my religion.' I said: 'You're a Christian. When was the last time you prayed? When was the last time you went to church — when your child was christened or when your mother died and you went to the funeral or somebody got married?' He couldn't remember. 'Do you go to church every Sunday?' No. 'Can I have a look at your Bible? Do you carry your Bible with you? If you're a Christian, surely you carry the Bible. You're in a war zone. You might need to look up the Bible to see how to behave in a war situation. Thou shalt not kill and all that.' When this heated conversation between two men from the Christian world stopped, the reaction of the Iranians was really interesting. I could tell they were amused but they were too polite to laugh. It was intriguing that the thing that upset my Christian colleague was that I appeared not to believe that Jesus was the Son of God. That was the crucial difference — because Islam does not claim that Muhammed was anything other than a human being.

K: And we are reminded five times a day through the loudspeakers at the mosque and the Call to Prayer.

GN: I picked up in Dubai a guide for expat British businessmen called *Don't They Know It's Friday?* There's a section that says — and I can imagine some pompous Englishman saying this: 'Oh and by the way chaps, when you're looking for your accommodation when you come to the Emirates, think about the location of the nearest mosque so that you're not woken every morning by the prayer call. Think about it when you're looking for your real estate.' Poor old English! Just fancy renting a wonderful villa near the famous Dubai Creek and you're just settling in nicely, you've brought your wife over from England and the kids are also there having a nice time, this is going to be quite a wonderful place to live — and suddenly at five in the morning they're woken by the Call to Prayer. 'How long has this been going on?' the startled wife asks. And he replies: 'Oh, fourteen hundred years or so.' 'And how much longer is it going to go on?' 'Oh! Probably forever!'

K: Yes, Muhammed is a messenger of God and we are reminded of this five times a day. He is not elevated like Jesus to another level. He is a messenger, but a human messenger.

GN: Earlier we talked about the jihad, but we didn't discuss the word 'fundamentalist'.

K: We didn't. But yes, 'fundamentalists', 'terrorists' and 'extremists' are the three most common words that are associated with Islam.

GN: I interviewed some Afghans once and I asked them if they were fundamentalists and their response was: 'All Muslims are fundamentalists!'

K: In that all Muslims fundamentally believe in God, in Allah as the one and only God.

GN: What's a 'casual Muslim', by the way? I heard someone here in Muscat being described that way. People do fall down on their religion and then have to repent. Is that what it's about?

K: Casual Muslims are those who follow Islam through inheritance and do not understand the many reasons behind it.

GN: Osama bin Laden — would you regard him as a Muslim who's got it wrong, or maybe somebody who isn't really a Muslim at all?

K: I have not associated with him.

GN: Are you saying you'd have to associate with him to know?

K: I have to know him to know about his belief. All I know is what I see and hear and read in the media. We are told not to judge. The verse in the Qur'an is to judge from what we see or hear. To an extent, we cannot make judgements on people. If someone says they know him, you should ask did you travel with him? Did you live with him? Did you have any association with him? Basically, in Islam, judging people is something we are told not to do — even to an extent that when we see somebody who's dead, and on one side there is a weapon and on the other there's been a glass of alcohol or even a needle injection, we are told not to make a judgement. If you do, you will be cast into hell's fire. You cannot really make that judgement for the simple reason that it could be that person was OK with his mind and was a true Muslim believer or that he was insane and that led him to commit some horrible deed.

GN: So you might regard bin Laden as someone who was a true Muslim but has lost his mind?

K: Right!

GN: What about Saddam? He strikes me as being very difficult to categorise as a Muslim who's just lost the plot?

K: What we say is that anyone as a general rule who does not follow the house of Islam is questionable. Of course, you cannot only categorise Saddam that way, but a lot of people who say one thing and do the other. There are amongst Muslims people who claim to believe in Allah and who claim to believe in the Five Pillars, but in reality they are not believers. They make a mockery of Allah. They deceive Allah and those who believe. But the reality is they deceive none other than their self.

GN: We discussed earlier people calling themselves Muslims who use Islam to get their own ends...

K: Use and abuse! For different reasons and throughout history we've seen people using Islam to gain their own political or economic benefit. At the moment, there's a lot of friction between Muslims themselves and between Muslims and non-Muslims, even between the sexes, with their sons and daughters. Often, this friction is created just to gain political power or to form a stronghold in a particular tribe or a particular society.

GN: Khalfan, are you optimistic or pessimistic about the way things are going to unfold within the Islamic world and between the Islamic and non-Islamic worlds?

K: I am very optimistic. I can already see an end coming.

GN: Tell me about that.

K: Historically there have never been two super powers. If one crumbles, the other one follows — and so the end of America is very near.

GN: And what will the world look like after that?

K: There will be other strong forces that will come to replace those two super powers; one could be Europe, that is, the United Kingdom, or we have the East, the Far East.

GN: China?

K: China or the Far East block.

GN: Not the Islamic world?

K: Islam as a faith.

GN: But not as a power block?

K: Not as a power block, we are not there yet as Muslims in terms of what we believe in, what we practise, but with the collapse of America definitely there will be a lot of peace around.

How has Khalfan, the professional Muslim observer, reacted post-Iraq? Again, Kirsty conducted a 're-interview' on my behalf.

Khalfan: The way this war has unravelled, three things have become very clear and they are going to drive the future. For the first time, the non-Muslim community is divided towards Islam. This is the first time the alliance of the non-Muslim community towards the Muslim community is split. It's the first time it is so evident that it's been publicly voiced — peace marches in Germany, France, Russia, China. Positions were taken and people in the West were being open about it. In the past, there were differences, but they kept it amongst themselves. But now, they are being aired openly and the relationship with the United States has gone sour. The second thing that has become evident is that the true image of America has been identified. Americans are now seen not as the liberators calling for peace, but that they came to the region to take control of it.

The world can see it — people in Melbourne, in Sydney, in France, in Istanbul, Korea, Japan, the United States itself, Britain — all those people marching were people saying no war. They understand the hidden US agenda — not to get rid of the dictator and not because Iraq has weapons of mass destruction. They are after the oil — and it's the first time the world comes to know that America is so arrogant that it wants to step outside the United Nations. They are the ones who are arrogant; they are the ones who are unjust. All these masks of America —

beauty, freedom, liberation, peace, democracy, all these glossy words — people everywhere have come to the realisation that there's a hidden US agenda. Muslims were advocating that message for a long time, but they were not heeded. The world has begun to realise that when we hear about terrorism, about threats and other things, there is a hidden agenda.

Khalfan's mate, Majid al Toky, was present at the re-interview. He chimed in with some thoughts of his own.

Majid: Maybe one could say that as long as you're playing ball, when you're playing the US game, you're a good boy. But if you disagree, you are a terrorist.

Khalfan: Irrespective of the consequences of the war, America has lost credibility. They've lost trust; their economic slump is beginning; others are reuniting, re-evaluating their positions. Europe identified that US threat earlier and got themselves together. They now have the Euro and the Common Market. The Europeans are grouping themselves together so that they won't be overpowered or taken over by American interests. And now, like France and Germany, the Muslim world is boycotting American products. This means that no longer are people relying on the governments to put a stop to this wave of terror, to keep control, our people are taking decisions themselves to do something about it.

Kirsty Cockburn: What about things that they need and can only get from America?

K: Need is the mother of invention. When people are so addicted to Coca Cola, we now have Mecca Cola, Zam Zam Cola. As long as it's not an American product! The minute they discover it is another brand people just buy it. Profits of Pepsi have dropped 70 per cent since the war. A number of US chain restaurants like Burger King, McDonald's, Pizza Hut, Kentucky Fried, have virtually closed down. People are exchanging their cars. They don't want American cars. They'd rather go for the Japanese or the German. people are no longer going to the United States for a holiday or to Britain, although Britain is not as serious. A lot of people are asking can they go somewhere else.

KC: On the score of American arrogance, do you think they imagined that things like boycotting would ever happen? Would they have gone into this if they thought they were going to be boycotted economically?

K: For the past thirty years America never heard the word 'no' from anyone. Now for the first time they're hearing it. They've paid a lot of money to try and regain their relationship with Egypt, with Turkey, with Pakistan and other Arab countries like Jordan. You can compensate governments, but it's much harder regaining people's confidence. Nobody would want to travel to the United States now because even if they open that door, it will contradict itself from the security point of view. The United States is exposed. It cannot afford to relax security and the last thing you want if you are going to attract people is to hassle them at airports, interrogate them and ask them to fill out six pages of forms. 'You want my money, you want to interrogate me? Sorry, I won't come.' So you see already that people are changing direction. These days, even what I call 'casual Muslims' are awaking to the reality. It's they who are becoming vocal with the anti-American sentiments, not just the religious people. Now people like me can rest their case.

KC: What about the future of Iraq post-Saddam?

K: I don't think the Americans will be able to settle in Iraq. They will try, but from the birth of civilisation, that place hasn't seen any rest. It's a place of unrest. Iraqis have lived through three decades of war and they know what hunger is. They don't know what luxury is.

KC: But here in the Gulf, in places like Oman, surely people thought Saddam should go?

M: They were saying Saddam was such a bad guy who killed people and now that they've got rid of him the Iraqis don't want their liberators either. My view is that Arab-Muslims get their perceptions from the media, from what they read and hear and they heard that Saddam was worse than anybody else in the region. So why is Gaddafi still in power in Libya? What about extremists in Egypt? Sure, Saddam was bad, but for a long while he was playing the ball with the Americans, so they left him alone.

KC: Khalfan, what do you think of what Majid has said?

K: If you're no longer on our side, we will show you how to be a bad boy and wish you to get out — and that's what they did. If you're not on our side, the American side, you're bad.

KC: What about the so-called clash between civilisations, the Muslim and non-Muslim worlds? Do you subscribe to that theory?

K: It's not about civilisation, it's about power. It's a battle of the rich playing silly games. It is no more than an economic struggle for power. An old Arab warrior once said: 'When I see my enemies, I attack the coward and show them how I execute people.' With the approach that America has applied in Iraq, they have sent a message around the globe. America is trying to establish a base in almost every Arab country, at the same time instilling terror into them.

KC: Are there any Islamic countries that are vulnerable to being bought?

K: I would reverse the question. Is there an Islamic country willing to stand and become independent? Now, for the first time in history, people, Muslim people, all people, have global connections. Using the internet, they can access information. Now, for the first time, people can interpret data as they see fit. They're not being kept in the dark, only fed information by governments or by the conglomerates.

KC: Where does religion fit into the equation? How will it be affected by the takeover of Iraq?

K: The way I see it, America has done Muslims a big favour. I have met a lot of Westerners who, after the September 11 incident, are keen to know more about Islam. They say we've read about Islam and we've seen Islam in the media and books but when we are encountered with Muslims, we see the opposite. That puzzles us. We don't see a match and that sends us a signal of curiosity, of wanting to know more.

When you watch CNN if you are a foreigner, you think all Arabs are terrorists. When you come here to Oman, you see completely different things. You see people saying 'peace to you' and smiling, no hatred. Even during the war, we had foreigners in our office who never considered leaving. 'We're staying,' they said, 'it's peaceful here.' They didn't feel there was any need to be worried. There was concern because they didn't know when it would all end, but in terms of their personal security, nobody was worried.

KC: To what extent do you think American actions are anti-Islam?

K: It is not anti-Islam per se, although the hidden agenda is to expand the Israeli territory. The only threat that would stop them from meeting that goal is Islam.

KC: What about the theory that the ultimate American motive is geopolitical, to use the war against Saddam and terrorism as the first cab off the rank to completely reshape the Middle East and the Gulf region in America's interests and image?

K: It's a case of divide and conquer. Can you imagine 1.2 billion Muslims if they were to gather force together and were united? What would that mean to the world — a shift in power, politics, domination, economy, education, peace, everything? Why remain just a lot of small countries, if, as a region, we share history, heritage, religion, faith? Europe is gathering force to be together, to unite, have common policy, security, economy, politics. We need to go and sort our own houses, our own home, the Arab-Muslim world.

M: The problem is that in not just the Islamic world, but the Arab world, we seem to be sitting and blaming the misery we have at the moment on other people, saying, 'Oh this is America's fault, this is the West's fault,' instead of looking upon ourselves and asking, 'What am I doing to my life, what am I doing to protect myself, what am I doing to satisfy my needs?' That is the problem. Once we start to look at ourselves, sort out our own way of life, build our own society properly, I think we will be able to look out and say we want this or we don't want that.

K: I was asked the same question on my radio program. I would like any one of you, I said, to point the finger, find something and point at it. I know what you're doing, you are good at blaming. When you point the finger at somebody else, in reality you are pointing three fingers at yourself. Before you blame somebody once, blame yourself three times. We are good at blaming; we are good at pointing fingers; we have this blame culture. We have to get out of it.

KC: Does that mean Muslims moving away from religion, from Islam?

K: No! It is part and parcel of religion. Our Islamic religion says that if you advocate other people to be righteous, you yourself must be righteous. How can you say things but not do them? We have to walk the talk.

KC: Is Western materialism affecting Muslims?

K: We have been influenced by the glamour of Western civilisation. Islam says that we have been made to be the agent of God on this Earth and that civilisations will be there for us if we have made a difference and co-exist with the differences. It's the differences that make us as we are. It's capitalising from each other, benefiting from each other. In the days of the Prophet himself, as he was advocating the message of the oneness of God, he co-existed with the Jews, the Christians, even with pagans. In the heart of Islam, he co-existed with them.

What we have seen, though, is the glamorous picture of the West. Maybe that has influenced Muslims a lot. Maybe the crime of taking that glamour was moral disintegration. Not everything that's glamorous is good. The good thing is that these days the educated Islamic elite are the ones who are making the comparisons. Those advocating boycotting Western and US products are not religious, they are Islamic people who are perceived in the West to be 'civilised'.

An example! If you go to mosques today — not twenty years ago, but today, 2003 — you see that mosques are filled, even for the early morning prayer, which is at 4:30, with not only the regulars; you see the working community — workers and professionals — and their kids. Twenty years ago, it was only the elders that went there for early prayers and they didn't have the persuasive skills to entice their kids to go to the mosque. The working community didn't care. They were raised that this was just basic tradition. But today they have gone beyond the obvious of why I have to pray, more to why I *should* pray, what do I get out of it? And seeing the benefit themselves, they say if this is the benefit I get, I'd better visit the mosque regularly.

KC: In the context of the post-war global situation, do you think the chances of terrorism are greater or less?

K: That depends on how America will react. If arrogance is committed, if human dignity is discredited, terrorism will increase — sadly, in the name of freedom. People will become more — not less — divided. It all depends on America's behaviour in the peace.

M: I have a problem using the word 'terrorism' itself. Oppositions will always be there — people who are in government and people who oppose them. Now if the other side is suppressed, they will retaliate, they will have to do something. Now what do you call that — human nature, a struggle or terrorism? Call it anything, I don't think that it will end. It will still be there, however powerful you are, because people still resist. In a small way, in a big way, in a courageous way, in a dangerous way, but still they resist. I can't see how you can eliminate terrorism, though it sounds a nice thing to achieve, a noble objective.

PART SIX

FINAL REFLECTIONS

They Won't Just Go Away:
Where to From Here?

Across the Arab world, the voices of liberalism will rise to say that the moment has come for change. Although part of the chorus will come from Western-educated Arabs, the most telling voices will be from reform-minded Islamists. They will have to wait for the dust to settle on Iraq before being heard. For now, their voices will be drowned in the cacophony of anti-Americanism. The United States may be calling for democracy in the Arab world but it has lost the moral authority for its words to be taken at face value.

Roula Khalaf in *The Economist*, 'The World in 2003'

Muslims — Whackos and Nuts?

I hope that in the next century we will come to terms with our
abysmal ignorance of the Muslim world. Muslims aren't a bunch
of whackos and nuts. They are decent, brilliant, talented people
with a great civilisation and traditions of their own, including
legal traditions. Americans know nothing about them. They are
people in that part of the world with whom we are simply out of
touch. That's a great challenge for the next century.

Insightful, or what? Those words were uttered a few years ago by
a US Supreme Court judge, Anthony Kennedy. He is not
alone in expressing such sentiments. It's the sort of thing you
would have liked to have thought of or written yourself!

John L. Esposito, a scholar of all things Arabic, said in his
book *The Muslim Threat: Myth or Reality?*: 'A series of world
events from the Ayatollah Khomeini and the Iranian revolution
to Saddam Hussein and the Gulf War — let alone the Taliban,
September 11 and Osama bin Laden — have reinforced mutually
destructive stereotypes in the Muslim world and in the West.'
Likewise, journalist William Pfaff commented in the popular
New Yorker magazine: 'There are a good many people who think
that the war between communism and the West is about to be
replaced by a war between the West and Muslims.'

And Karen Armstrong, a prolific writer on religion was
prompted by the Islamic flashpoint of our times to rework the

introduction to her epic biography of the Prophet. Armstrong
went so far as to urge that 'at this dangerous time' the world
seriously needed to hear the story of Muhammed, the Muslim
messenger. Why now? From Washington to Baghdad and beyond,
Armstrong's answer should be heard by everyone. The world
needed to hear the true story of Muhammed and Islam, she said,
because 'Muslim extremists must not be allowed to hijack the
biography of Muhammed and twist it to suit their own ends.'

You mightn't be a religious scholar like Karen Armstrong, but
how many of the questions that follow here have you asked — all
of them, some of them — most of them, I'll bet. What exactly is
Islam? For that matter, what is a Muslim? Why do they believe
what they believe? What, in fact, do they believe? What is their
working definition of right and wrong, of good and evil? Of
Heaven and Hell? How are the extremists different?

And why what appears to the rest of us to be their seemingly
unapologetic oppression of women? Why the veil? Why the
abaya, the flowing cover-all cloak? Why the stories of Muslim
hands being cut off as punishment for sometimes petty crimes?
Why do we hear of Muslim adulterers being flogged? How
prevalent are 'honour killings' of women and girls who stray or
are thought to have strayed? Why do Muslims fight not just wars
but holy wars — jihads, as they call them? At a deep-seated
human level, why are they so different from those of us who are
not Muslim, who don't live in their emotional and spiritual
homeland of Islam? How wide are the differences in belief
between Muslims, Jews and Christians? How can all three
possibly have the same origins? Why have these so-called great
faiths been at each other's throats, religiously and physically, for
century after century? How can all three religions call Jerusalem
their holy city?

And if people like Saddam Hussein and Osama bin Laden are

not true Muslims by Islam's own standards, why should those who are be tarred with something like the same brush?

Hopefully, as this journal has unfolded, answers to at least some of these questions will have emerged.

Cultural Burglary

As we found for ourselves, among the temperate everyday folk of the Arab-Muslim world a great deal of anger, resentment and anti-Western vehemence persists. In fact, it permeates Muslim thinking. Why? It can't be merely cultural or economic envy. Are there more rational explanations? Brian Beedham of *The Economist*, like others, reckons there are, if, that is, we bother to look.

'A millennium ago,' Beedham says, 'Islam was a sparkling civilisation next door to a crude medieval Europe. The crude Europeans then bloodily sacked its holy places in Jerusalem, borrowed Islam's science, its mathematics and its arts to bring about their Renaissance, rose to dominate most of the rest of the globe, and then scooped up the majority of Muslims into their European empires.'

Beedham was not the first nor will he be the last to point out the radical skewing of history that has plagued the Islamic peoples and altered our view of them for, not years, but centuries. Two other calmly intelligent writers on Islam, Jonathan Bloom and Sheila Blair, in their work *Islam: A Thousand Years of Faith and Power*, set out to counter the intensely negative Western media images of Muslims as 'turbaned terrorists and stern-faced mullahs exhorting the faithful to shun the temptations of Western civilisation'.

'It's not too much of an overstatement to say,' they comment, 'that at a time when unwashed Europeans in northern forests wore leather jerkins and ate roast game and gruel when they weren't beating each other over the head with clubs to solve disputes, bathed and perfumed Muslims inhabited splendid palaces with running water and sanitation systems, dressed in silken robes and downed haute cuisine off fine porcelain while sitting on plush carpets discussing the subtleties of ancient Greek philosophy.'

It's a confrontingly different perspective on history, you'd have to agree. If we can possibly get September 11 and the Iraq disaster out of our justifiably anxious minds for a moment, our too often distorted view of Muslims is probably sufficient cause for their pretty heavy anti-Western sentiment, if not their anger and hatred. The centuries-old prejudice towards Islam from so-called Western civilisation would 'get to' most normal human beings. When you consider the monumental shift in power and influence, from them to us, that's taken place over a few hundred years, whatever you call that shift — cultural burglary is colourful but not inappropriate — it's enough to upset people, Islamic or otherwise, pretty badly.

The World was Never Going to be the Same Again Anyway

For a while, both before and after September 11, our worst fear was that some massive culture clash — World War III? the New Crusades? — was inevitable. But is that fear, as human as it might be, exaggerated, maybe an ignorant overreaction? On the other hand, given the serious, even menacing differences between us that have become so obvious in the first half of 2003, are our best hopes of a lasting, peaceful co-existence between the Muslim and non-Muslim worlds unrealistic, even dimwitted folly?

Whatever your individual response, we've all been living, rather uneasily if you're a Westerner, in the shadow of what used to be the architecturally fabulous World Trade Center in New York City. In the immediate aftermath of September 11, we were petrified by the thought of what might happen next. What did in fact happen was not our worst fear, another similarly devastating attack, but the so-called war against terrorism, beginning in Afghanistan. We, the West, were on the front foot. The US responses to September 11 initiated by George W. Bush, albeit with a touch of 'the Hollywoods', appeared to stop any further homicidal attacks like those on New York or Washington, at least for the time being. Our hunch was that there was no way the WTC and the Pentagon were accidental targets. To the entire Arab-Muslim world, not just the tiny minority of extremist misfits who actually carried out the attacks that obliterated close to 3000 individuals, those two places were utterly symbolic of what Arab-Muslims regarded as the unbridled economic, cultural and military power of the US in the post-communist Global Village.

But, as consoling as the absence of any other anti-American terror attacks might have been, in terms of cooling the Islamic heat directed at America, what has the war on terrorism actually stopped? The Taliban were turfed out of power in their sad haven of Afghanistan, but the pursuit of Osama bin Laden and the Al Qa'ida perpetrators of the September 11 atrocity drags on even now, embarrassedly and inconclusively. In the process, Saddam Hussein somehow replaced bin Laden as an even more current 'evil man of history'. Saddam is almost certainly the only man to have that dubious accolade thrust upon him not once but twice — remarkably, the first time by Father Bush and then by the Son. A pre-emptive war to remove Saddam and his alleged weapons of mass destruction in Iraq has loomed and then actually occurred. As a result, many in the West now fear the spectre of an even angrier Arab world and, distressingly, more and worse terrorism against Western targets — including Australia, which joined the Coalition of the Willing, despite vociferous opposition from the unwilling within the country.

Meanwhile, as all this raged, what many in both the Muslim and non-Muslim camps maintain is the root cause of Arab anti-Western antagonism, the protracted and deadly carry-on between the Palestinians and Jews in Israel and the Occupied Territories, continued in its awful 'eye for an eye' stop-start fashion. After the occupation of Iraq began, the intifada and the Jewish response to it had become almost like that half-time entertainment at a major match.

The seemingly endless Arab–Israeli stoush is pitiful, it's futile, but it's a more telling reason for the trouble and strife in the Middle East than the world's pet explanation: control of the region's vast and lucrative oil reserves, currently in Arab-Muslim hands exclusively. Oil — including Iraq's — has always been a hugely significant geopolitical issue for both those who have it and those who don't. But with or without the oil war, with or without Saddam, with or without terrorism, Arab-Muslim suicide bombers would still take their own and Jewish lives senselessly and Israeli tanks would still pound Palestinians in the Occupied Territories for the same old reasons: belief, land and identity. Those three ostensibly innocuous things — belief, land and identity — go close to explaining the inexplicable in the Gulf and the Middle East.

Think about it. In a tit-for-tat way, desperate young Arab suicide bombers still descend to the desperate depths of dying for a cause rather than, as they see it, living for nothing. With monotonous, blood-spattering regularity, they blow themselves to pieces at bus stops and in milk bars in Jerusalem and Tel Aviv, taking frightened Jews, old and young, with them. The murderous retaliation from both sides is painfully regular and tragically pointless. But try telling them that. The suicide bombers see no other way to demonstrate what they believe, to secure the land they cherish and to acquire the identity they seek. Similarly, the Israelis who bulldoze scungy Arab homes and wretched villages looking for bomb-makers are doing it in the name of their separate Jewish belief, their Holy Land and their Semitic identity. Deep down, the whole thing is almost shallow. You could say that it's simply and ultimately about race, religion and real estate. That explanation might be simple, but the solution is obviously a little more complicated.

As these things prevailed, comfortably far away in the Middle East, for those of us in Australia the whole sorry mess suddenly came much, much closer to home. In October 2002 the entire nation found itself struggling to come to grips with the shock and then the ongoing trauma of innocent Australian deaths, incidental or otherwise, at the hands of Al Qa'ida-inspired Indonesian Islamic extremists, or maybe even insidious forces far less obvious, on the idyllic tourist island of Bali.

In the context of the Bali bombings and the subsequent trial of the Indonesian perpetrators, it is crucial to recognise that when a terrorist falsely embracing Islam claims religious martyrdom — as Amrozi, the notorious 'smiling assassin' did on receiving the death sentence — he is out of kilter with his professed Islamic faith and law. In fact, what he did was breach a Qur'anic tenet. Killing 'non-combatants', as all the Bali victims were, is forbidden by the Qur'an. No matter what Amrozi would like to believe, he is not a holy warrior. He will never be an Islamic martyr. Besides, Muslim martydom is bestowed on Muslims by Allah, not by man. Sorry, Mr Amrozi, no dark-eyed virgins in Paradise for you, my atrocious friend! It's Hell, not Heaven that awaits you, the September 11 killers and Palestinian suicide bombers who take out innocent Jewish citizens.

And while we're on the point of martydom, Uday and Qusay Hussein, Saddam's psychopathic sons, might have had themselves a viciously merry time on Earth, but martyrdom and the joys of Heaven were not theirs for the taking either. Not that anyone in the real Islamic world should or would consider either of those nasty pieces of work genuine Muslims. They were Muslims in name only. Like the entire rogues' gallery — their father, bin Laden, the Taliban, Al Qa'ida, Amrozi and company — they bowdlerised and exploited the Islamic faith. They did not follow it; they used and abused it. But don't take my word for it. Ask any real Muslim who knows far more about these things than a Western blow-in!

In this disturbing new international environment, wherever we are, in Australia or elsewhere, we're all learning to live with two global threats. One is the spectre of frontier-free terrorism, whenever and wherever it occurs. The other is the war against terrorism, whenever and wherever it's waged. The third worry is that each of these threats, real or perceived, is as potentially devastating as the other. Muslims or non-Muslims, what will eventually be the greatest threat to our comfort, our freedom, our cultures and our ways of life — terrorism or the war against it? Who said that the chicken-and-egg theory of history doesn't apply?

Which Good versus Which Evil?

As the tragic enormity of what the Americans call '9/11' set in, the preposterously loaded phrase, 'Good versus Evil', was trotted out. Repeatedly we heard it in Western attempts to explain the religious, even the moral, rift between Muslims and (at least) American Christian fundamentalists. Like his father before him during the Desert Storm conflict, George W. Bush used this phrase pejoratively, clearly reflecting his 'born again' Texan view of the world. For weeks we also heard plenty about a new Axis of Evil — apparently the pariah states of Iran, Iraq and North Korea. These three nations, we were told, were the fosterers, the financiers and perpetrators of both old and new wave international terrorism.

As provocative and potentially explosive as these twin epithets of Good versus Evil and Axis of Evil were, they both faded as recollections of two world wars and predictions of a possible third one came flooding in, mainly from the more sceptical Europeans. And then, just as we were getting used to living with the apparently unlivable — a terror-plagued world we were told would 'never be the same again' — our attention was diverted. This time we cowered under the growing storm cloud of a US-led military attack on Iraq, with or without United Nations approval and involvement. What's that old adage? The only thing we've learned from history is that we've learned nothing from history!

Once Saddam was speedily vanquished, the fruits of victory, we were told, would be twofold. Miraculously, the threat of global terrorism against America and its allies would immediately subside, and suddenly democracy would sprout and grow in the entire Arab-Islamic world. Not only that, the Israelis and the Palestinians would end their mutual bloodbath, stop trying to drive each other into the Mediterranean and instantly transform themselves into a peaceful two-nation state. How did we know all this? George, Tony and John told us. And they wouldn't lie or deceive, would they? They're Christians. It's against their religion to tell fibs. It's other religions that lie. Look at Saddam and all that lying and deception he went on with about weapons of mass destruction.

But the fact is fear and insecurity pervade the globe. The distrust and misunderstanding between the Muslim and non-Muslim worlds, persist. Should we be surprised?

The thought lingered in many minds that there was a distinctly religious undercurrent to all of this. The vociferous American right-winger Patrick Buchanan, of all people, in an article for the New Hampshire *Sunday News* headed 'Is Islam an Enemy of the United States?' wrote: 'To some Americans, searching for a new enemy against whom to test our mettle and power after the death of communism, Islam is the preferred antagonist. But to declare Islam an enemy of the United States is to declare a second Cold War that is unlikely to end in the same resounding victory as the first.'

Ignorance is not Bliss!

On 13 September 2001, two days after the shocking events in New York and Washington, the author was asked by a mass-market magazine in Australia to pen a reaction piece to the terror attacks. 'What are you going to tell your children?' the magazine's editor asked. 'Are you worried for them? Are you worried about the future?' Reasonable questions that we should all be asking.

'The US terror attacks were unspeakably inhuman acts,' I began. 'At the personal and emotional levels, most of us were left speechless. But now that the dust has settled, the shock is easing and the dead are being counted, what should our reaction be? Anger? Vengeance? Recrimination against the entire Arab world? Most importantly, what do we tell our kids?

'The hatred that leads to acts as terrible as crashing hijacked passenger planes into New York skyscrapers and the US defence headquarters in Washington doesn't just happen. It certainly doesn't happen because the Arab–Islamic world is innately homicidal or born with a hatred of everything and everybody Western, particularly Americans. It is, in fact, born out of huge difference and ignorance.

'Having travelled in and reported from many Arab and Islamic countries for twenty years or more, including our Asian neighbour Indonesia, the level of mutual ignorance — them or us, us of them — is mind-boggling. It's the sort of ignorance that has Arab children cheering the deaths of innocent Americans and Westerners baying for Arab blood in revenge.

'Let's put this into perspective. These people do not feel or think the way we do. Their values are different. Their definition of right and wrong, good and evil — even God — is different. They are culturally and emotionally different. Like us, they eat, sleep, make love, have children, work, play and grow old — but not much else is the same. They even die differently. Their heaven and hell bear no resemblance to ours. At best, they don't understand us. At worst, their extremists hate us. Why? Because they think we hate them. For our part, regarding them as barbarians and not taking them seriously as humans is the sort of arrogance that snuffs out lives in seconds. That's what we saw on TV.

'Is terrorist behaviour wrong? Yes. Is it inexplicable? No. Only when we get down to working on our ignorance will be begin to develop a relationship that doesn't breed the hatred and contempt for human life that reduces skyscrapers to rubble and turns passenger planes into human missiles.

'What do we teach in our classrooms that might mean future generations of Australians will see the Arab–Islamic world as different — not degenerate? Ignorance is not bliss. It can have awful results. Ask the families of those who went to work at the World Trade Center or caught a plane to Boston on September 11 2001 — and never came home.'

Two weeks later, with the world still reeling, the author found himself on his feet at the Australian National University in Canberra, launching a new degree in International Relations. Warming to his earlier theme, he argued that 'in the long term, only an understanding of the Muslim world, not retaliation, will help solve the problem of terrorism'.

'Retaliation does not guarantee that other terrorists will discontinue attacks on America and other countries,' I told my audience of students, academics, bureaucrats and the media. 'Unless we are working at another level to find out why these people are doing what they are doing, there will be no guarantee that retaliation will achieve anything. The plus [of retaliation] is that it can have an immediate impact — but that is not a guarantee. It might even spawn people with more fanatical attitudes than bin Laden and co.

'Western leaders should sit down with moderate Muslims, as their help is needed in the long term to stop terrorism. Terrorists and fanatics are only a minority of Muslims.

'Speaking as someone who has spent a lot of time over the years in Islamic countries, I believe there is so much mutual ignorance we need to work on. The events of the past few weeks have shown how desperate is the need for better international relations. It is the total lack of understanding of the levels of difference between ourselves and Islam that has caused this.

'While a war is inevitable and the terrorist attacks were wrong, the long-term fight is against ignorance. Mutual understanding will come a lot closer to solving the problem of terrorism than any military operation in Afghanistan or elsewhere in the Islamic world.'

Militant Muslim Moderates

Most rational observers in the Muslim world will ask you what the connection is between Saddam Hussein and the war against terrorism. Indeed, is there a connection? Where are the weapons of mass destruction he's supposed to have stockpiled? In short, where is the evidence — full-stop? Is it possible is that neo-conservative Washington is hellbent on the ultimate in self-fulfilling prophecies — a 'Clash of Civilisations' between the Islamic and non-Islamic worlds?

So, how do we put this sort of 2003 Doomsday scenario into a rational, unemotional view of Islam? For starters, Saddam Hussein claimed to be a Muslim — but few Muslims the author has met over the past two decades see him that way. During his dictatorship of his sad and shattered land, the garish Saddam murals, statues, posters, paintings and portals were inescapable. They left no doubt, phoney popularity polls and elections aside, that he was comfortably ensconced as a demagogue, a political one-man show. But a demagogue Muslim? Most Islamic scholars have disputed his claim, other than those in Iraq, a place where dissent was a rare commodity.

Observers with a generally more tolerant view of moderate Islam have always found Saddam's claim to the faith impossible to stomach. If Saddam is, as he claims, a Muslim, then everything else about him flies in the face of the very essence of Islam.

The overwhelming majority of people around the globe calling themselves Muslims are utterly opposed to Saddam, let alone what he has done and stands for. So why are they reluctant to talk this through? One Muslim contact explained it to me as their 'collective humiliation at the hands of the West'. They don't believe that we non-Muslims take them seriously as human beings, let alone their seemingly alien religion that most in the West know precious little about.

The Islamic moderate is in no way a terrorist, but resents what he or she perceives as Western arrogance. With moderates, the matter rests there. But a tiny minority of Muslims, the immoderates, the terrorists, are prepared to take matters as far as they can, as far as premeditated death — their own and targeted enemies in Israel, Munich, New York, Washington, Yemen, Kenya, Tel Aviv, even Bali.

Why Muslims Wouldn't Want to Go to Hell

When extremists, widely dubbed as 'Islamic extremists', carry out their atrocities, if they do it in the name of Islam, they are doing so falsely. According to the Qur'an, their wildest dreams of the Muslim afterlife will not come true. Quite the opposite. For killing innocents, not Heaven but Hell awaits them. And by all accounts, the Muslim Hell is a particularly unattractive place; at least as nasty as any other religion's idea of Hell. Yahiya Emerick says, 'No dancing with the Devil here!' A peek into the Qur'an should be enough to scare off most evildoers, Muslim or otherwise.

There are, the Qur'an says, seven layers to the Muslim Hell, each one worse than the one before. Muhammed remarked that the fires of Hell are seventy times hotter than any fire on Earth. The Qur'anic descriptions are certainly graphic — endless columns of fire, snakes, scorpions, clothes made of burning pitch, fountains of burning oil, thorny fruits, renewable skin so that bodies can be put to the torch more than once, no communication with anyone other than screams and moaning. The punishment depends on the crime — nails to scratch the faces of faultfinders, iron bars to rip out the cheeks of liars, razors to cut off the lips of gossipers, snakes to bite the greedy and disfigurement for anyone guilty of 'dressing to excite', if you get the drift. Fountains of pus and blood, fetid boiling muck the only refreshment. Could go on, but you get the picture. You might be reading this close to mealtime?

Then again, Hell, Muslim or otherwise, was never meant to be a five-star health farm for people with attitude problems. But there's an Islamic twist! Other religions' Hells, we've always been led to believe, are for ever. No way out. But some Muslim sinners can apparently spend time there copping their punishment, repent, show renewed faith in God, be released and can make it to Heaven after all. In the religious stakes, that's an offer almost too good to refuse. The catch is, though, you've got to be a Muslim, and a sinful Muslim, in the first place.

Not Exactly a Muslim's Muslim

Is Saddam the ultimate Evil Man in History, not once, not twice but now maybe three times? There have certainly been a few contenders for that title in the past, most of them hung in the US 'rogues gallery' — Marx, Lenin, Trotsky, Beria, Stalin, Hitler, Mao, Ho Chi Minh, Castro, Che Guevara, Yasser Arafat, Gaddafi, Milosovic and not forgetting Osama bin Laden. How could we forget Osama? Or have we already done so? Not bad company though for a bloke like Saddam, with poor taste in hats and a penchant for incredibly nasty weaponry.

Saddam notwithstanding, Muslims are so often depicted as inherently and historically violent, war-mongering people, inspired by a faith that condones and encourages such behaviour. It's true that they have a history with a militaristic pattern. At various times in the nearly 1400 years since Islam's arrival on the scene, militarism was the order of the day for many faiths, ethnic groups, races and even nations. But did the Muslims start the Crusades? Who fired the first shot in anger, the Palestinians or the Israelis? And why are weapons of terrifying mass destruction less destructive in the hands of a nation claiming to be acting 'in God's name' than in the hands of individuals, groups or countries mounting terrorist acts or murdering minorities on behalf of Allah? There are nasty misdirected people calling themselves Muslims, and there are also nasty, misdirected people calling themselves Christians or Jews.

There have been something like 480 major wars around the world since the year 1700. That breaks down to more than a war-and-a-half every year for 300 years, as silly as that statistic sounds. In virtually every one of those conflicts, both sides have claimed to have either God, Allah, Gott, Dieu, Deo or a heap of other popular names for the deity on their side. What is it with religion? An attack on religion becomes an attack on the people — and vice versa.

It's worth pointing out that where the ongoing tension between Muslims and non-Muslims throughout the world is concerned, the Arabic word 'jihad' does not really mean holy war, the tag so often slapped on it. Officially, religiously, it is the term Muslims use for their non-stop, personal struggle to maintain their religious commitment and remain faithful to Allah, their one true God.

It Always Comes Back to Palestine

In the early 1980s, the Israelis planted and exploded a massive car bomb in the crowded West Beirut district of Lebanon's amazingly resilient capital. West Beirut was, and still is, populated largely by Palestinian refugees and their supporters. Needless to say, this heavy concentration of Palestinians explained the Israelis' choice of location for their bomb. It worked — horribly. An entire block of apartment buildings was destroyed by the blast and more than 150 Arab-Muslims were killed.

There was still plenty of graphic bodily evidence of the carnage among the rubble and on what remained of walls and staircases when the author and a 60 *Minutes* television crew began filming 48 hours later. The unmistakable sickly smell of death, along with lingering smoke and incendiary fumes, still hung in the air.

The PLO's headquarters for the region was in the same street. In fact, it was directly across the road from where the car bomb went off. Astoundingly, the building it was in was unscathed even though it was probably the Israeli target. My reason for being in such an unlovely location was to talk to PLO officials about their cause in the Middle East and, in particular, to get an interview with the PLO chairman, Yasser Arafat — who at that stage, in fear of his life, was constantly moving around the PLO-friendly parts of the region, like Tunis, Amman and Beirut. In those days, prior to any suggestion of peace accords in the Middle East conflict, he was regarded outside his section of the Arab-Muslim world as a terrorist. In Israel, even now, he is regarded in exactly the same way.

West Beirut was also close to Sabra and Shatilla, the sites of two infamous Palestinian refugee camps on the outskirts of the city. Later in the 1980s, in an air raid on the camps, the Israelis killed an estimated 3500 Palestinian men, women and children. Israel's defence minister at that time, the man who ordered the attacks, devastating even by the brutal standards of the region, is the present Israeli prime minister, Ariel Sharon. Given their blood-spattered history, Muslim Palestinians, indeed Arabs generally, have never forgotten or forgiven the Israelis, and Sharon in particular, for this attack. Sharon's was a commanding role, and he's never come even come close to anything resembling a statement of regret or apology. The same has to be said about his Palestinian counterparts. Ever since, 'fight to the death' vows have been swapped incessantly by Sharon and Arafat. Over the years, each has promised to drive the other into the Mediterranean. Indeed, recently the Palestinians, still under Arafat's chairmanship, and the Israelis, with Sharon as prime minister, have drawn gory parallels between Sabra/Shatilla and the 2002 Israeli ground and air attacks on places like Jenin and Gaza, on the one hand, and on the other, Palestinian suicide bomber responses.

But in Sabra and Shatilla a different kind of peace was shattered — peace within the Muslim family itself. And this non-Muslim was actually caught in the reverberations in West Beirut. Sitting on the balcony of the PLO's third floor office, leaning against the rail, looking across the street at the utter devastation from the Israeli car bomb, jotting down reactions, the air was suddenly alive with loud and insistent automatic rifle fire. Without any warning, bullets whistled up the wall of the building housing the PLO. Call it white-hot fear or a survival instinct, I instantly dived a couple of metres sideways through the open balcony door, landing under a low coffee table in the middle of the cramped office. The rest of the folk in the office, all PLO officials, burst into peals of laughter.

Unlike me, they knew it was harmless friendly fire and that it hadn't passed as close to me on the balcony as I'd imagined. More than a little shaken by the experience and embarrassed by the Palestinians' mirth at my expense, I asked the obvious question. What's that all about? The explanation gave me my first inkling about the shaky dysfunctionality of the Muslim family. The Arabs with the guns down below in the street, I was informed, were celebrating the assassination of Egypt's President Anwar Sadat. Why? Because, like us, said my PLO hosts, they believe that he sold out the Palestinian cause by taking part in peace talks with the Israelis and the Americans. So there are Muslims and there are Muslims. But there is probably no such thing as a 'typical' Muslim.

God — the Sticking Point?

The *Sydney Morning Herald*'s Paul McGeough is the author of an eminently readable 2003 politico-travel work, *Manhattan to Baghdad*. He's one of the few Australian journalists to cover the Iraqi War from Baghdad, and in an article tagged 'God Must Be On The Side of the Just — But Which Side, That's The Sticking Point', he clearly had similar thoughts about the whole 'God thing' to the author and other commentators.

Like McGeough did in Baghdad, I've witnessed many Fridays, big prayer days, outside mosques in any number of Muslim places, as bare-footed devotees sorted through thousands of sandals in the specially provided cupboards on their way out after that all-important hour or so every week when the local imam leads them closer, they believe, to their God. Like Paul, we saw how orderly the whole sandal-finding process was. How do they manage to get their own back so easily and without any fuss? It happens like clockwork.

In February 2003, in the post-September 11 'war on terrorism' and the early build-up to the military incursion into Iraq, the imam at Baghdad's al-Aadham Mosque talked with McGeough about how he'd told his followers that in the good versus evil stakes, 'God is angry with the American evildoers.' The anti-war protests around the world at the time were clear proof of God's anger. The protesters, he reckoned, agreed with Iraq. 'Right is on our side. That makes us stronger, safer. This evil will end badly for the US.' As McGeough noted, didn't that sound like the sort of religious utterance that had become pretty much the hallmark of George W. Bush's presidency?

Like ourselves, McGeough wondered if God was 'being asked to play both sides of the street' in the shambles that was Iraq. More to the point, he asked, did the Iraqi imam and the US president pray to the same God? At this last question, he says, a flurry of activity and consultation exploded within the imam's small army of turbaned advisors. Eventually, the imam replied. 'There is only one God for all humans. We are Muslims and we believe in the same God as Christians and Jews. But Bush misrepresents God. We are right and America is wrong. They can't even get the support of the UN Security Council for their evil intentions.' Nor God's support either? That's the big one.

Catholics couldn't be blamed for being just a little confused about this religious tug-of-war, as McGeough quaintly described it. The Pope, their boss, had already said no to war. War, he had warned, was a defeat for humanity — no matter who wins.

'Where's God when you need him?' asked the man from the *Sydney Morning Herald*. 'The invocation of his name has a particular resonance in this part of the world. This is the earth on which Jesus and Allah [I suspect Paul meant Muhammed] walked. Mecca and Jerusalem are just down the road from Baghdad.' As he was flying over Saudi Arabia, that other US-backed rogue Islamic state, McGeough mused that neither the Iraqi imam nor the American president doubted that God was on his side — 'but perhaps he's sitting this one out.' What have we said earlier in this journal? You've got to feel sorry for God, or Allah — or whoever it is up there or wherever it is that he, or they, hang out!

A New World Order?

Each year the British weekly magazine *The Economist* publishes a look at the year ahead. In 'The World in 2003' the preview's editor, Dudley Fishburn, wrote that the delicious irony of the year would be that the single most democratic part of the Arab world would not be a nation at all, 'but the battered remnants of the entity of Palestine'. Fishburn made the point that in January 2003 almost three million Palestinians voted — 'more openly and fairly than anywhere else in the Middle East other than Israel' — for a parliament. 'If a non-existent nation, riddled with terror from without and within, can align the Muslim faith with the ballot box,' he asked, 'how can it be impossible elsewhere in the Middle East?'

He's got a point. This infant Palestinian democracy could well lead to Yasser Arafat, the old, sick, long-entrenched, obstinate former PLO guerilla leader, being booted out and replaced by a modern, probably younger Palestinian leader, less set in his political ways and objectives. The end of the Arafat era would certainly make possible a clean start for the whole Middle East peace process. The use of brute force by both sides has failed miserably. For decades, the Israelis have been surrounded, as Fishburn says, by 'hard, hostile and illegitimate' Arab-Muslim regimes. Ironically, it was this that made Israel safe from Arab invasion. US protection was guaranteed. But with even half-decent, even quasi-democratic Muslim neighbours, that same sort of billion-dollar American protection would no longer be automatically forthcoming.

That, in turn, would make it impossible for the Israelis to keep up their relentless territorial expansion and their construction of more and more deliberately provocative Jewish settlements and 'walls'. They would also have to curb their heavyhanded oppression of the Palestinians living in the squalor of the Occupied Territories. And the futile, persistent killing by pathetic Arab suicide bombers would have to decline. In other words, the vicious eye-for-an-eye cycle these two ancient Semite nations have been caught in might break. They might even get around to remembering that they have religious origins in common — Adam, Eve, Abraham, Moses.

But surely we're not so madly optimistic as to suggest that, over time, peace might break out in the world's most troubled region? Yes and no. If the US distortion of the Palestinian–Israeli death struggle was to be removed or dissipate, with it would almost certainly go the principal reason for the universal anti-Americanism in the Islamic world.

But, even if this worked out in the best possible way, then the real work would begin. The basis of a new world order would have to entail an unconditional acceptance of difference — Muslims of non-Muslims, and non-Muslims of Muslims. That sort of world order could well turn out to be one in which deranged Islamic terrorists will not fly planes into New York skyscrapers in order to kill Christians and Jews; one in which Jewish and Arab-Muslim kids are able to return to the days when their tribal ancestors in the unholy Holy Land squabbled over land, but were not committed to driving each other into the Mediterranean.

In the meantime, once the heat and dust in Iraq have settled, the next great war to be fought is that thoroughly just and justifiable one — a war against the mutual ignorance between Muslims and non-Muslims. As we have seen so often and so recently, ignorance is not bliss.

They Won't Just Go Away!

As we've said earlier in this journal, Muslims account for almost one in four of the world's 6 billion people. Despite everything that's happened in the past — and even more recently — that might have slowed its progress, Islam remains the world's fastest growing religion — other, of course, than Hollywood and McDonald's! 'MacWorld versus Jihad,' as American Ben Barber's clever title has it.

Arab-Muslims, the dominant Islamic group within these covers, make up around 20 per cent of the world's Muslims, but their international clout is far greater than their actual numbers. Forty per cent of Muslims live in south and south-east Asia. Indonesia, on Eurocentric, would-be multicultural Australia's doorstep, has the largest Muslim population in the world. The figures vary according to source, but these days there would have to be close to 215 million Muslim Indonesians. In an irony of ironies, most Western Muslims reside in the United States, where they represent just 2 per cent of the population, which sound spiddling but that's actually one in 50 Americans or 6 million American-Muslims!

The list of the world's Islamic countries — including those with almost entirely Muslim populations — more or less in descending order of number, include: Indonesia, Pakistan, India, Bangladesh, Turkey, Egypt, Iran, Nigeria, China, Algeria, Ethiopia, Morocco, Afghanistan, Iraq, Sudan, Uzbekistan, Saudi Arabia, Yemen, Syria, Tanzania, Russia, Malaysia, Mali, Tunisia, Senegal, Niger, Azerbaijan, Somalia, Kazakhstan, Guinea, Burkino Faso, United States of America, Tajikistan, Congo, Libya, Turkmenistan, Jordan, Cote d'Ivoire, Chad and Cameroon. Separately, it's a line-up probably not worth worrying about — but together?

Islam is not going to go away, despite what those in the West who feel threatened by it would like to hope. Nor is the problem of the non-Muslim world's relationship with it going to evaporate overnight. If anything, post-September 11, post-Saddam, even post-terrorism, that relationship is always going to be more, not less, problematic. Islam's sheer numbers alone leave the rest of us with no choice but to learn to live with the ongoing certainty that we are not going to wake up one morning and find the world's 1.25 billion 'former' Muslims at Mass, doing yoga or tai-chi, repeating the Jewish Torah or meditating à la Zen Buddhists. Sorry!

As William Allen, editor-in-chief of *National Geographic*, put it: 'From the sands of the Sahara, to the mountains of Afghanistan, to the Pacific islands of Indonesia, Islam is here to stay.' Or, if you prefer, Islam is an empire, 'more far-reaching at its zenith than Rome's', as Tim Abercrombie, another *Nat Geo* man, aptly describe its global reach. Fourteen hundred years of religious debate and rivalry have not and will not change the apparently permanent state of Islam. But exactly what kind of Islam it becomes in the short, medium and long term — violent or benign, moderate or extreme — is a seriously different matter.

For decades now, most Muslims, particularly in the Arab world, who we've spoken to have told us they are incensed at the United States for what they see as the unfair, unequal, unjust and prejudiced support of Jewish Israel against the Muslim Palestinians in the Occupied Territories. Not only that, they resent the continuing American military presence in Saudi Arabia, the land of their holiest of places — Mecca, the Prophet Muhammed's birthplace. They believe that it is United States support for the hardline and repressive Saudi Royal family that has spawned terrorists like Osama bin Laden over the years. They also believe, like Hosni Mubarak, the Egyptian leader, that the war against Saddam Hussein in Iraq probably created a hundred more bin Laden clones each day of the Coalition of the Willing's invasion-cum-occupation.

Now, they dread that the Western military conquest of Iraq will result in the spontaneous combustion of worse anti-American and anti-moderate Muslim terrorism. Significantly, they fear that the war against Iraq was merely the curtain-raiser to further United States military intervention and political incursion into the affairs of other 'unacceptable' Islamic states like Syria and Iran. Who's next, they ask, in the Bush-led, neo-conservative crusade to reinvent the Middle East in America's image by foisting America's idea of democracy and freedom on the Arab-Muslim world.

Commentators all over the world queue to make the same sort of points. 'Muslim societies have a longstanding love–hate relationship with US popular culture, and these days those intense feelings may be closer to revulsion than respect,' says Don Belt, another long-time *National Geographic* observer. You get a similar view from Muslim commentators, like cleric Imam Anwar al-Awlaki: 'To many Muslims, especially in traditional societies, American pop culture looks like old-fashioned paganism, a cult that worships money and sex,' he says. 'For such people, Islam is an oasis of old-fashioned family values.' As Belt and so many others point out: 'Islam is not a political system. It's a way of life, a discipline based on looking at the world through the eyes of faith.'

It cannot be denied that public floggings — and worse violations of human rights and decency — are still carried out in some Islamic nations. Muslims agree that these things happen. Muslim moderates accept that this sort of human misbehaviour is wrong, just as, they would argue, capital punishment in Texas is wrong. But the thing that moderate Muslims all over the world do not want to see is their way of life internationally 'flogged'. In the long run, it's all a question of identity, of self-image — and religion. Whether or not they make a big thing of it publicly, being a Muslim is an absolutely essential part of their identity.

And that's what all moderate Muslims are trying to tell us via their view of the world from Islam: 'Don't take away my identity. Don't tell me what to be or how to be it. Assist me, don't assimilate me. Acknowledge that, whatever either of us might think, my Allah is your God.'

It has to be said that you come away from this sort of immersion in the 'world from Islam' convinced that religion — theirs or anyone else's — has a hell of a lot to answer for! And speaking of Hell, so many on both sides of the Islamic divide have got so many things so disastrously wrong recently, it must be bloody crowded down there!

Salam! Shalom!

Disclaimer:
This Way We Offend Everyone!

There will, of course, be Muslims, Jews, Christians — in fact, believers of various shapes, colours and sizes — out there in Humansville who will find something, big or small, serious or flippant, to be offended by in this discourse. So be it! But the whole idea was not to offend the sensitivities, but to stir the senses. Religion is a touchy subject; it always has been and it probably always will be. It is, after all, about belief and belief is about what we are or at least think we are. It's ultimately about identity.

If God is, maybe he or she might eventually get around to telling us how close or how far each of us is from the truth. If he or she is not, then we're on our own, folks! And if the frighteningly obvious Muslim/non-Muslim divide is any indication, we still have quite a few things to learn. In the meantime, wouldn't it be more useful if we could put aside being Muslim, Jew, Christian or whatever, and started being human beings? Does it really matter who's right about a question that doesn't really have an answer? If we strip away the prejudice and mutual ignorance, none of us is right — but a heck of a lot of us have clearly got it horribly wrong.

What was it that the late humanitarian John Lennon used to warble on about imagining there was no heaven, hell, countries, nothing to kill or die for, and 'no religion'? Now that's a very different world. Imagine us all living in peace, as the old Beatle would say.

In April 2003, at war with Iraq, George W Bush in Washington asked God 'to continue to protect America'. At precisely the same moment, in the packed mosques of Baghdad, Iraqi Muslims were praying to God for exactly the same protection. How can this be? Are we suggesting that there are two Gods — and they are at war? Surely not. Nevertheless, as things are in the world right now, both Muslims and non-Muslims are carrying on as though there are, in fact, two deities — God and Allah, both of them protecting their believers from the others. It just doesn't make intellectual, religious, philosophical or any other kind of sense. Until we come to grips with this completely irrational and dichotomous 'God-thing' that's been dividing the world for getting close to 1500 years and still does even now, the threat of an oft-predicted 'clash of civilisations' — military, terroristic, religious or otherwise — remains.

Maybe the final word should go not to a Muslim, but to a Jew, Yitzhak Rabin, the former Israeli Prime Minister assassinated, in the name of God, by one of his own. 'Enough of war. Enough of bloodshed. Enough.'

Acknowledgments

This personal journal came together as a result of a lot of contact with lots of Muslims, over a long period of time and during any number of trips to a considerable aggregate of Islamic countries.

My thanks and acknowledgment goes to anyone and everyone in the Muslim world who has contributed — deliberately, indeliberately, over a period of time or merely in passing — to the build-up of my experience and knowledge of their culture, religion, values, their aspirations and fears. As another human being, I learned heaps from my many Muslim friends and contacts about being different. Most of all, I learned that one of our most pressing global needs has to be greater tolerance and acceptance of the differences between us — not necessarily unconditional — but tolerance and acceptance nonetheless.

In particular, big thanks are due to Michelle Sabti in her two absolutely crucial roles, so willingly offered — firstly, as Kirsty and my point of reference with the Sheikh Mohammed Centre for Cultural Understanding at Jumeira in the UAE and via her work on behalf of Dubai Tourism Authority (www.dubaitourism.co.ae).

Thanks too to my dear friend, Hassan, for being far more than a driver; Abdallah for taking me into his home and family; Ranya Kadri and Dr Adic Asad for their years of friendly help and for introducing Serge to Jordan and Islam; to Khalil for being Serge's Muslim mate; Costanza, Fritz and the boys for their help and friendship in Jerusalem and Napoli, their personal Muslim and non-Muslim worlds; Doug and Nancy Andrews from Emerald Beach near home for sharing their Abu Dhabi friends and experience; Charl Laubscher and Rosalie for turning their home over to the author in Al Ain — and for all those good productive times eating, drinking and talking; Steve Margolis and Valmae for the same reason and for Steve for allowing me to pick his Muslim-alert mind; Maura Angle from work for being so thoughtful enough to set us up with her brother Sean and his family in Muscat; to Sean and Renata for becoming our friends and lending us theirs including Sheik Aflah Bin Hamed Salim; Shawqi Sultan and his wife Hayat and their friend Sadek Sulaiman; also, Majid Al Toky and Tahiya, beautiful Omanis and their friend Khalfan Esry; back in Oz, Mez and Gary O'Neill for putting me up and putting up with me; David and Gillian Helfgott for a beautiful place to write close to home and the UAE Ambassador to Australia, Khalifa Alfalasi.

And to all those Muslim folk who filled in so many gaps.

Thanks also to Geraldine Hunt and Carl Matto of *Emirates Airlines* in Melbourne for being there to help through a hectic itinerary; to Christopher and Lyn Heysen from the Western Australian Trade Office in Dubai for help and a bed; Dubai Tourism students Athba, Alia, Maryam and especially Hessa Abdullah Ali Alhumairay, her sister and father for their hospitality; Peter Deakin and Lynda Hunter from the Victorian Government's Dubai office for their invaluable assistance; Peter Lindford, Australia's Senior Trade Commissioner and Consul-General in the UAE; Beata Jankowska-Smith for her travel assistance and contacts; Susan Rae, Austrade's Business Development Consultant in Oman; Ian Fairservice from Motivate Publishing for his knowledge and experience; Yanal Abaza from Dubai's 'Royal Mirage'; Catherine Armstrong for all her friendly offers of help; Tracy and Mav, my old mates at 'Foreign Correspondent'; swiftly supportive SBS Television Library and John Tullow, ABC News; Peter 'Trig' for keeping the lap-top firing and Carol Wells for that massive transcribing job. As always, the NMI Promised Land 'team'.

Source Reading

Akbar S. Ahmed, *Discovering Islam: Making Sense of Muslim History and Society*, Routledge & Kegan Paul, New York, 1989

—— *Islam Today: A Short Introduction to the Muslim World*, I.B Tauris, London, 1999

Abdullah Yusuf Ali, *The Qur'an: Text, Translation and Commentary*, Tahrike Tarsile Qur'an Inc, New York, 2001

Karen Armstrong, *Muhammad: A Biography of the Prophet*, HarperSanFrancisco, New York, 1992

—— *A History Of God: The 4000 Year Quest of Judaism, Christianity and Islam*, Ballantine Books, New York, 1993

—— *Islam: A Short History*, Weidenfeld & Nicolson, London, 2000

—— *Muhammad: A Biography of the Prophet*, Phoenix Press, London, 2001 (1991)

Benjamin R. Barber, *Jihad vs McWorld: Terrorism's Challenge to Democracy*, Ballantine Books, New York, 1995

Ramzy Baroud (ed.), *Searching Jenin: Eyewitness Accounts of the Israeli Invasion*, Cune Press, Seattle, 2003

Jenny Baxter & Malcolm Downing (eds), *The Day That Shook the World: Understanding September 11*, ABC Books, Australia, 2001

Don Belt (ed.), *National Geographic: The World of Islam*, National Geographic Society, Washington D.C., 2001

Jonathan Bloom & Sheila Blair, *Islam: A Thousand Years of Faith and Power*, TV Books, New York, 2000

Geraldine Brooks, *Nine Parts of Desire: The Hidden World of Islamic Women*, Transworld Publishers, Sydney, 1995

Thomas Cahill, *The Gifts of the Jews: How a Tribe of Desert Nomads Changed the Way Everyone Thinks and Feels*, Lion Publishing, Oxford, 1998

Camerapix, *Spectrum Guide to Jordan*, Camerapix Publishers International, Nairobi, 1994

Ergun Mehmet Caner & Emir Fethi Caner, *Unveiling Islam: An Insider's Look at Muslim Life and Beliefs*, Kregel Publications, Grand Rapids, 2002

Connector: Your Complimentary Monthly Guide to the UAE, vol 11, issue
         2, November 2002, Connector Publishing, Dubai

Jonathan Dimbleby & Donald McCullin, *The Palestinians*, Quartet
         Books, London, 1980

Dubai Explorer, 5th edition, Explorer Group Ltd, British Virgin Islands
         and Explorer Publishing, Dubai, 2001

Yahiya (J.A) Emerick, *The Complete Idiot's Guide to Understanding Islam*,
         Alpha Books, Indianapolis, 2002

John L. Esposito, *Islam and Politics* (4th edn), Syracuse University Press,
         New York, 1984

—— *The Islamic Threat: Myth or Reality*, Oxford University Press, New
         York, 1999

Dudley Fishburn (ed.), *The World in 2002*, The Economist Newspaper
         Limited, London, 2001

Foreign Affairs March/April 2002, volume 81, number 2, Council on
         Foreign Relations, 2002

Foreign Affairs: Middle East Countdown, January/February 2003, volume
         82, number 1, Council on Foreign Relations, 2003

Nathan P. Gardels (ed.), *At Century's End: Great Minds Reflect on our
         Times*, Lincoln James Associates, Singapore, 1995

Edward Henderson, *Arabian Destiny: The Complete Autobiography*,
         Motivate Publishing, Dubai, 1988.

Patricia Holton, *Mother Without a Mask: A Westerner's Story of her Arab
         Family* Motivate Publishing, Dubai, 1997 (1991)

Tony Howard & Di Taylor, *Treks and Climbs in Wadi Rum, Jordan*,
         Cicerone Press, Milnthorpe, 2001

Mike Hywed-Davies & Julia de vere McIlroy, *Oman: Once visited never
         Forgotten*, Modern Colour Printers, Oman, 1991

Shirley Kay, *Enchanting Oman*, Motivate Publishing, Dubai, 1999

Thomas Kiernan, *The Arabs: Their History, Aims and Challenges to the
         Industrialized World*, Sphere Books, London, 1975

Christopher Kremmer, *The Carpet Wars: A Journey Across the Islamic
         Heartlands*, Flamingo, Sydney, 2002

Anton La Guardia, *Holy Land Unholy War: Israelis and Palestinians*,
         John Murray, London, 2001

Bernard Lewis, *The Middle East: A Brief History of the Last 2000 Years*, Touchstone, New York, 1995

—— *What Went Wrong: The Clash Between Islam and Modernity in the Middle East*, Weidenfeld & Nicolson, London, 2002

Lonely Planet, *Jordan and Syria: a Travel Survival Kit*, Lonely Planet Publications, Melbourne, 1987

Lonely Planet, *Turkey*, Lonely Planet Publications, Melbourne, 1990

Lonely Planet, *Iran*, Lonely Planet Publications, Melbourne, 1992

Lonely Planet, *Egypt and the Sudan*, Lonely Planet Publications, Melbourne, 1994

Lonely Planet, *Jordan, Syria and Lebanon*, Lonely Planet Publications, Melbourne, 1997

Lonely Planet, *Jordan, Syria and Lebanon: Travel Atlas*, Lonely Planet Publications, Melbourne, 1997

Lonely Planet, *Oman and the United Arab Emirates*, Lonely Planet Publications, Melbourne, 2000

Lonely Planet, *Tunisia*, Lonely Planet Publications, Melbourne, 2001

Rosalyn Maqsood, *Petra: A Travellers' Guide*, Garnet Publishing, Reading, 1994

V.S. Naipaul, *Among the Believers: An Islamic Journey*, Penguin Books, Harmondsworth, 1981

Seyyed Hossein Nasr, *Islam: Religion, History, and Civilisation*, HarperCollins Publishers, New York, 2003

Wendy Northcutt, *The Darwin Awards: Evolution in Action*, Plume, New York, 2000

Joanne O'Brien & Martin Palmer, *The State of Religion Atlas*, Simon & Schuster, Sydney, 1993

Ahmed Rashid, *Taliban: The Story of the Afghan Warlords*, Pan Macmillan, London, 2001

Robert Redenbach, *Safe Passage: Navigating Conflict in a Changing World*, Redenbach Training International Pty Ltd, Mudgeeraba, Qld, 2002

Scott Ritter & William Rivers Pitt, *War on Iraq: What Team Bush Doesn't Want You to Know*, Profile Books, London, 2002

Stuart Robinson, *Mosques and Miracles: Revealing Islam and God's Grace*, City Harvest Publications, Queensland 2003

Malise Ruthven, *Islam in the World*, Oxford University Press, New York, 1984

The Sultan Qaboos Grand Mosque: The Inauguration, Apex Publishing, Oman, 2001

El Hassan Bin Talal (Crown Prince of Jordan), *Christianity in the Arab World*, Parkway Publishing, London, 1995

Wilfred Thesiger, *Arabian Sands*, Motivate Publishing, Dubai, 1959 (1994)

Tribute: 32nd Renaissance Day 2002–2003, Apex Press and Publishing, Oman, 2002

Shelagh Weir, *The Bedouin*, British Museum Publications, London, 1990

Jeremy Williams, *Don't They Know It's Friday? Cross Cultural Considerations for Business and Life in the Gulf*, Motivate Publishing, UAE, 1998

The World Mathaba, *For Resistance Against Imperialism, Zionism, Racism, Reaction and Fascism*, Second Mondial Congress, 1987